THE GROOVY HAND LETTERING WORKBOOK

Linda Scott

Skittledog

This unique and
kick-ass lettering book
belongs to:

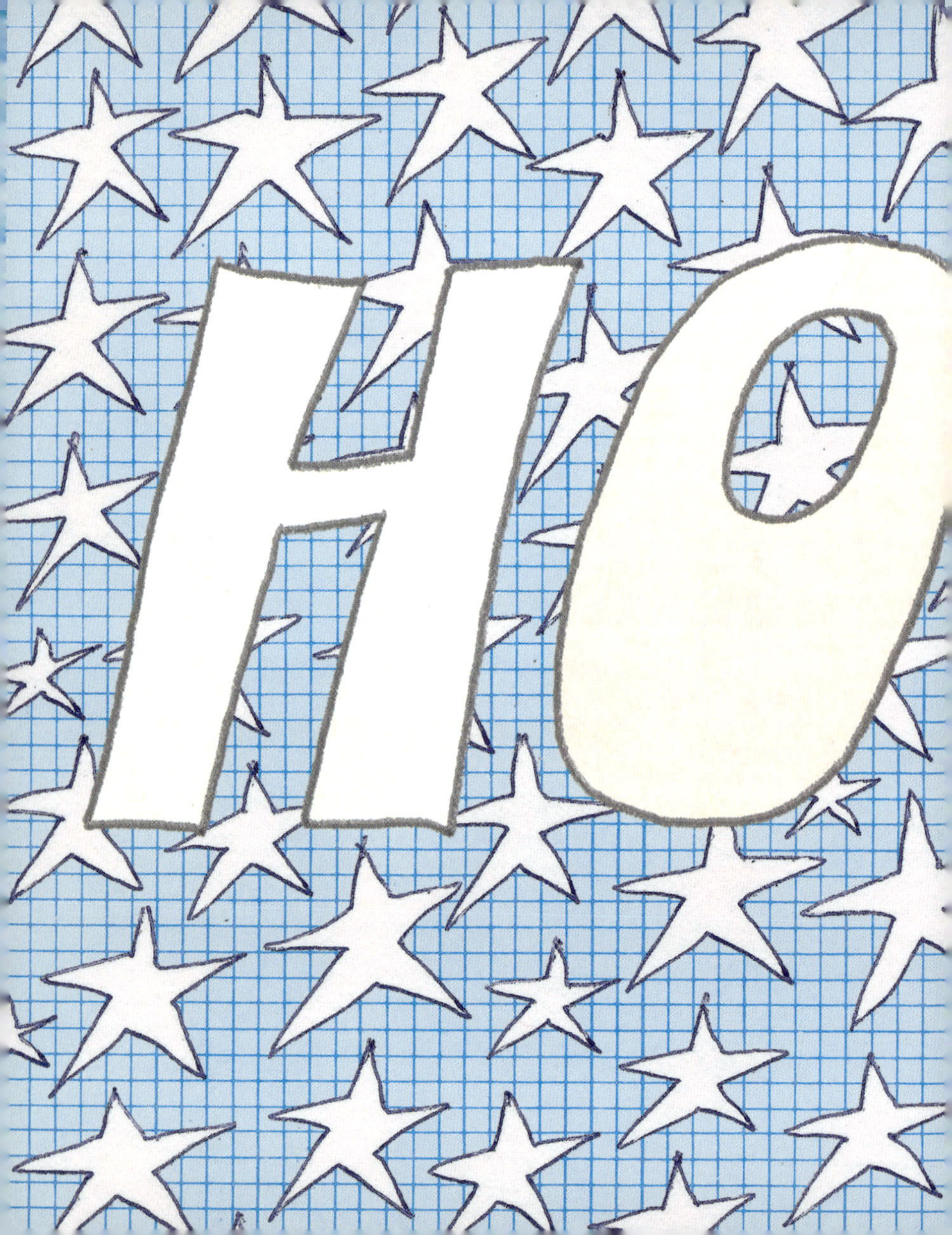
HO

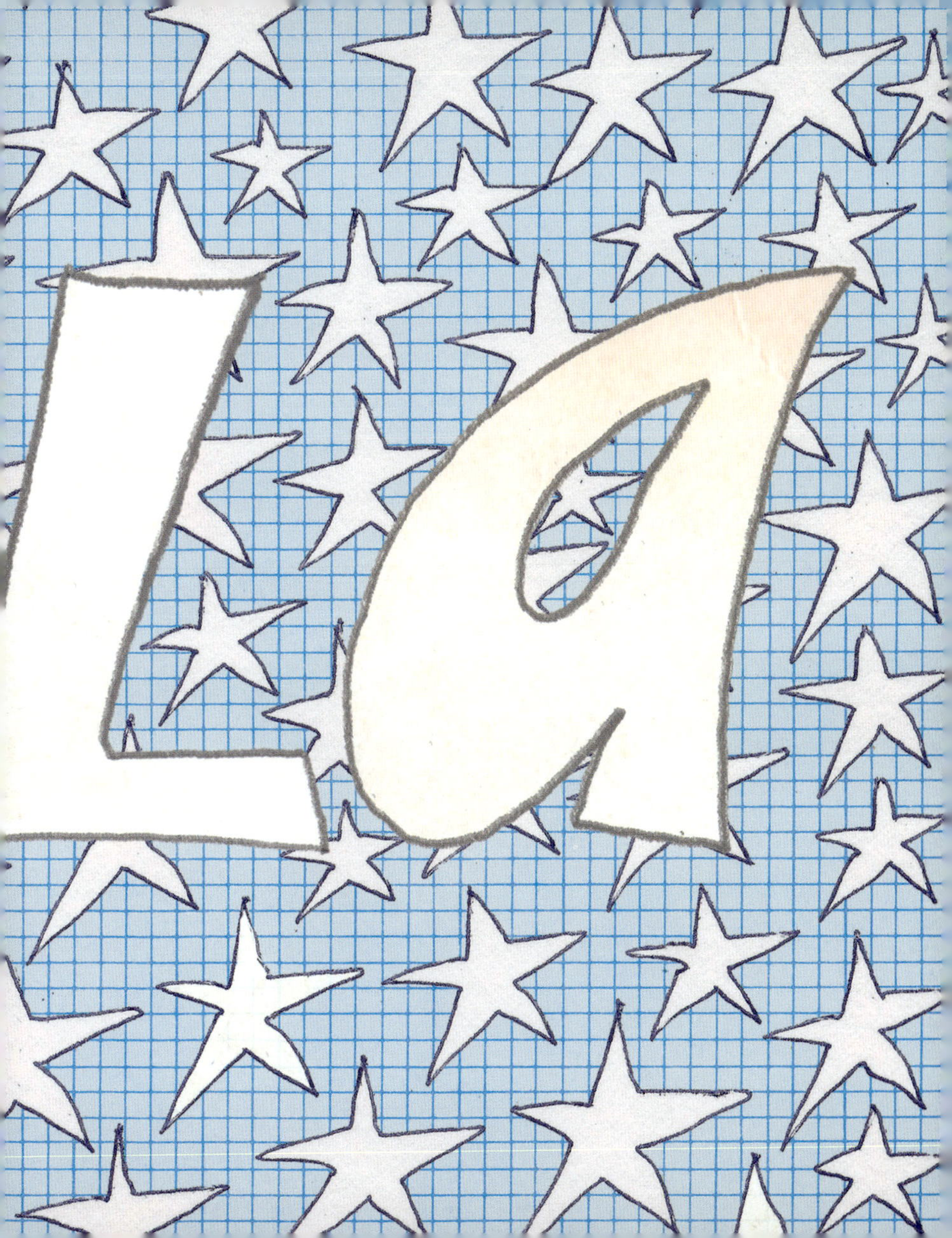
LA

CONT

ENTS

WHAT IS GROOVY HAND LETTERING?

Put simply, this book is all about words. It's a celebration of their beauty and the messages they deliver, whether silly, important, political, sensitive or philosophical...it really doesn't matter. What I'm interested in is the power behind the letters and words. When we write something down, we're committing it to a kind of permanence that isn't true of the spoken word. There's enough hate, upset and unfairness in the world already, so here is an opportunity to add your words in a joyful, beautiful way.

Think what you can do with wonderfully written words: you could find a lost cat (for real - this is how it all started for me) or stand up for something you believe in. Party invites, love letters or birthday cards can all be elevated to such glorious items that the recipients will never throw them away. Get ready to have your handiwork live forever on fridge doors and pin boards, like a scattered exhibition. Hand-drawn letters show that you really care.

In the 1960s and 1970s, people used the word 'groovy' in a positive way to describe the vibe of that era. It stood for moral excellence: love, peace, togetherness, inclusivity and freedom. All the good stuff that we're still fighting for now. And they communicated these ideas through wonderful hand lettering that still has influence on the design landscape today.

HOW DO I USE THIS BOOK?

This book is in four parts, each offering skills, ideas and activities built around different foundation alphabets: basic block, 3D letters, bubble writing and freestyle. Each section offers how-to knowledge, practice alphabets, fun and creative styles to try yourself, plus loads of activities, including colouring pages.

But, most importantly, this book is now YOURS. Each page is ready for your creative input, so make each one your own. Even if a page seems full already, add to it some more! This book is a collaboration between you and me. Please share your wonderful creations with me on Instagram @lindascott. I can't wait to see it all.

I have an inkling that in buying this book, you're already a creative of sorts, so get ready to have your voice heard - or seen - through the magic of creative lettering. This is the start of a life-long journey of creativity, so buckle up and get ready for a great ride.

Linda

TOOLS OF THE TRADE

Everything you need can be found around the home or at local stationery shops; I don't use expensive materials. I love pens - all types of pens - they're pure magic. My favourites are dual **felt-tip pens** that have a fine tip at one end and a brush tip at the other. I even like the discarded and semi dried-out pens that live at the bottom of the drawer...you know what I mean. These old pens can produce really interesting textures; let them live out their full lives, and then recycle them at a pen bank (you can find these at shops and in schools).

Pencils, of course, along with **coloured pencils,** are perfect for starting your lettering work and gorgeous for shading.

Black marker pens totally rule. They are essential for big, bold lettering, outlining and filling in areas quickly. **Fine liners** are equally essential for more detailed outlining and finer lettering work in general.

I often work with **highlighters** too. These are great for, well, doing what they're supposed to do, adding highlights to work, but are also excellent for dynamic block colouring too.

Chalk pens are the royalty of pens, total game-changers. You can use them to work onto dark papers, photographs, glossy papers, anything at all. If you don't have any (they are a bit pricey), then a white correction pen gives the same effect.

The **ball-point pen** is the absolute queen of pens. I can't tell you how versatile and fun they are to work with. Save them from a life of shopping lists and essays and get lettering with them!

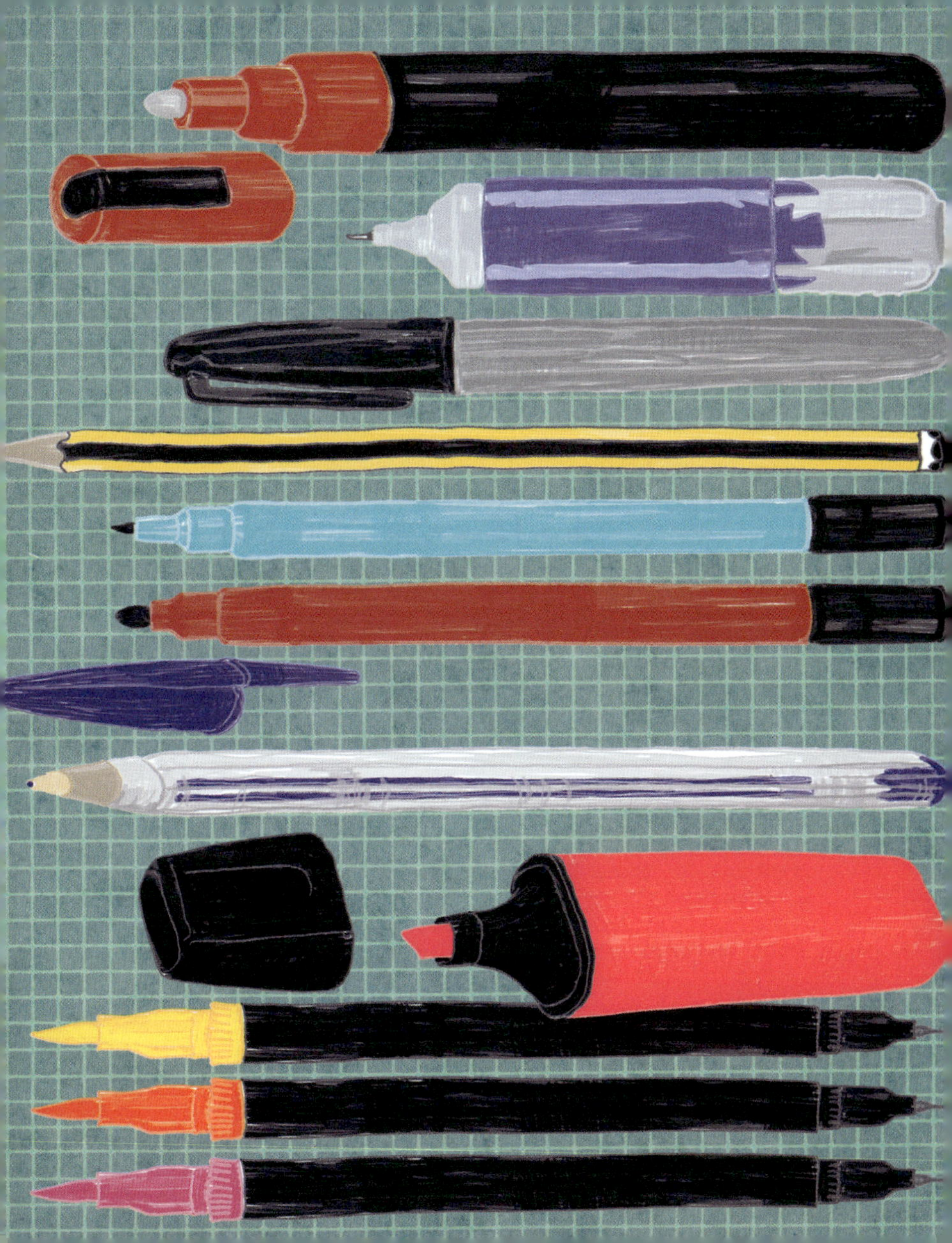

MY TIPS FOR NAILING GROOVY HAND LETTERING

Relax: The best hand lettering I come across is wobbly and wonky. These carefree outcomes are totally unique and charming and could never be successfully replicated digitally with a computer. Take that, tech bros!

Step away: From the screen...computers, phones, tablets, the whole lot of it. Take a break from incessant digital life and get busy with your drawing tools.

Save: Paper - all of it. Wrapping paper, brown paper (drool), notes, letters, magazine pages, anything. Save it all, smooth it out and save it in a box, drawer, shelf, wherever. All sorts of papers look magic when you doodle over the top of them and add your hand lettering.

Keep: All your pens. Stick them in a shoe box and vow never to throw them away until they're totally finished!

Look around: Everywhere, all the time. Notice and pay attention to hand lettering on T-shirts, flyers, posters, cards, menus, anything at all. Start a visual library in your head or, better still, take photos.

Scrapbook or journal: Whatever you call it, keep doing it. Whenever you come across any written or printed hand lettering that makes you smile, keep it. Stick it into a book and you can look back on it time and time again.

Practise: All the time. Every day, ideally, on shopping lists, to-do lists, thank you notes for friends or colleagues, etc. Trust me, the more you practice, the easier it all becomes. And lastly...

Have fun!

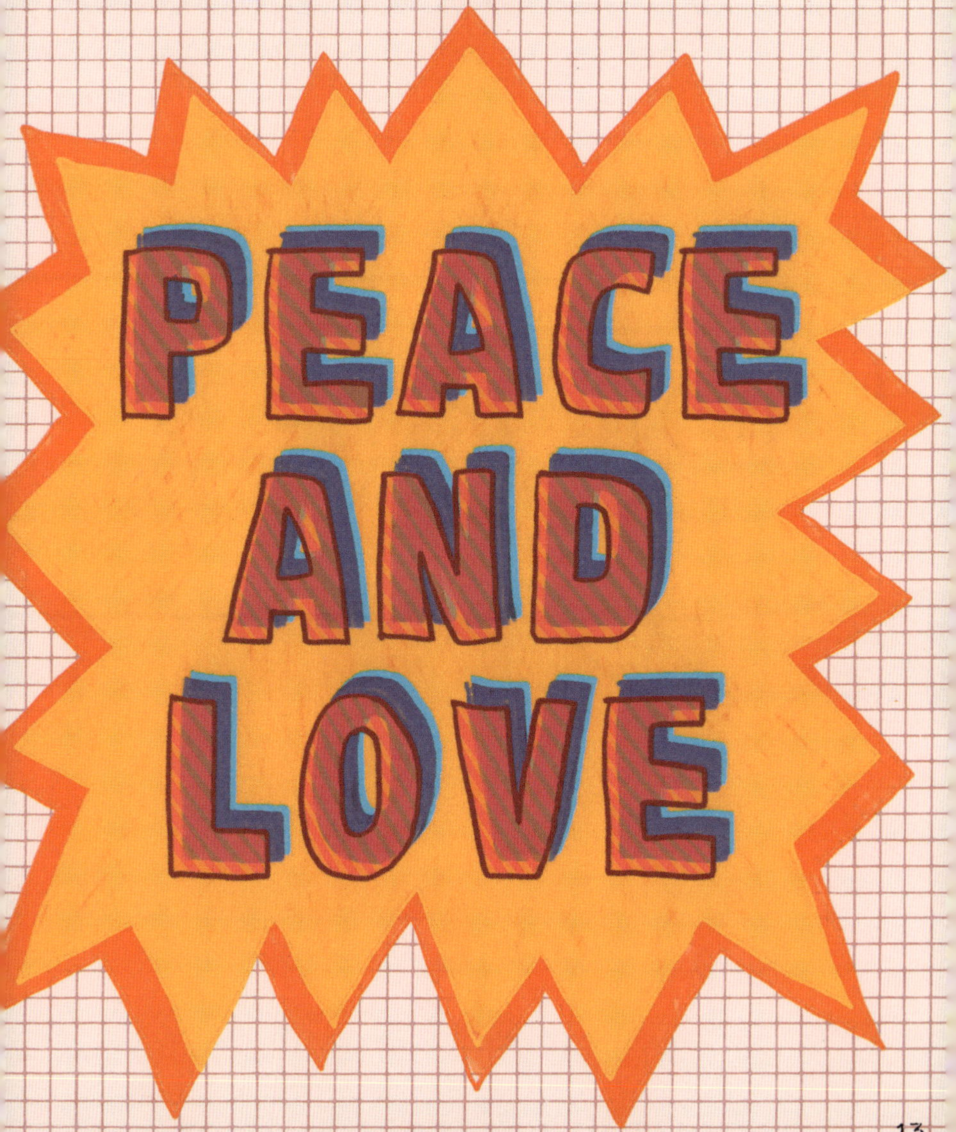
PEACE
AND
LOVE

BLOCK

ETTERS

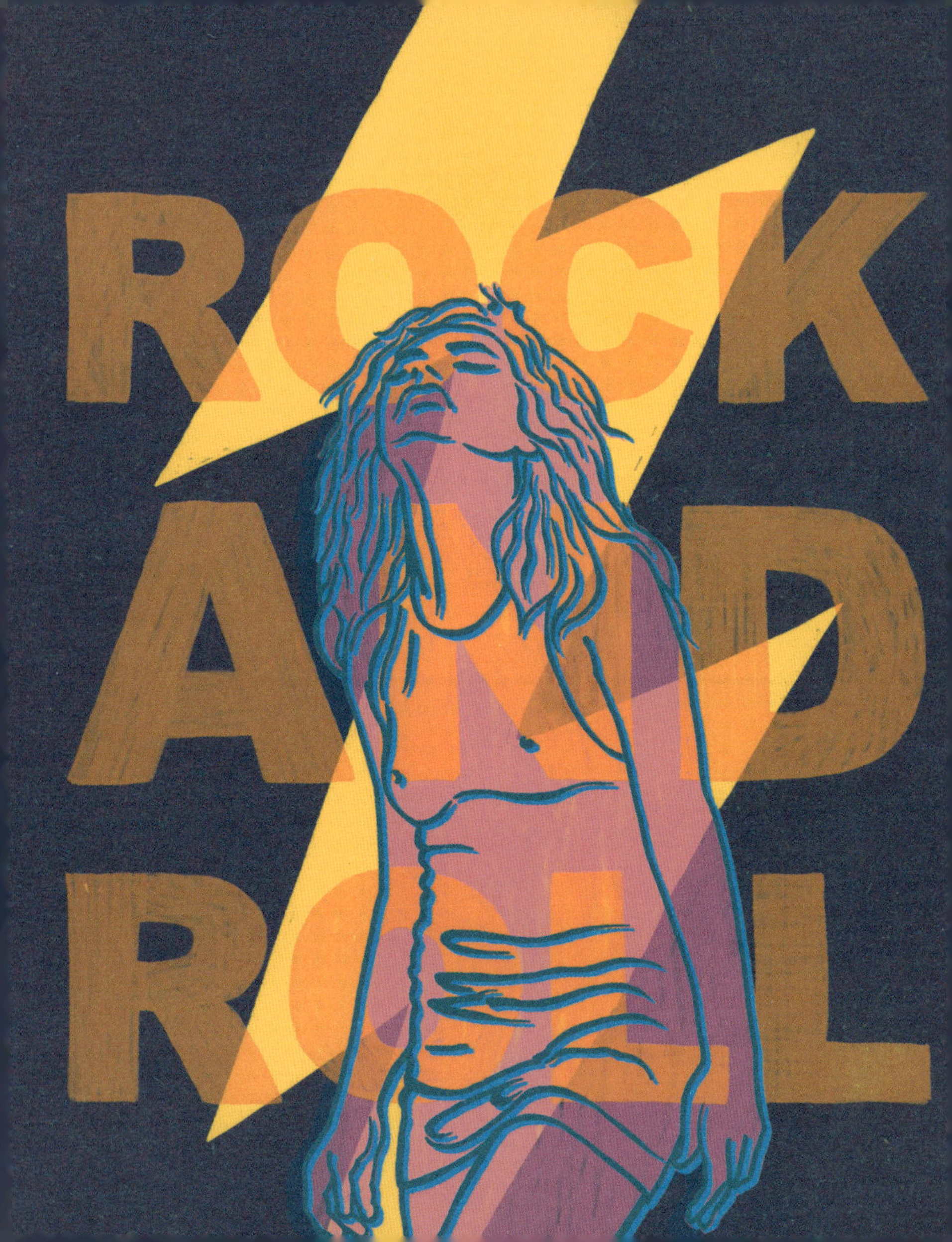
ROCK
AND
ROLL

Block letters totally rock! Learn this basic block alphabet to get started. Turn over to find out how...

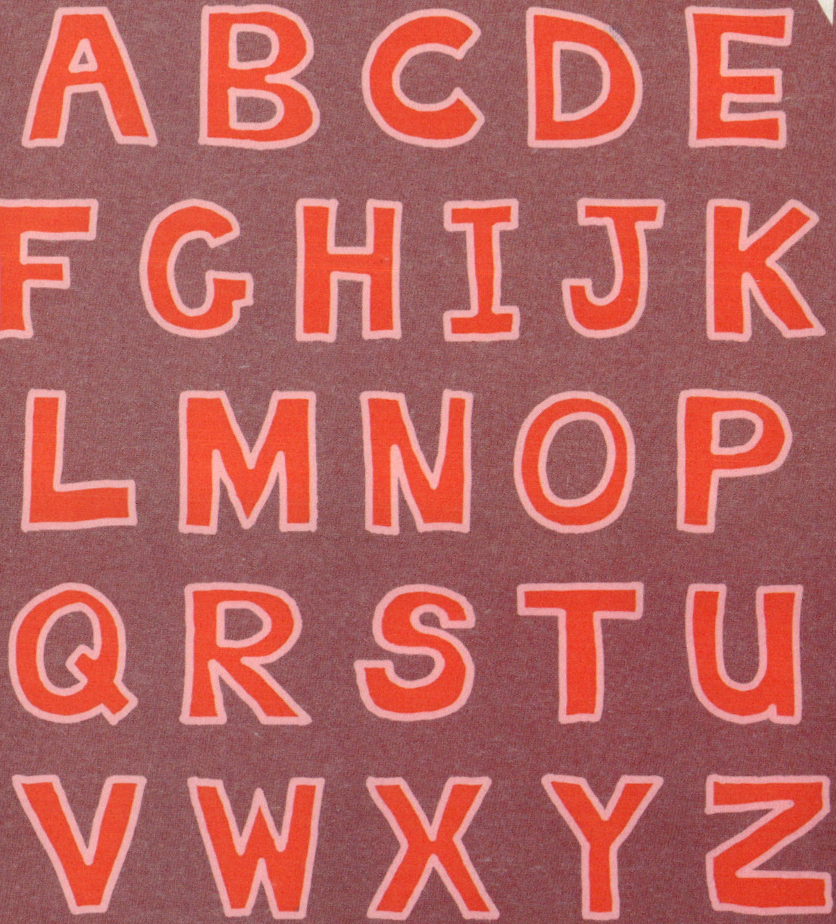

First draw the letter shape with a thin pencil line. Next, build the thicker block outline around it, line by line, using a pen. Erase the pencil lines afterwards.

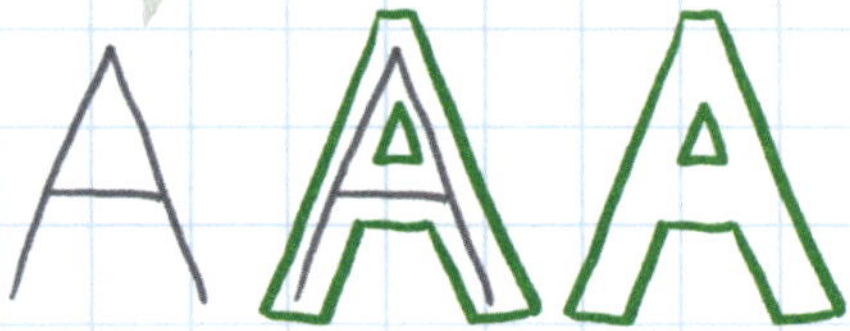

Carry on practising here and you'll soon get the hang of it.

Once you've mastered the block lettering technique, you can take on the world with your words.

Write a message that's important to you on this placard.

Block letters can be tall and skinny...

A B C

G H I J

N O P Q

U V W

...or squat and chunky. You decide!

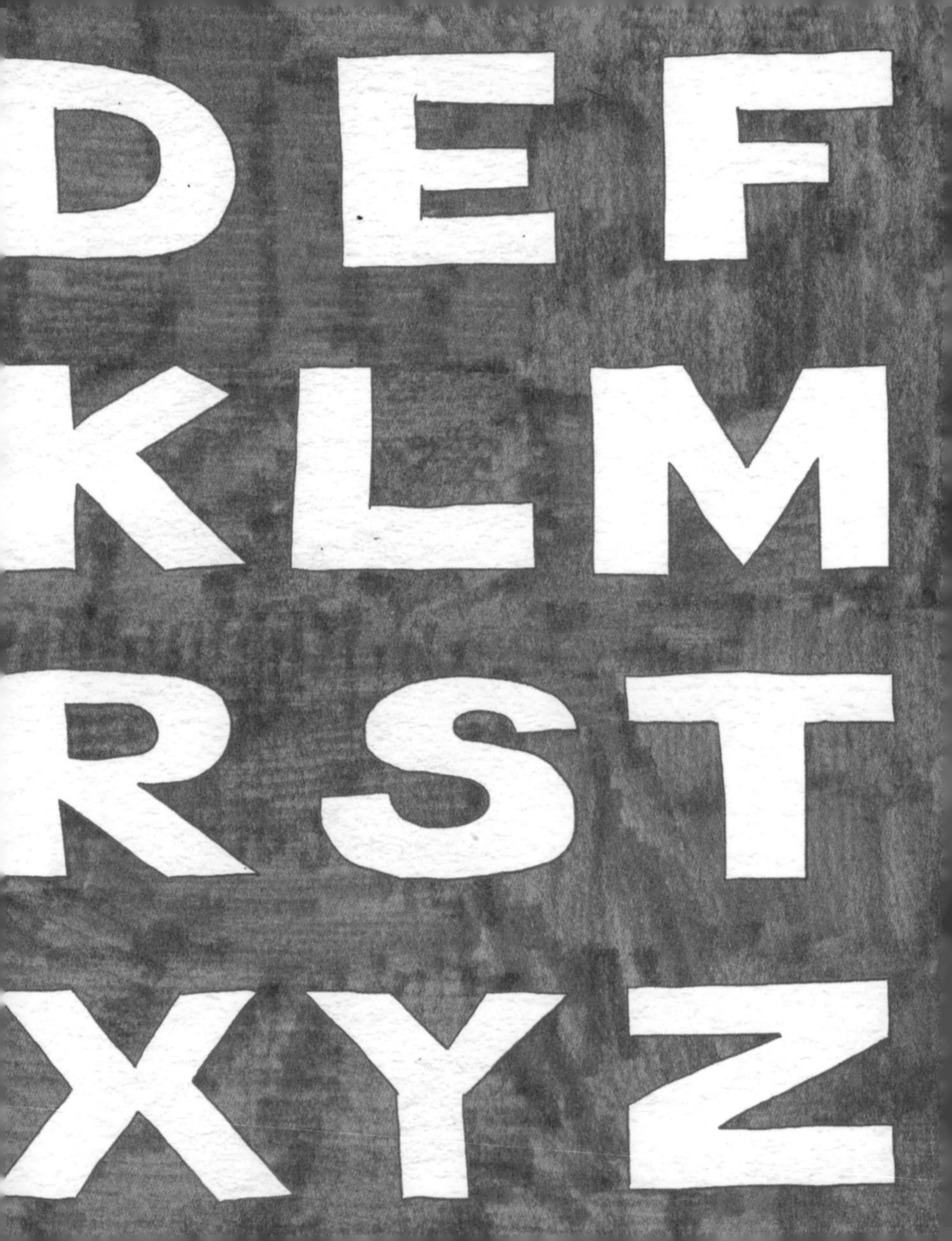
DEF
KLM
RST
XYZ

Mess about with your block letters: mix up sizes and shapes, make them as wide as you can or as tall as you can.

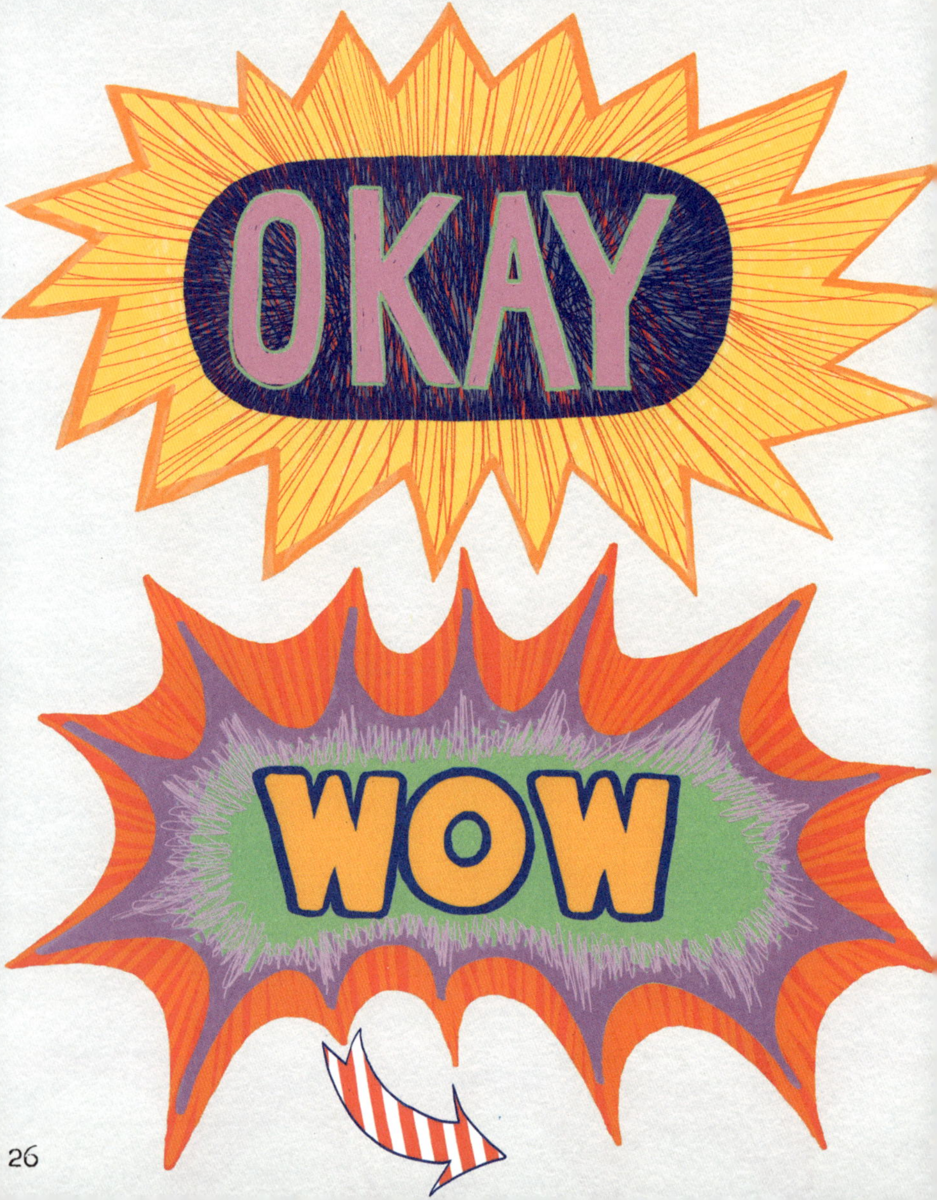
OKAY
WOW

Give your words some power – drop word bombs into these shapes.

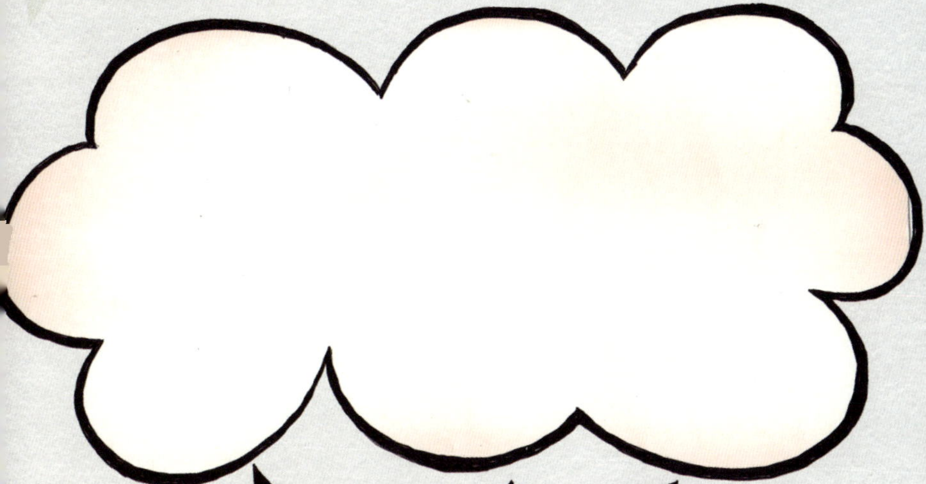

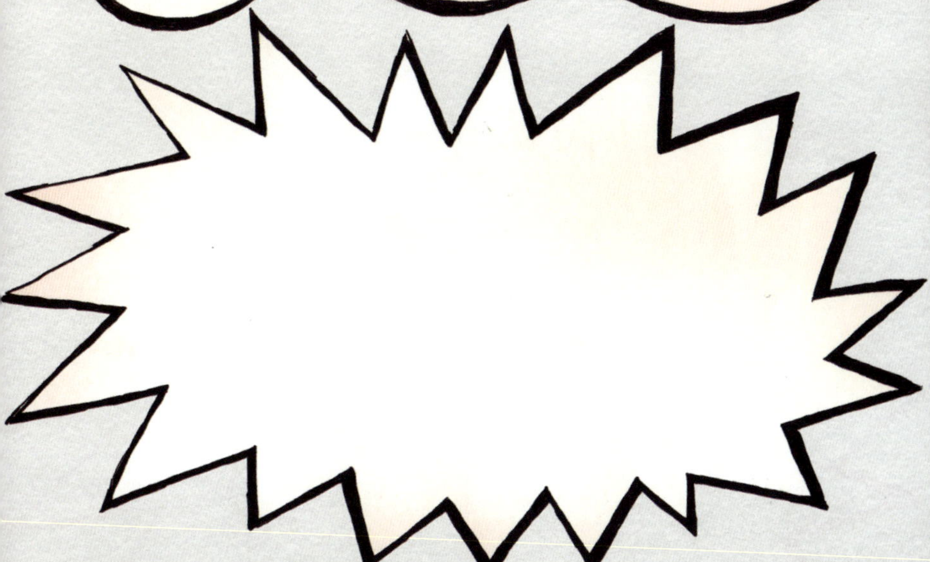

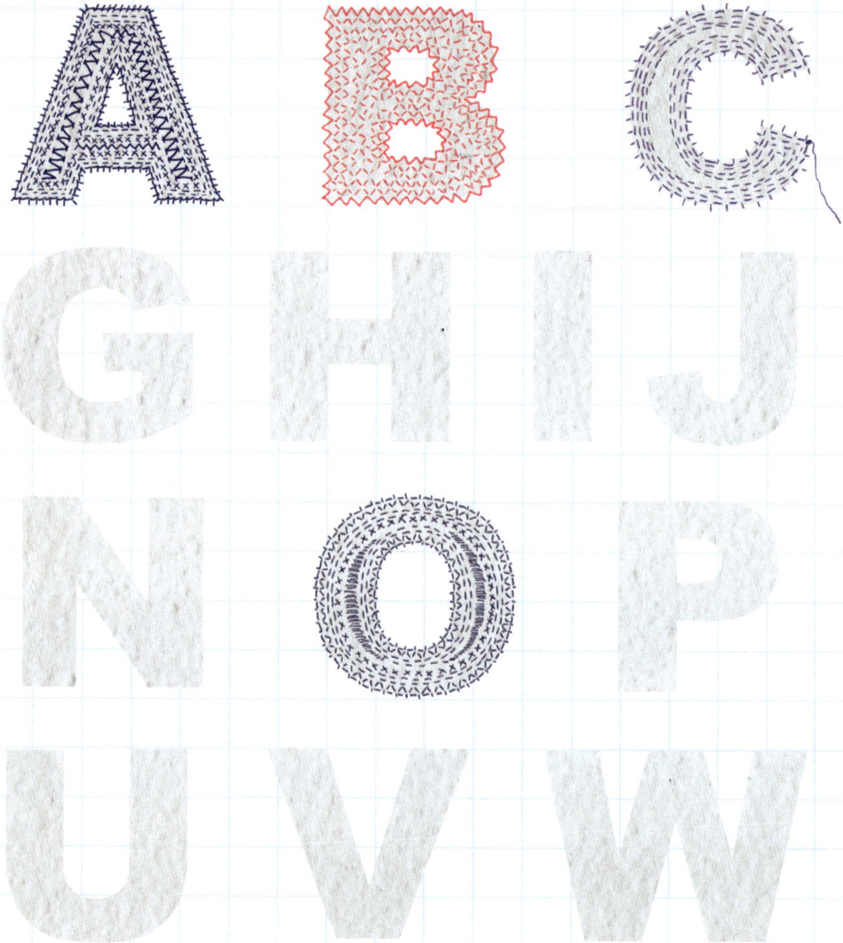

Embellish block letters by adding tiny lines to look like stitches. Fill in the empty ones above.

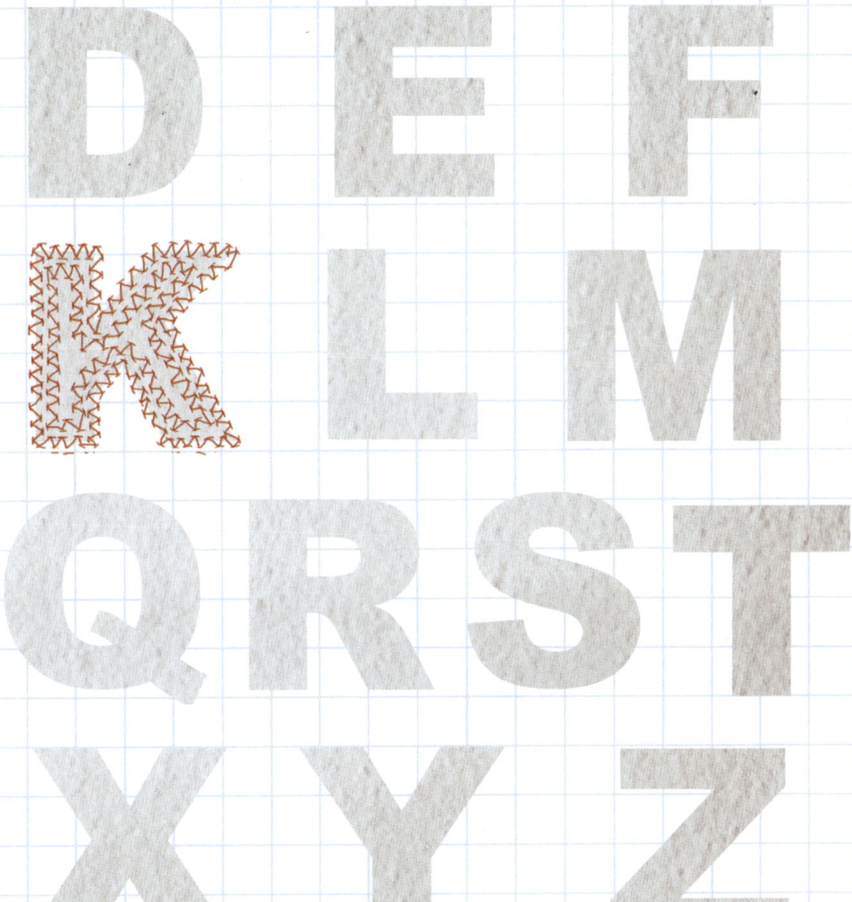
D E F
K L M
Q R S T
X Y Z

I ♥ T-SHIRTS

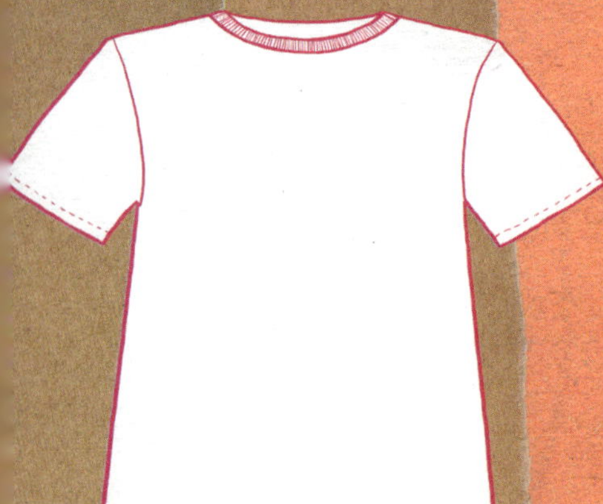

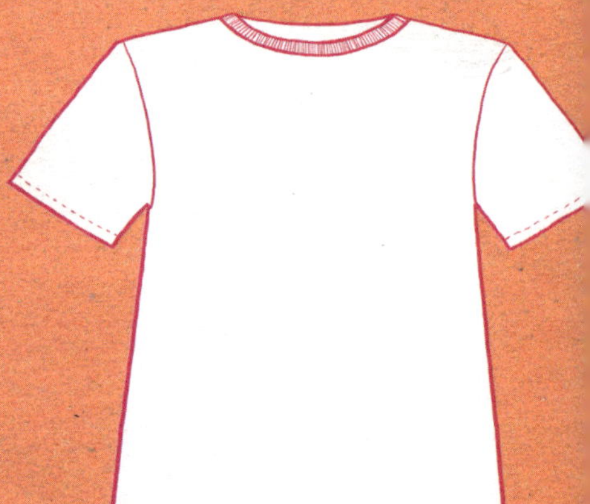

Give these plain T-shirts a slogan. Practise on the mini versions first.

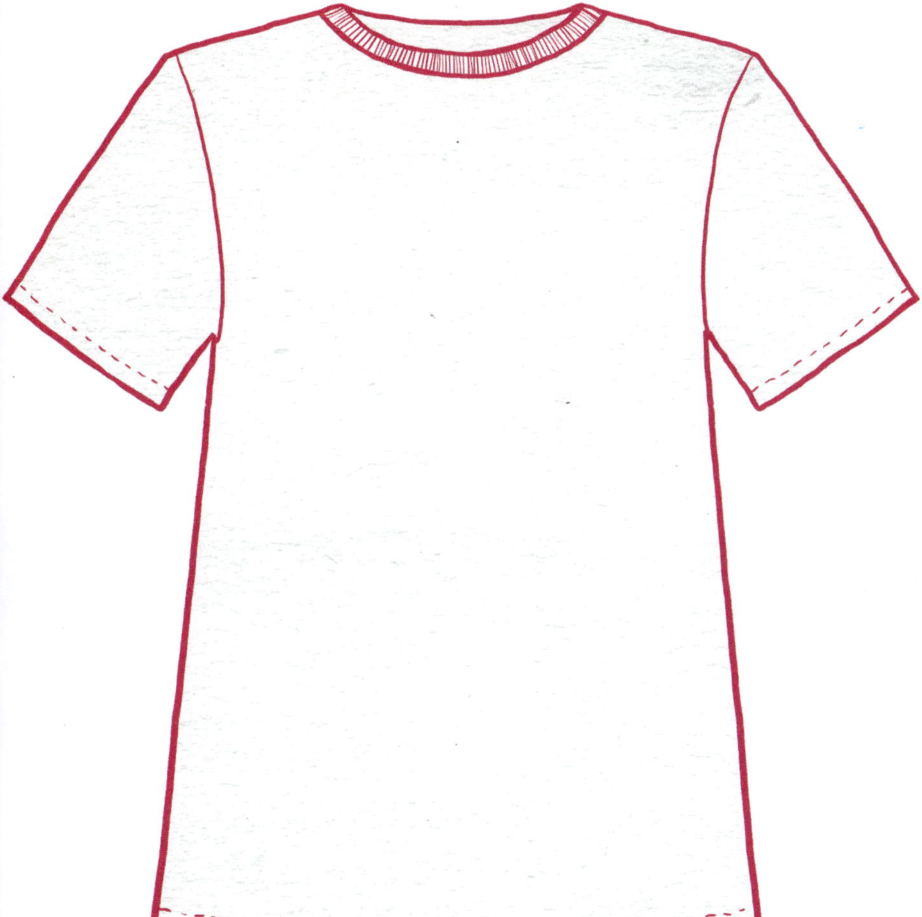

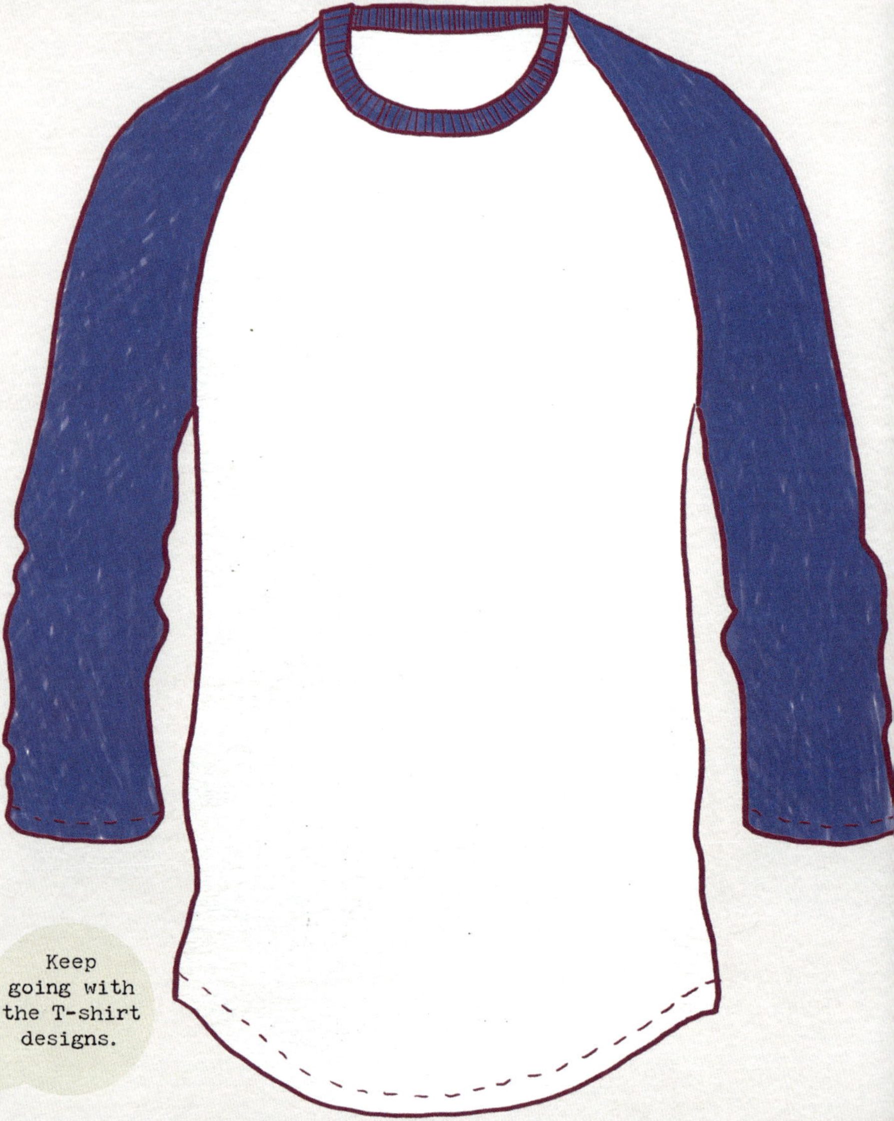

Keep going with the T-shirt designs.

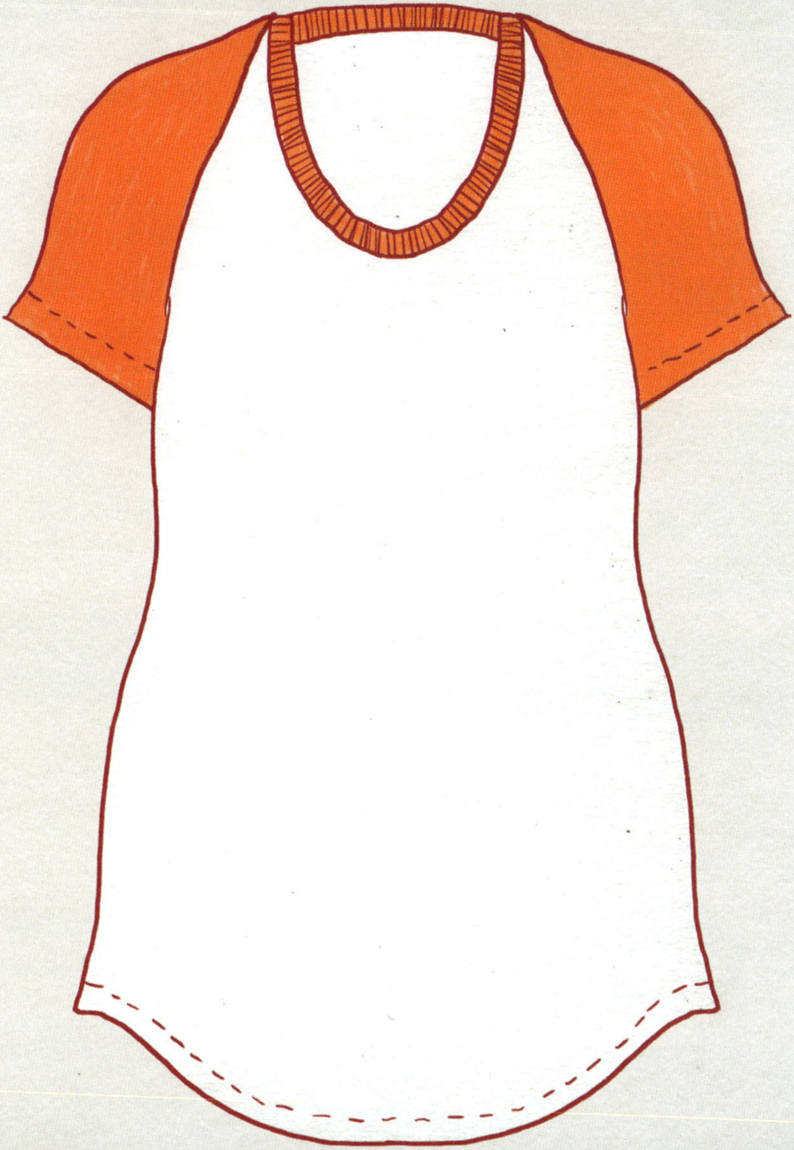

Try filling in the empty letters with patterns and doodles...

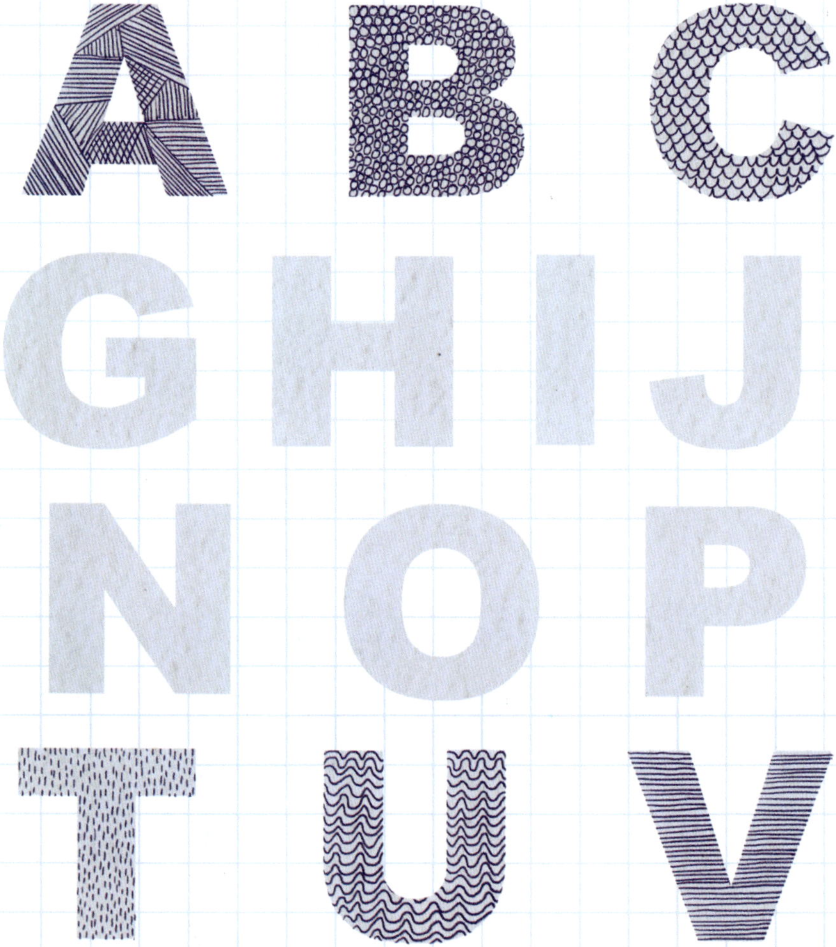

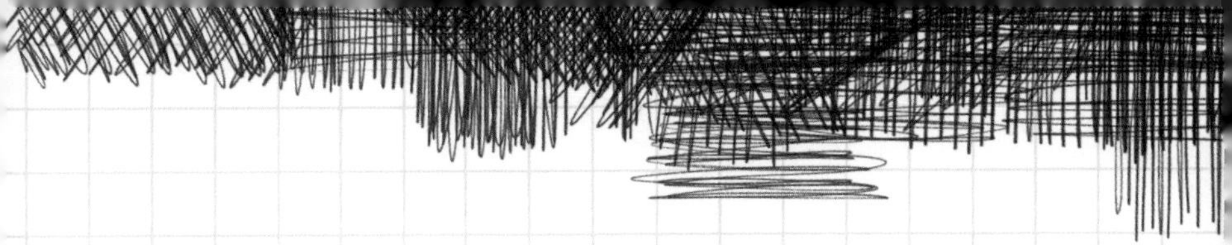

D E F

K L M

Q R S

W X Y Z

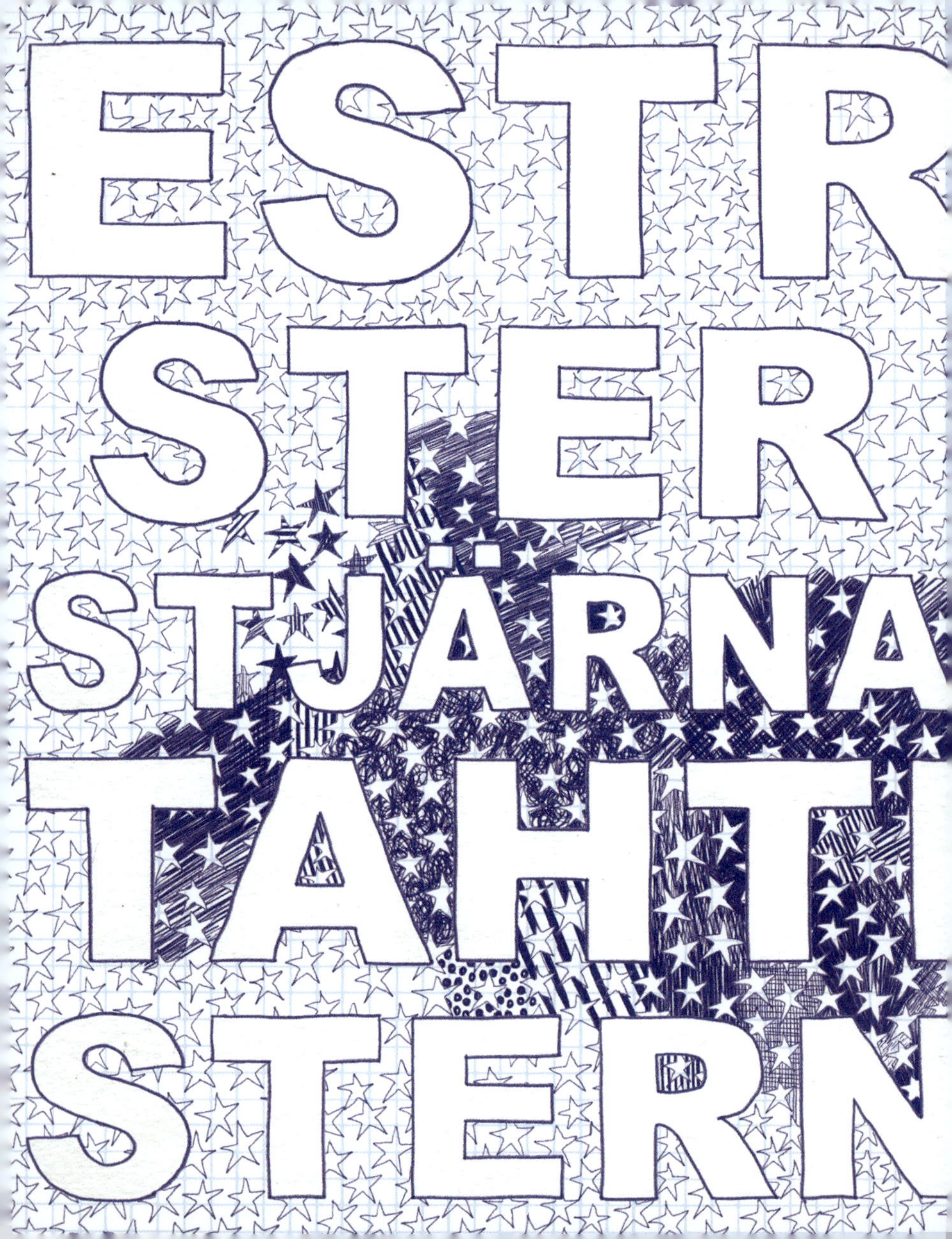
ESTR
STER
STJÄRNA
TAHT
STERN

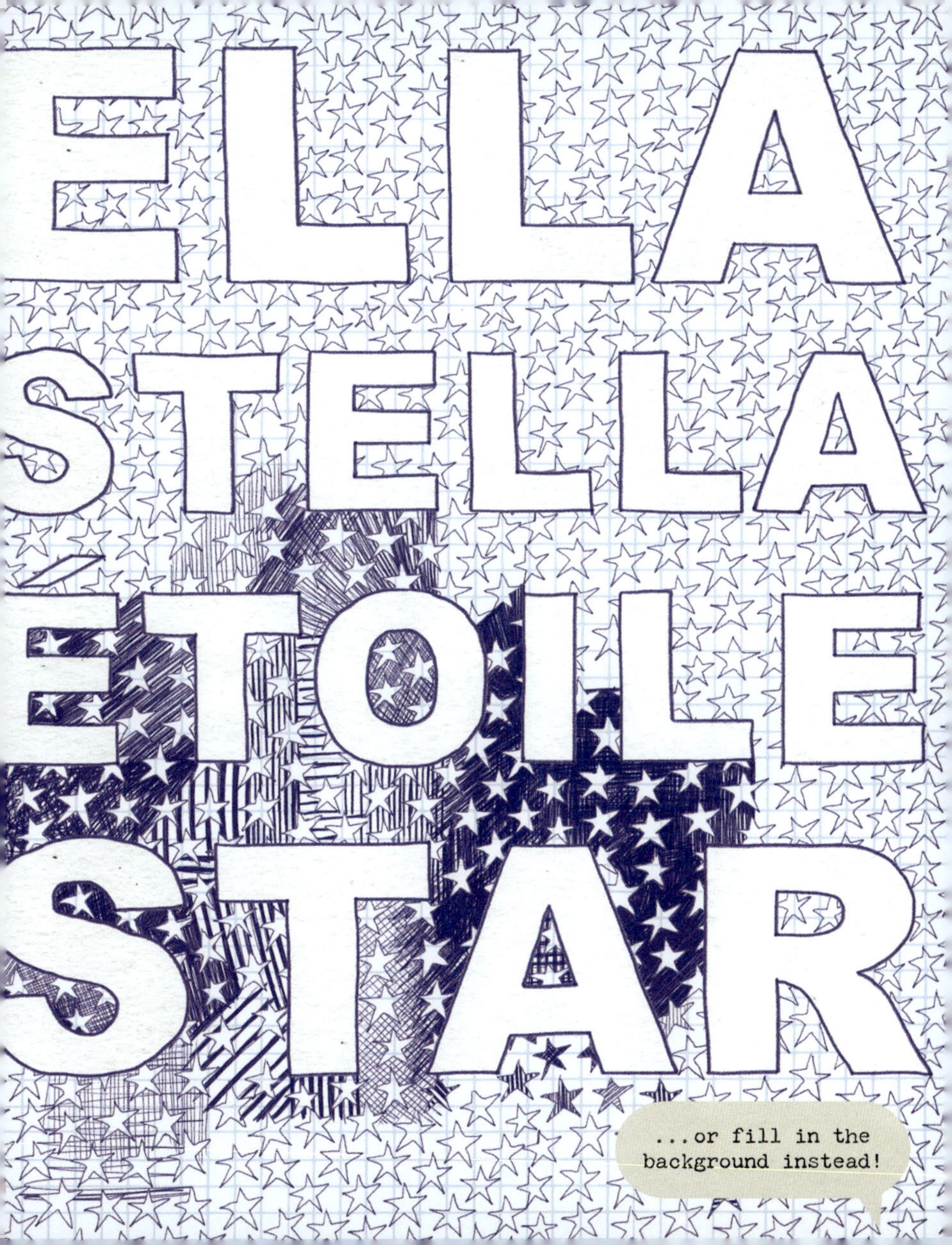

...or fill in the background instead!

Doodle patterns over the whole background on this page...

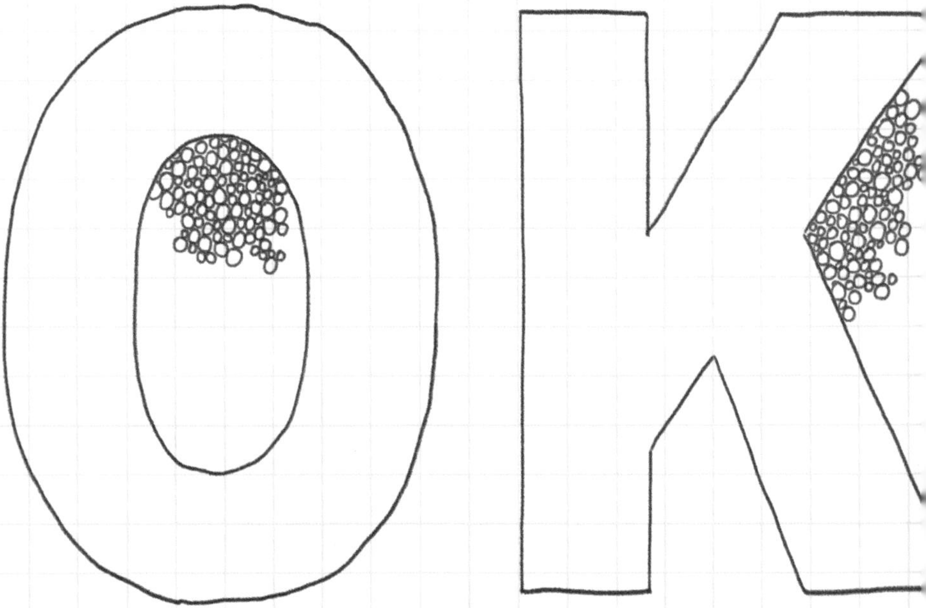

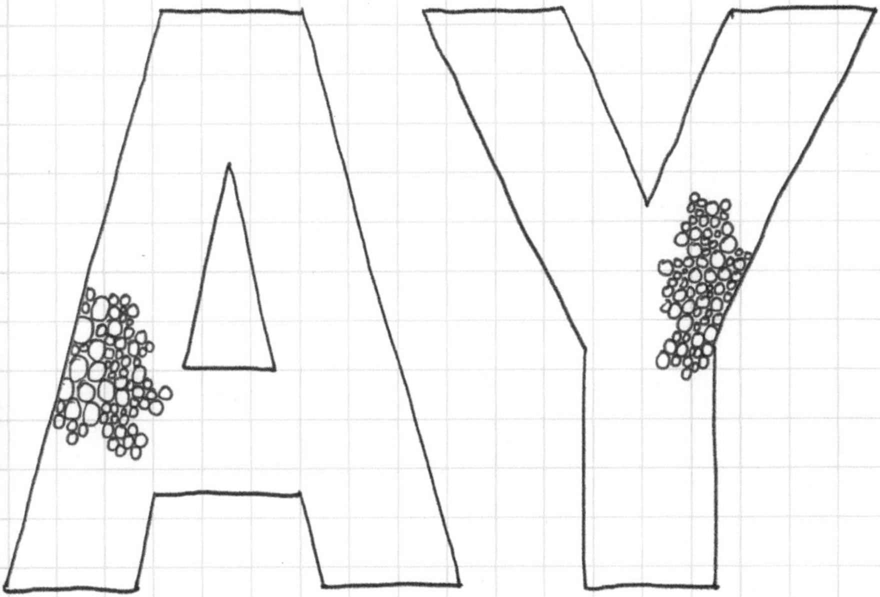

...swap over and doodle inside
the letters on this side.

Draw tiny stars and then connect them up to make a constellation.

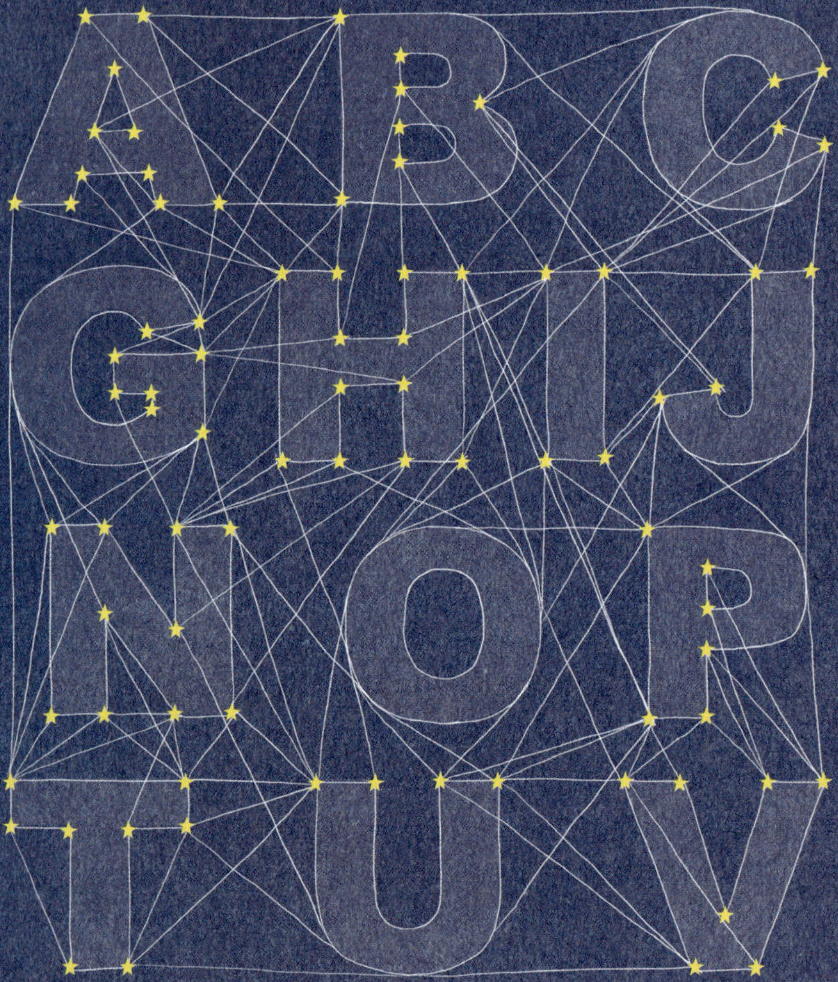

Chalk pens or pencils, or paint pens in light colours work best.

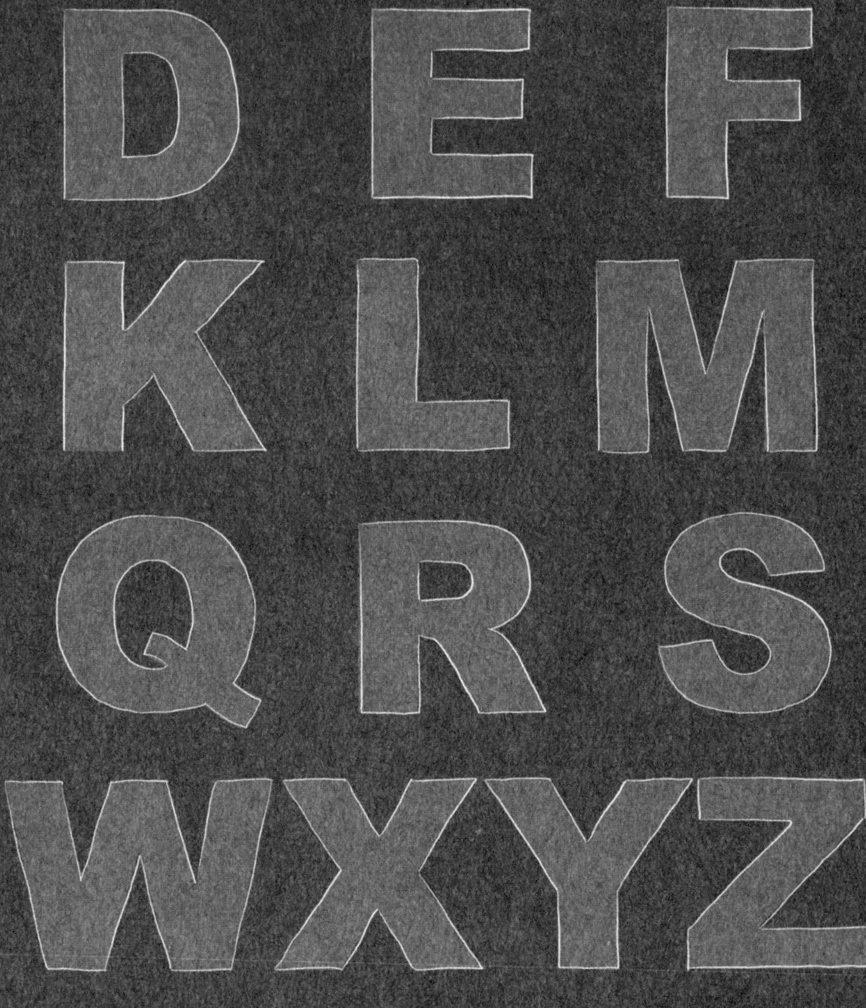

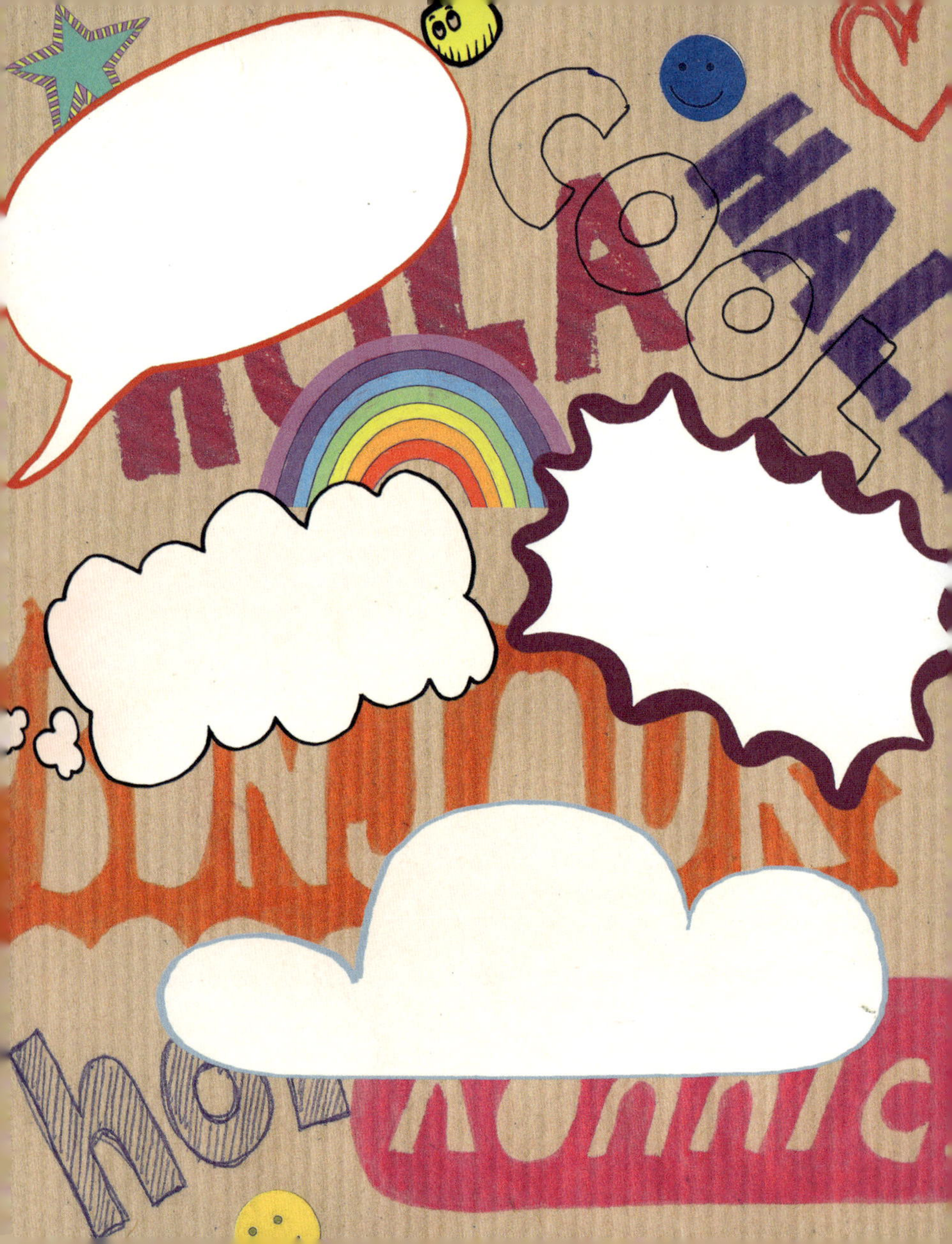
COOL

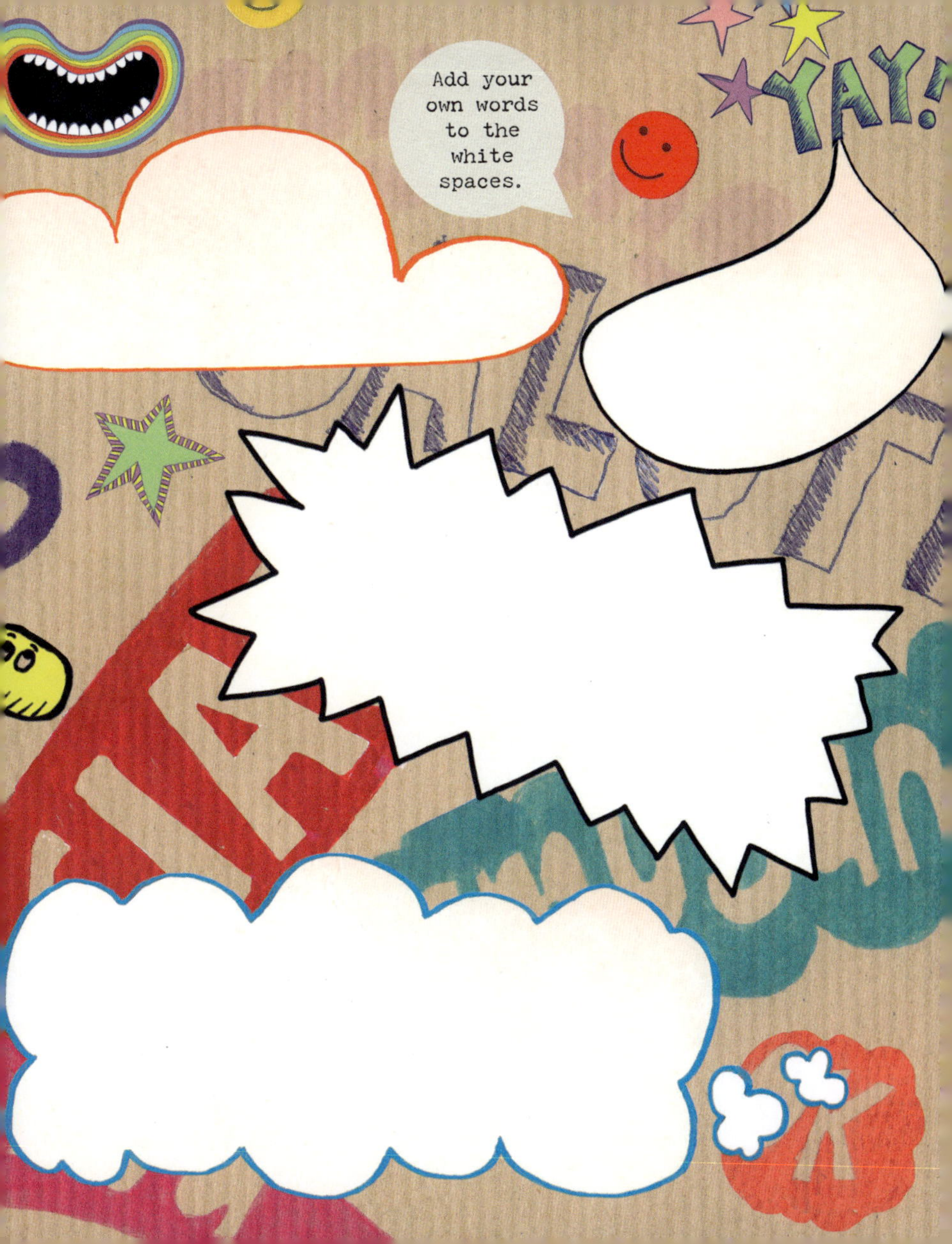
Add your own words to the white spaces.
YAY!

Layer up! This simple technique gives block letters cool drop shadows.

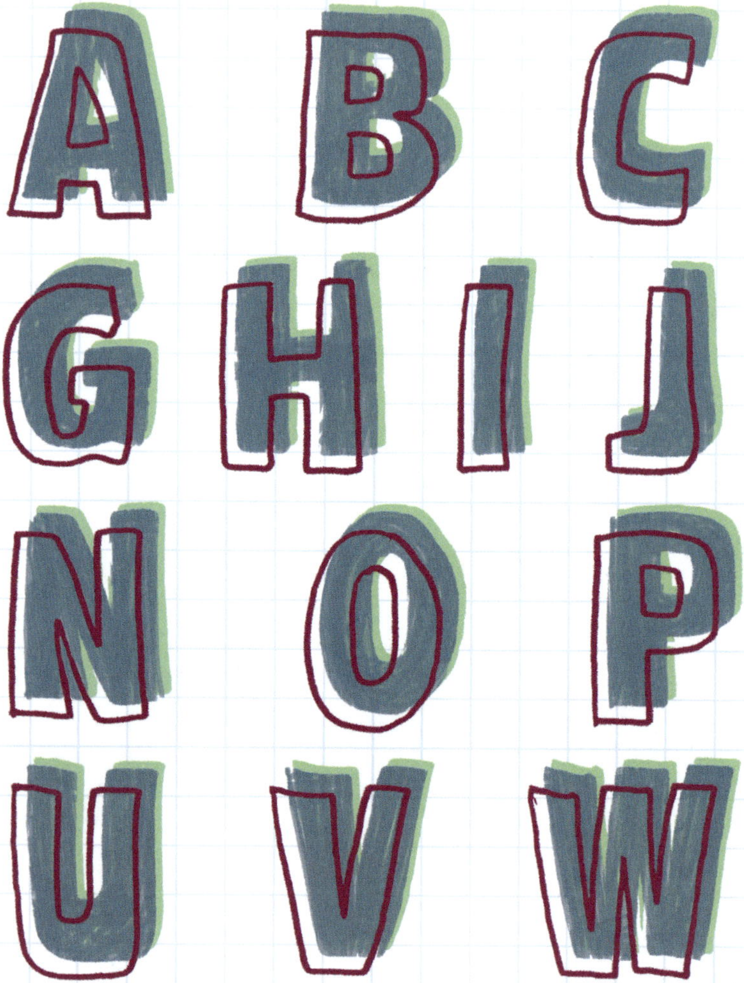

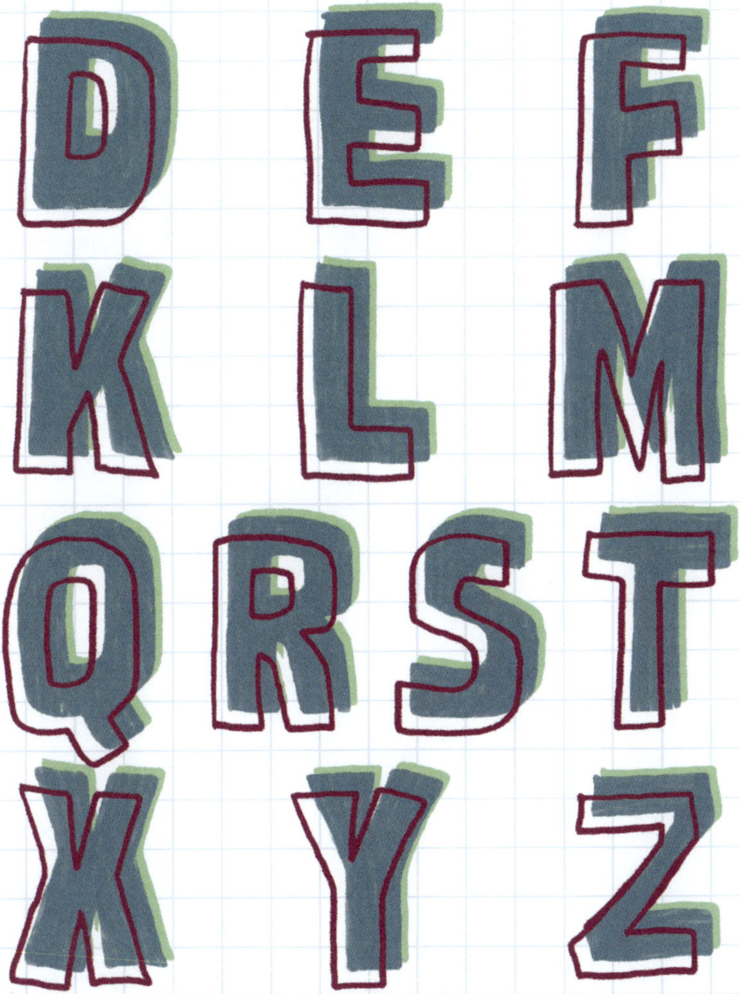
D E F
K L M
Q R S T
X Y Z

Now you try! Draw two offset block letters in different colours with the lighter shade underneath. Finish off with an outline.

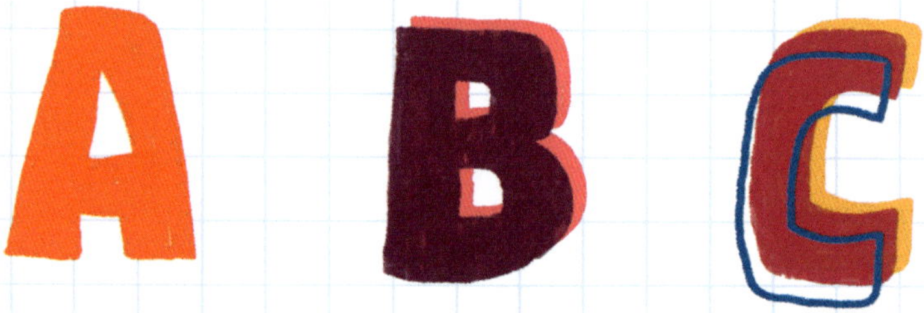

Practise with these letters. Coloured pencils or wax crayons work well with a letter outline in felt-tip pens or paint pens.

D E F

Finish drawing in the shadows being cast by the lamp.

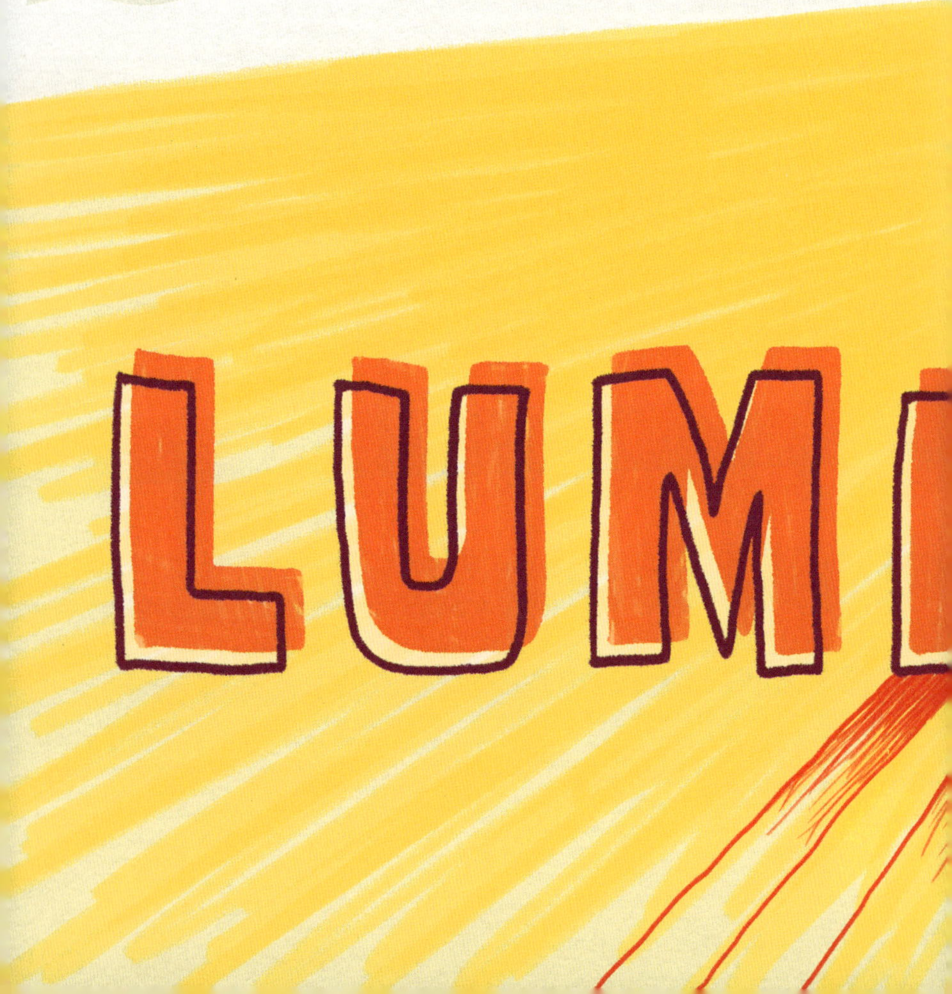

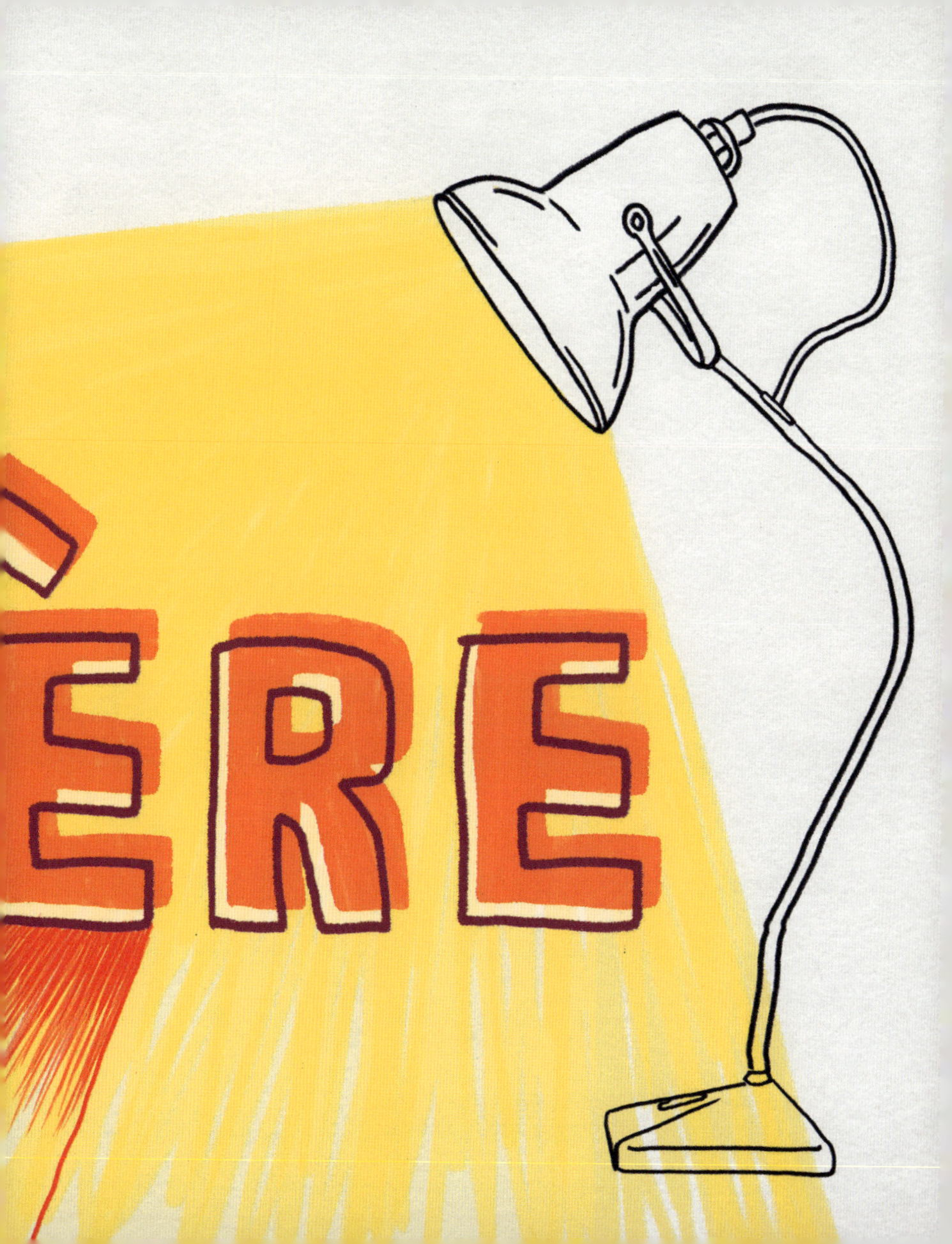
ÈRE

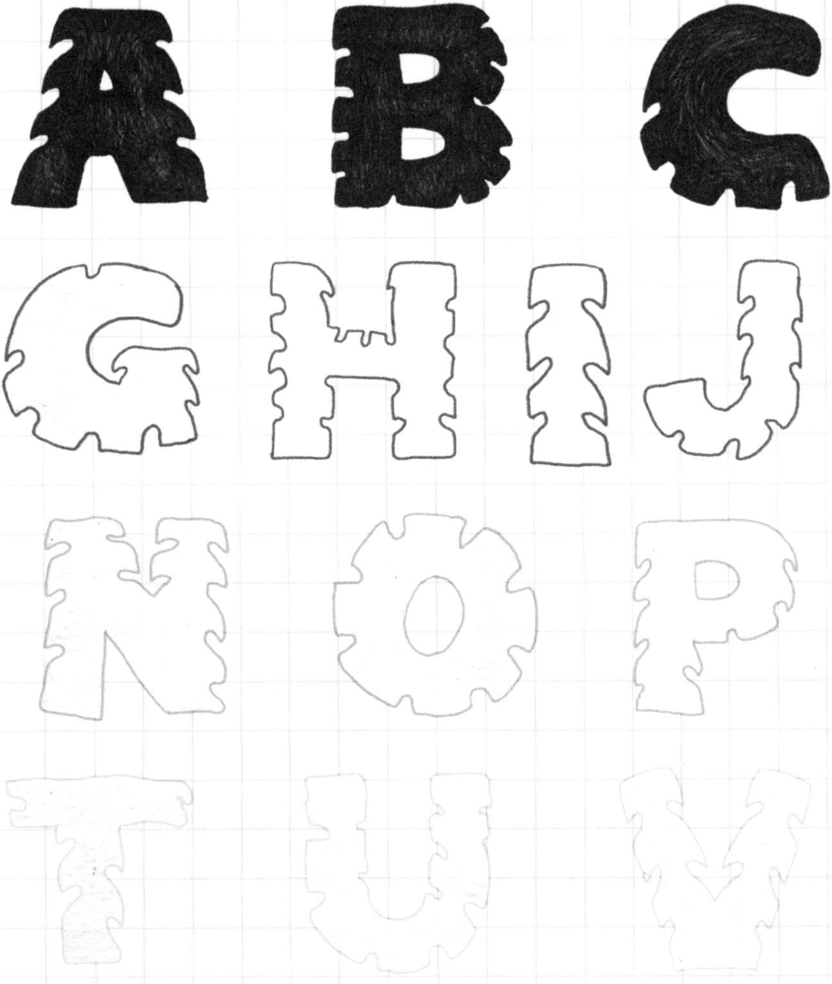

Turn basic block letters into leaves.
Finish off the empty ones above.

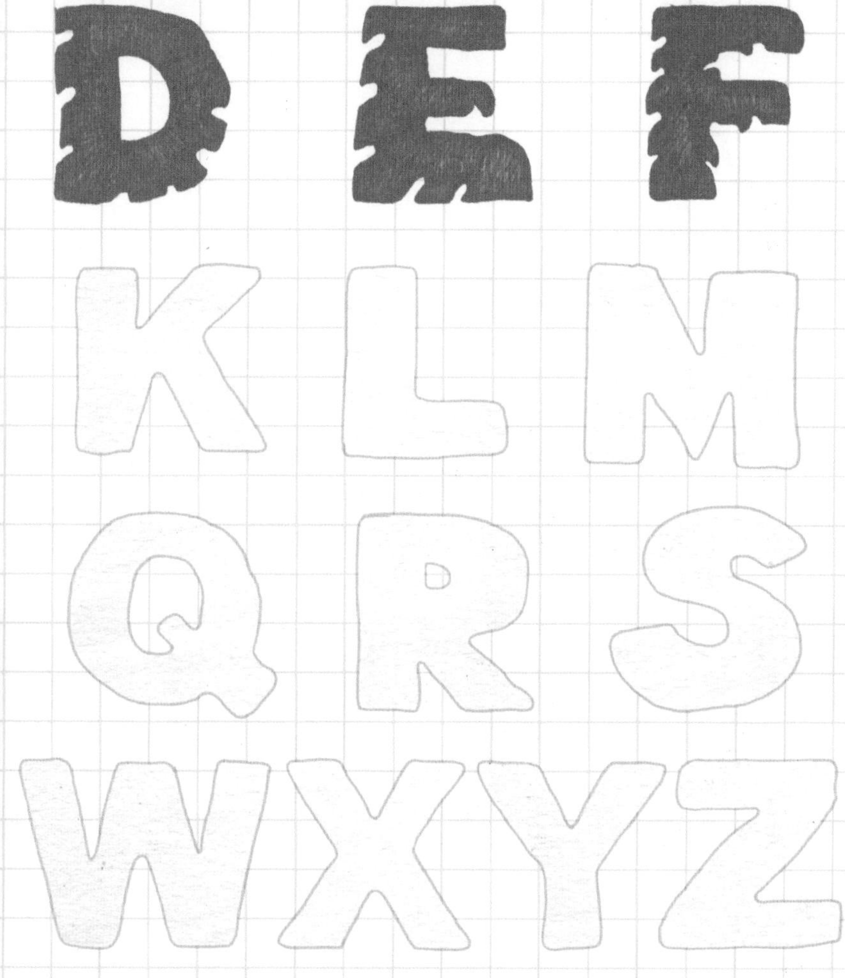
D E F
K L M
Q R S
W X Y Z

Collage block letters onto the page. Or just colour them in.

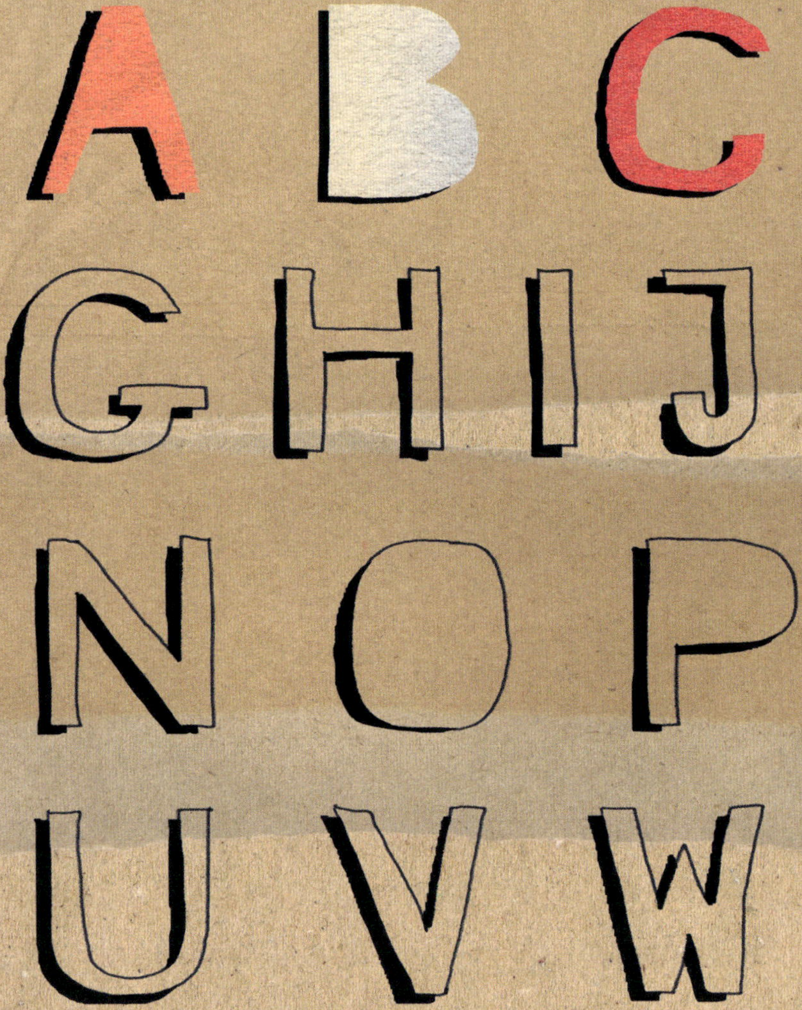

Forget about cutting out the counters (the holes inside the letters).

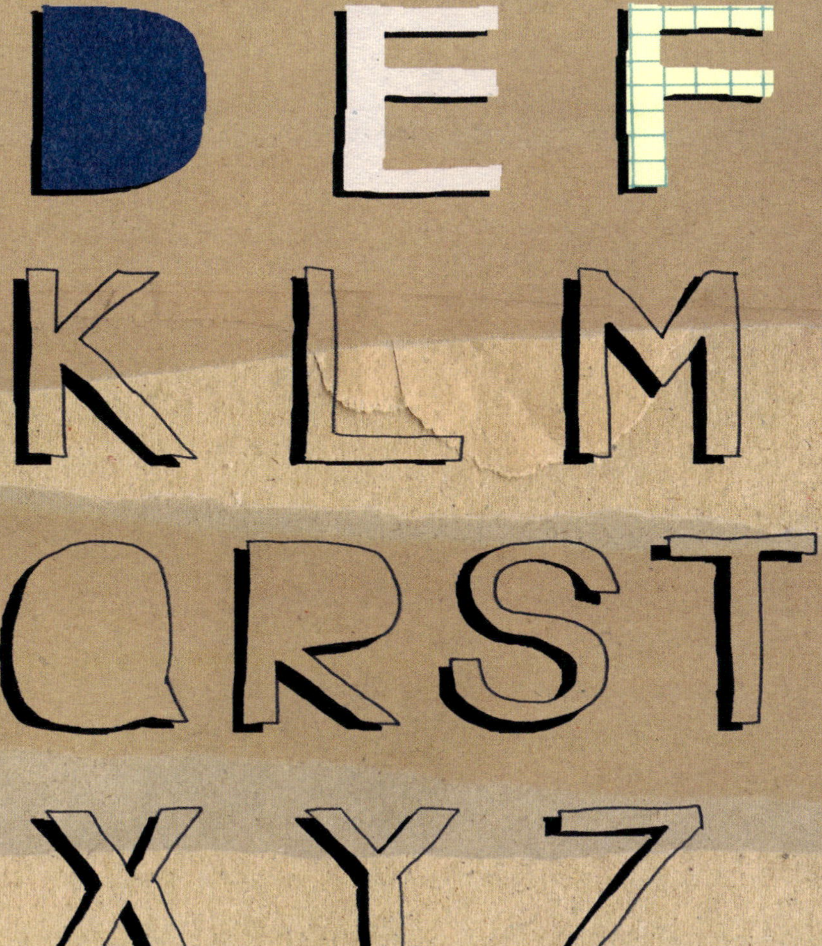

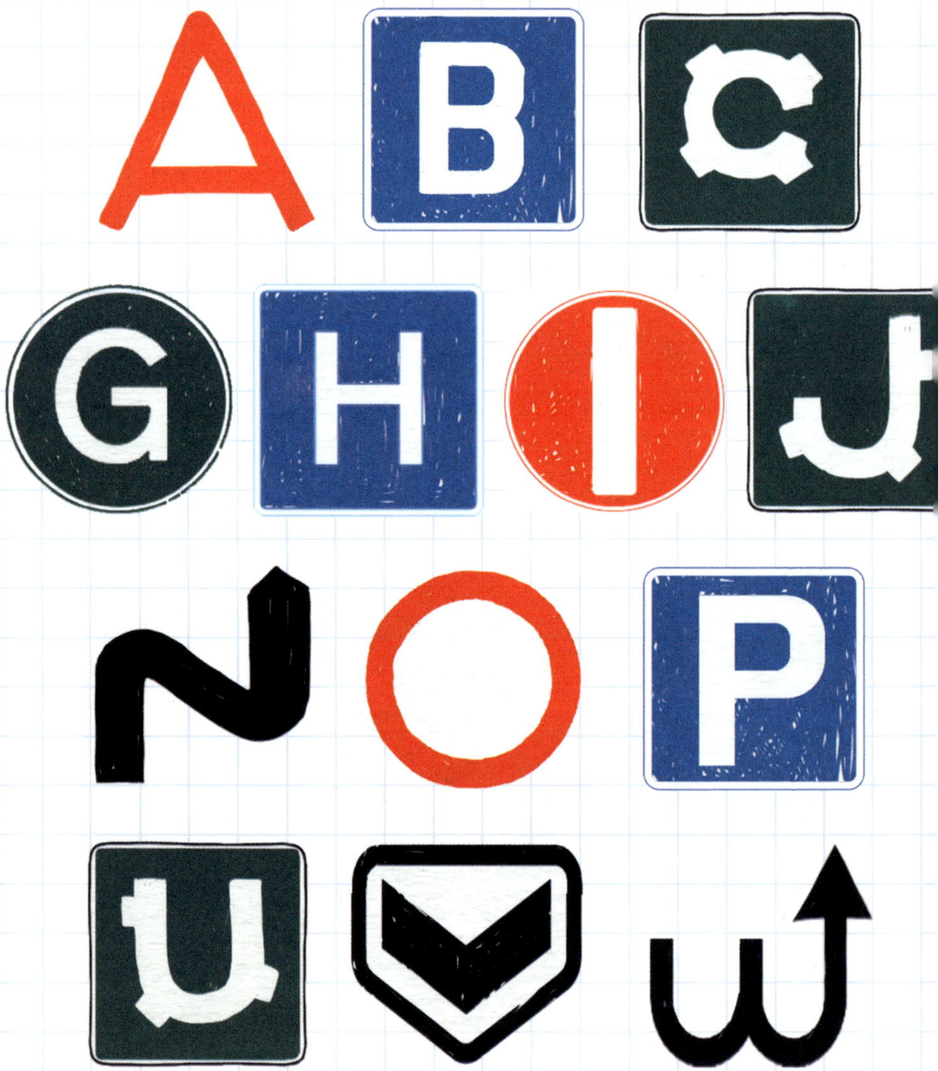
A B C
G H I J
N O P
U V W

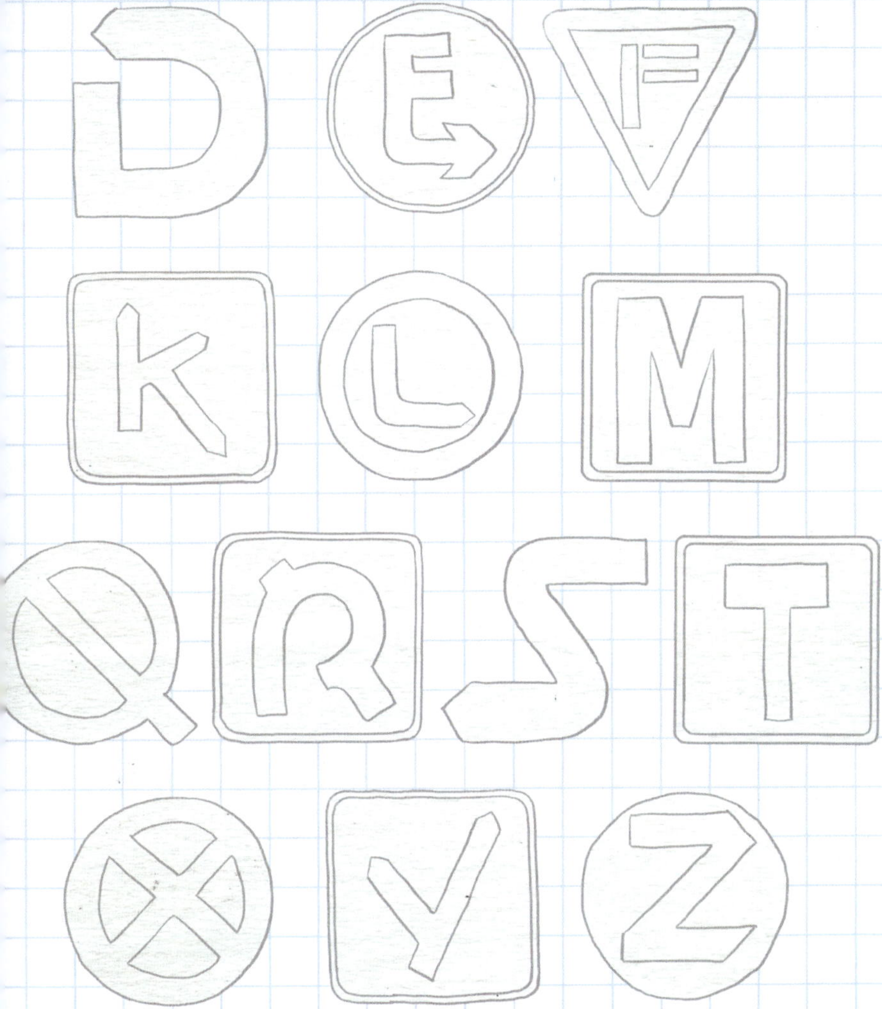

Once you really look, you'll see that block letters are all around you. Give these signs some colour.

Now try spotting them yourself, and draw them here.

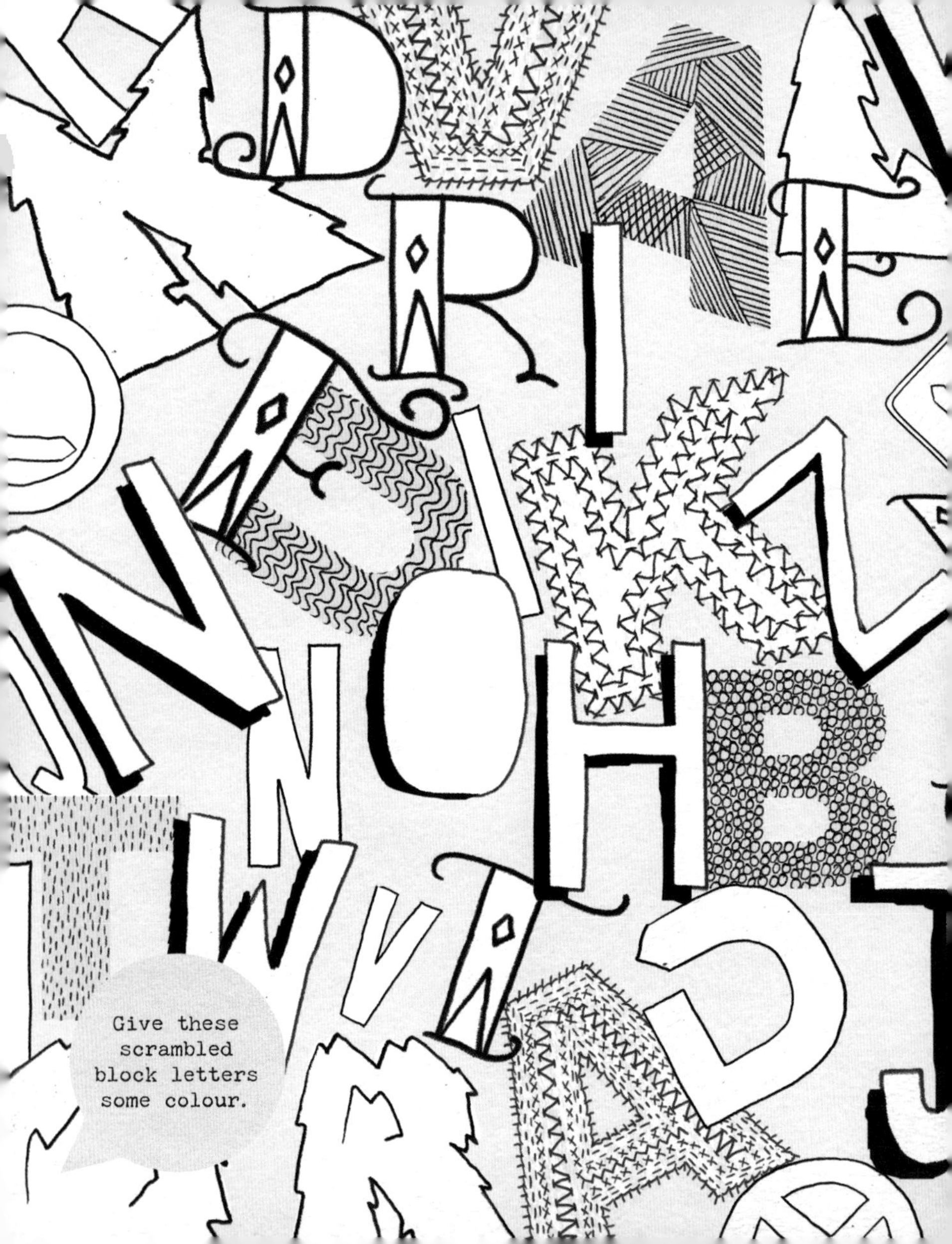
Give these
scrambled
block letters
some colour.

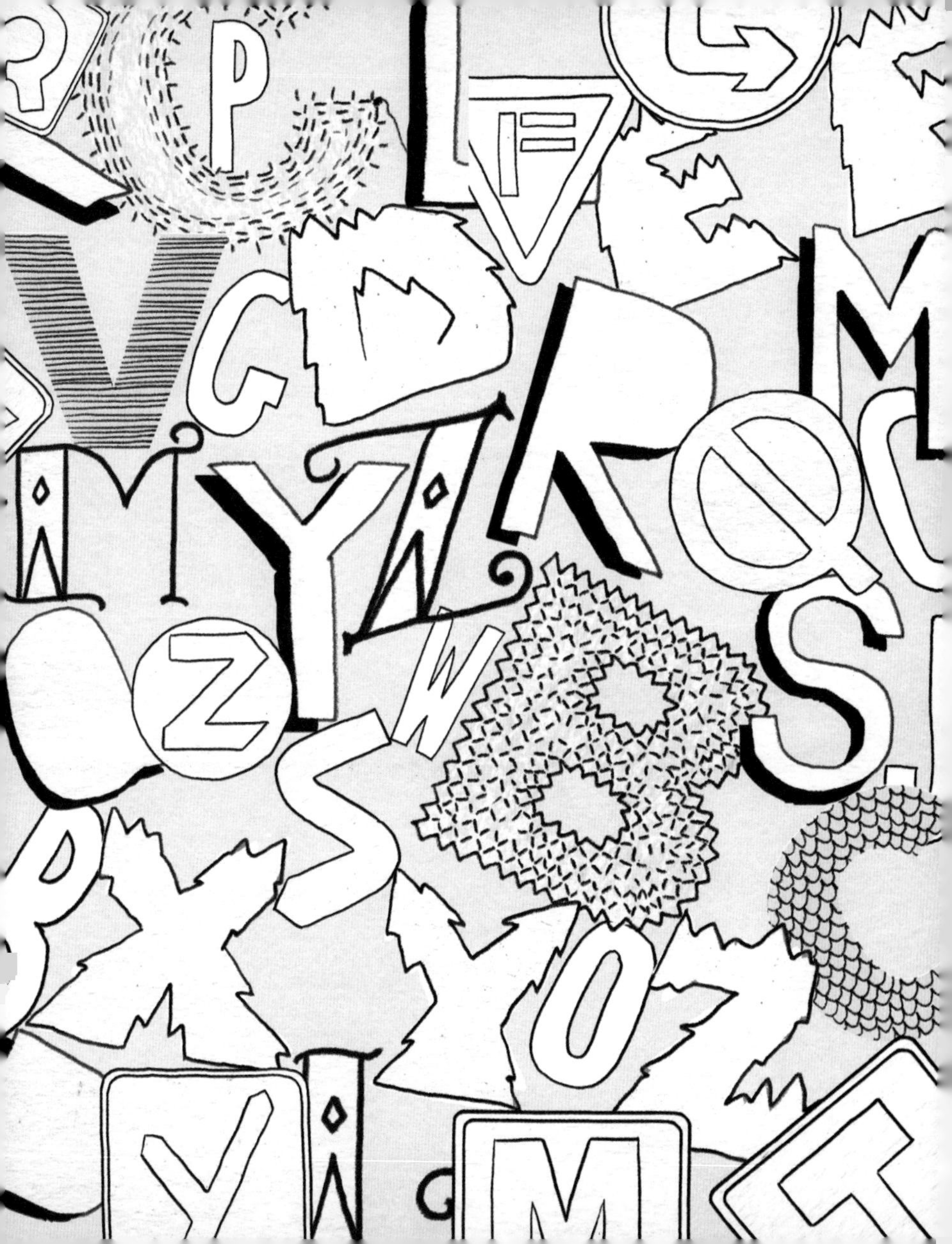

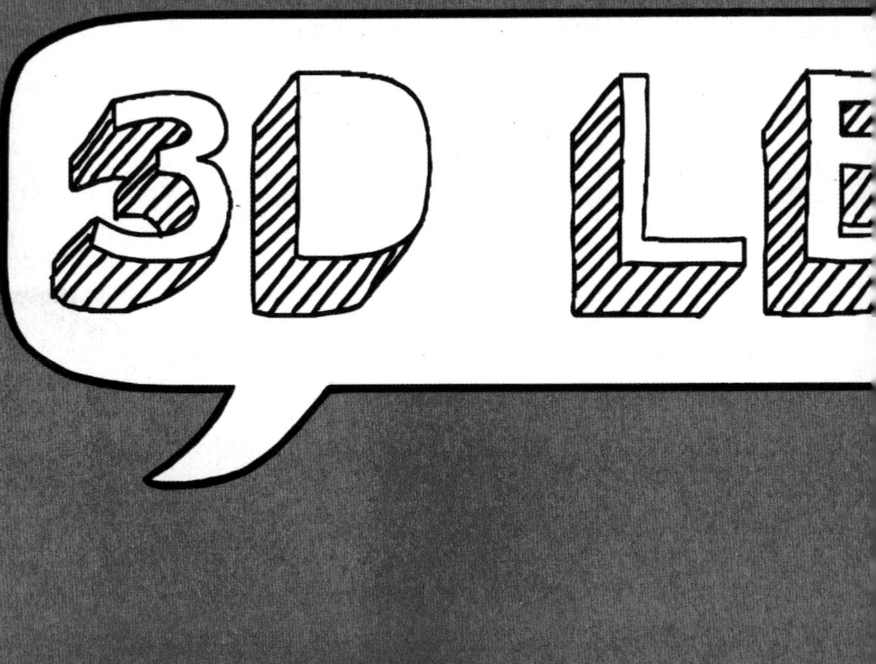
3D LE

TTERS

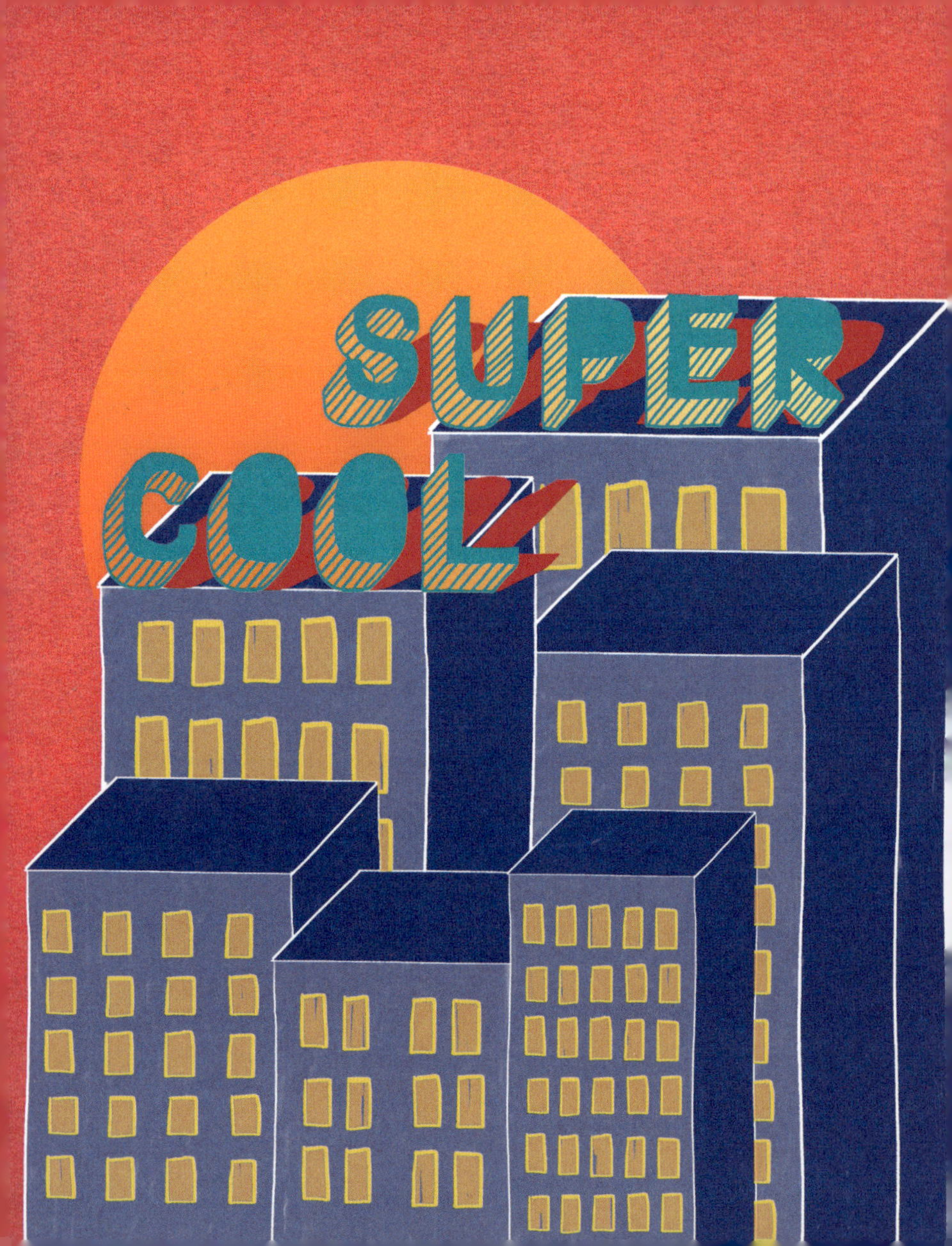
SUPER
COOL

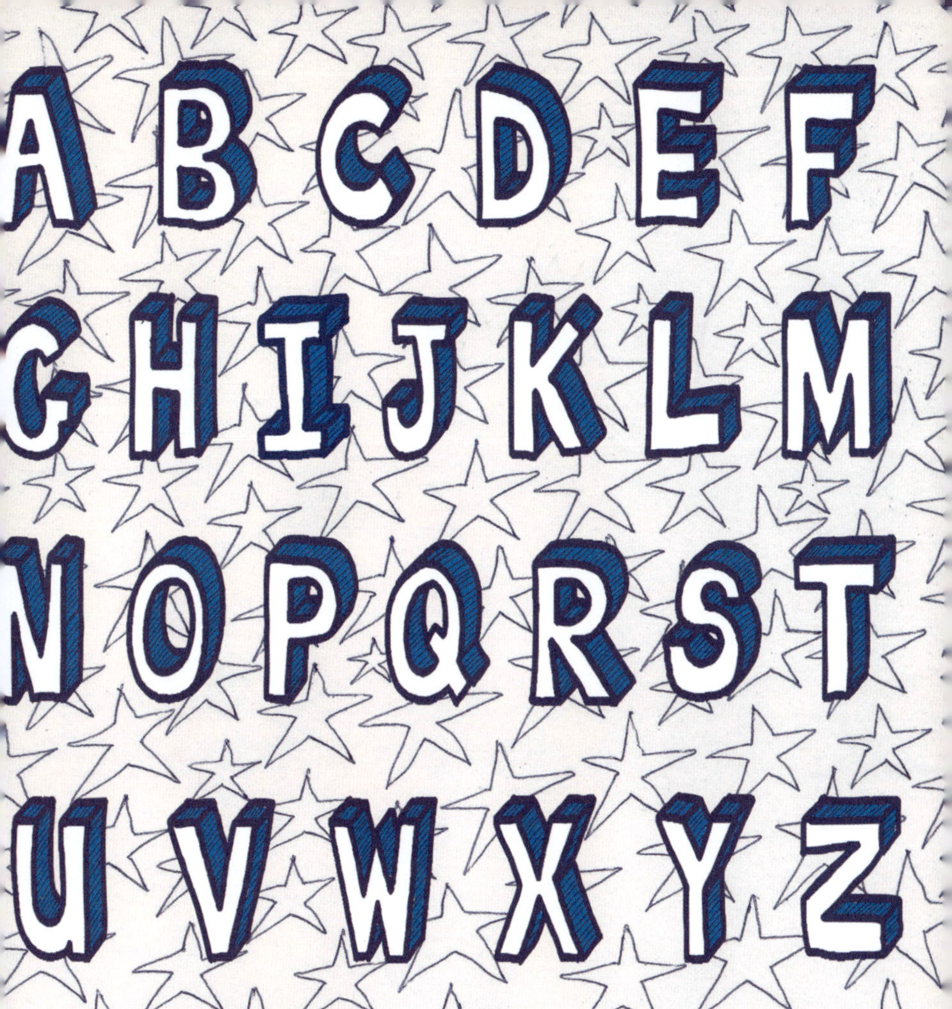

3D letters are magic! Turn over to find out how to draw this basic alphabet.

Draw a basic block letter, then add a diagonal line going in the same direction from each 'front' corner. If there are no corners, then imagine where they could be.

Draw in the outer line and then add some stripes to emphasize the depth of the letter.

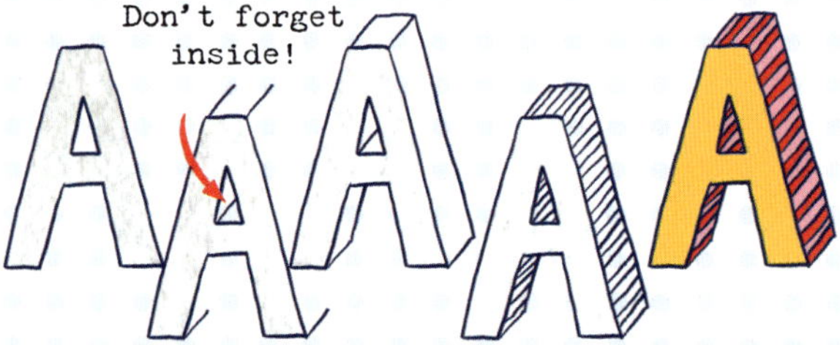

Once you have mastered the 3D technique, experiment with the thickness of the letters. You can take them in any direction and to any depth.

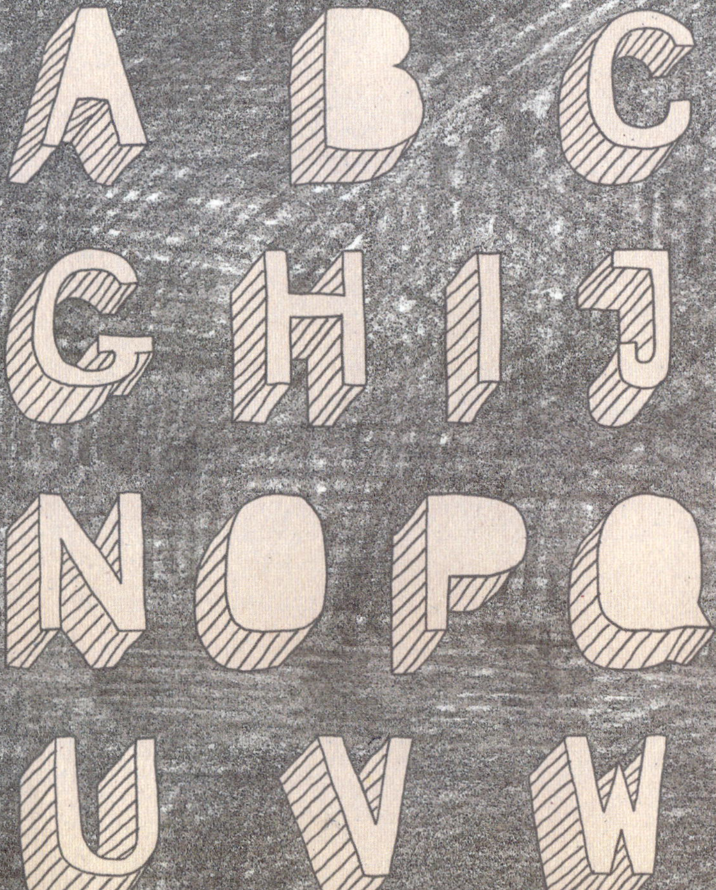

Add some colour and extra detail to this alphabet.

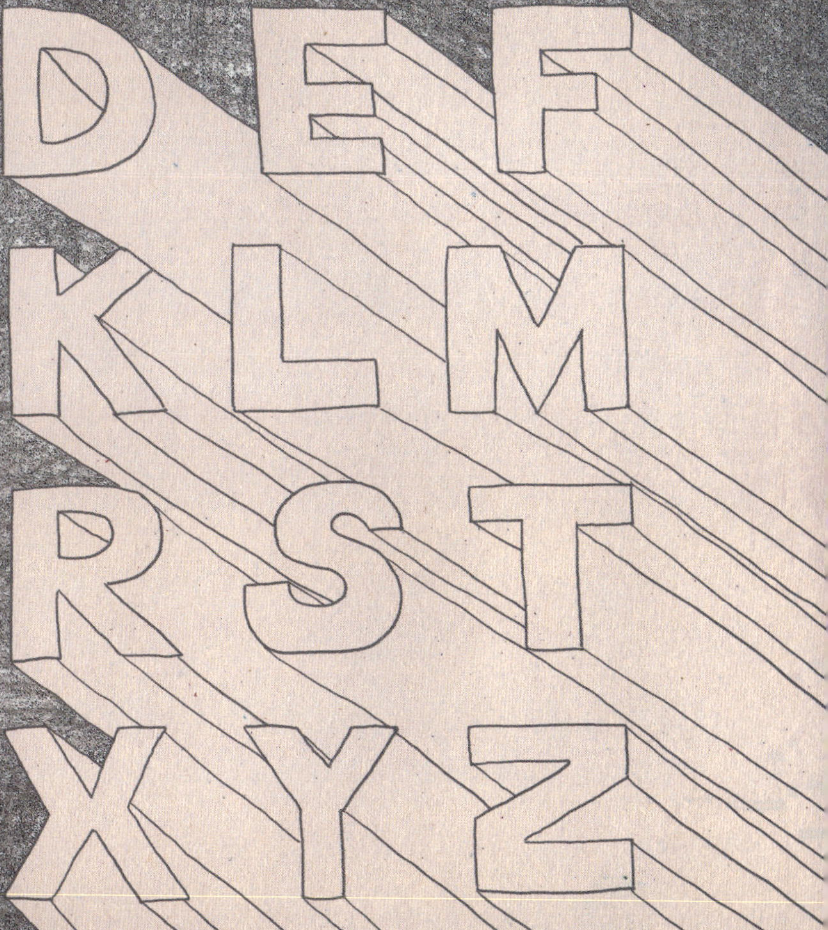

Practise some different directions for your 3D letters here. How DEEP can you go?

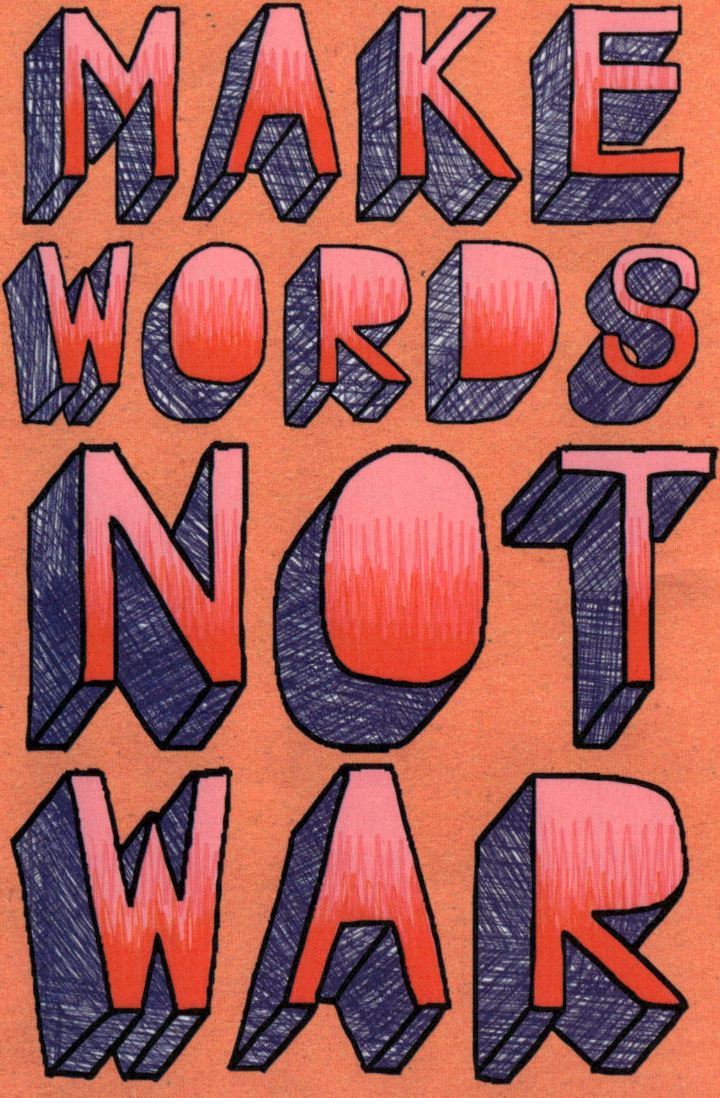
MAKE
WORDS
NOT
WAR

GO

Remember
that your
words
matter.

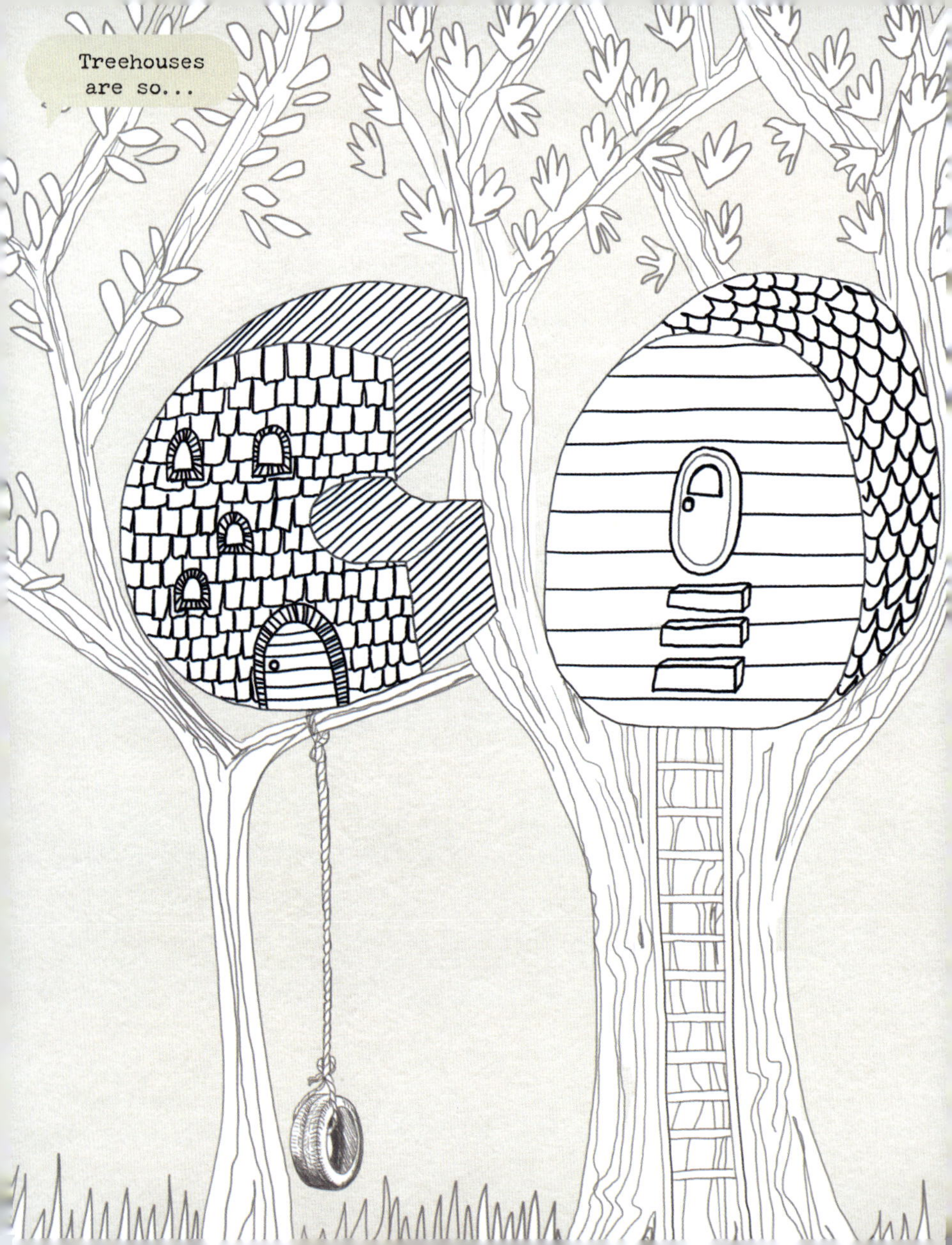
Treehouses
are so...

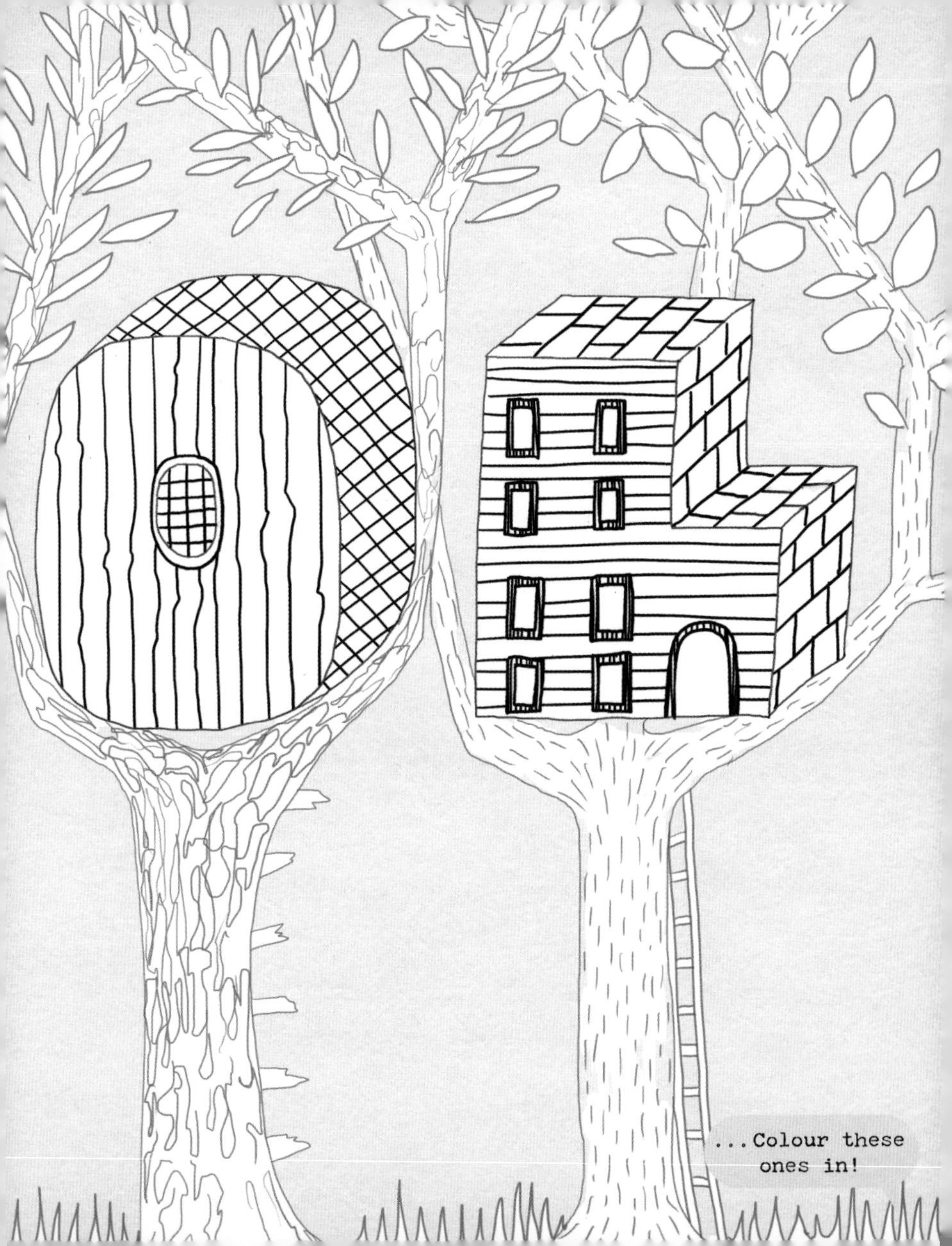
...Colour these
ones in!

Turn 3D block letters into rock letters by giving them texture, cracks and crevices. Fill in the blanks.

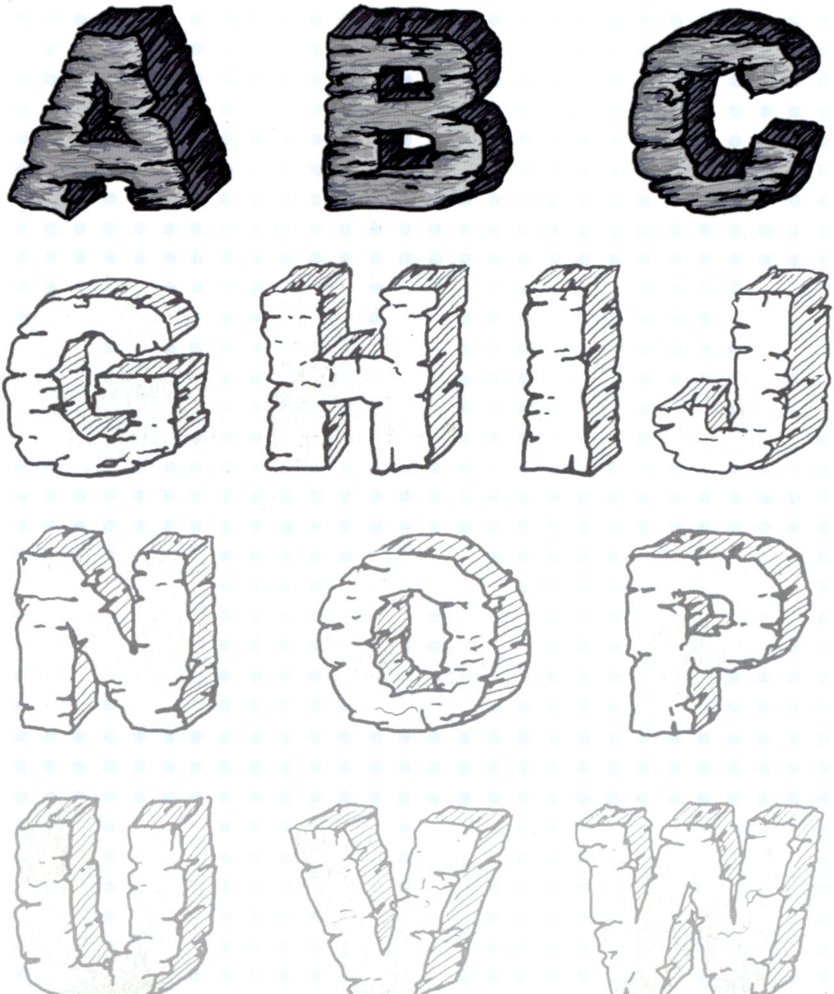

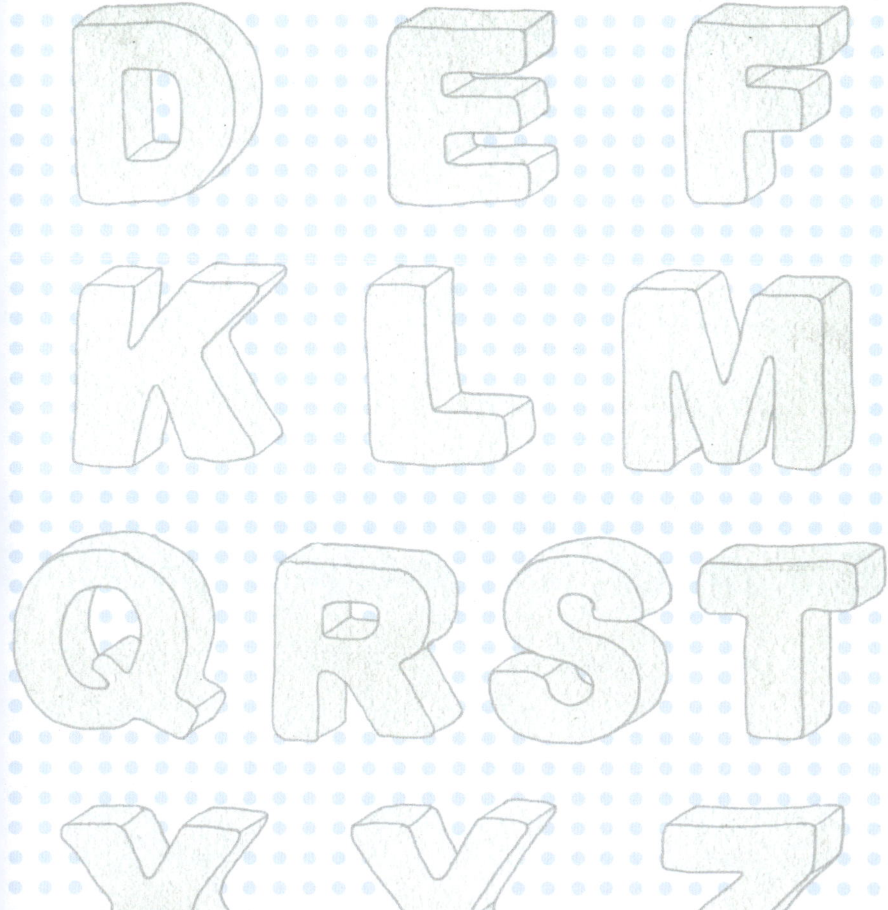
D E F
K L M
Q R S T
X Y Z

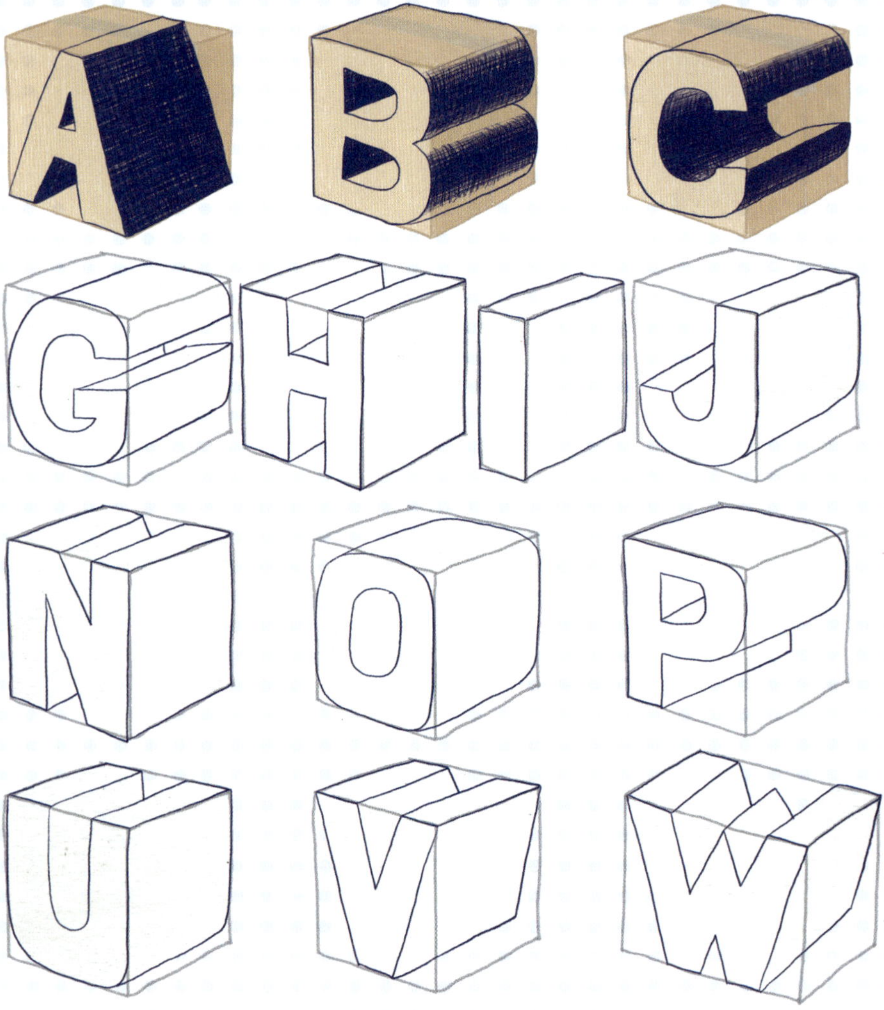

Imagine your 3D letter sitting inside a box.
Finish these ones off with a ballpoint pen.

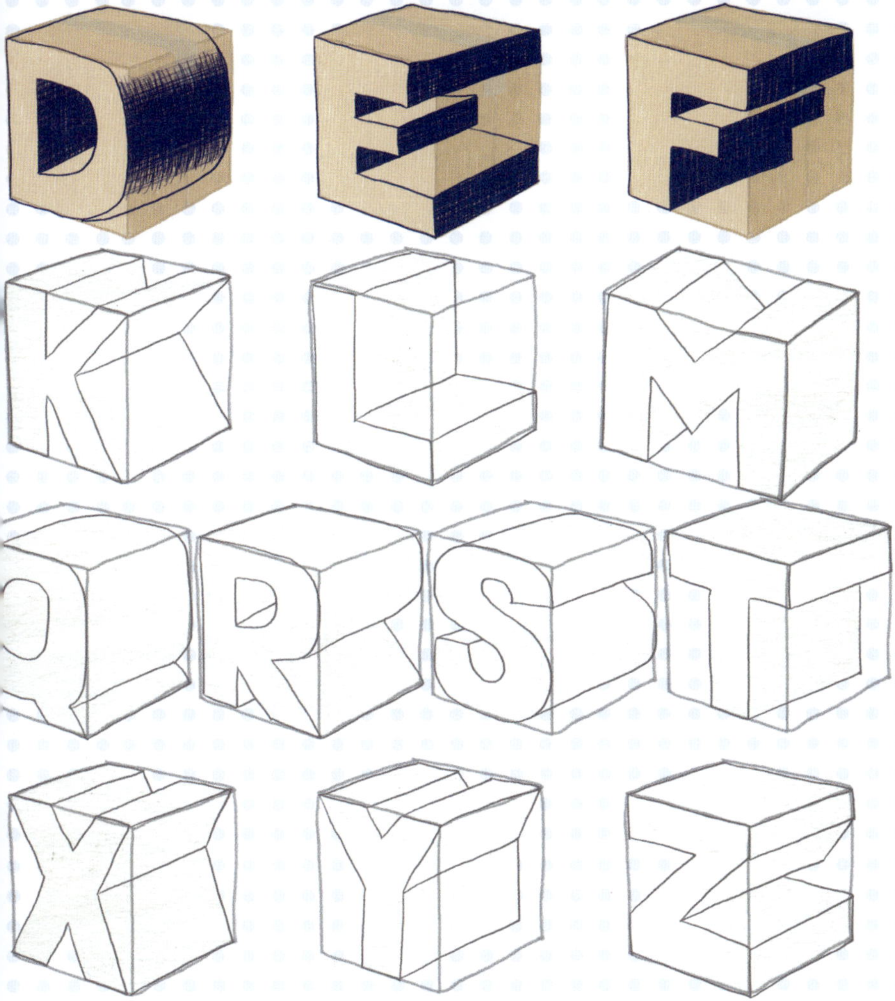
D E F
K L M
Q R S T
X Y Z

Draw your 3D letters into the empty boxes: supersize or tiny – you decide.

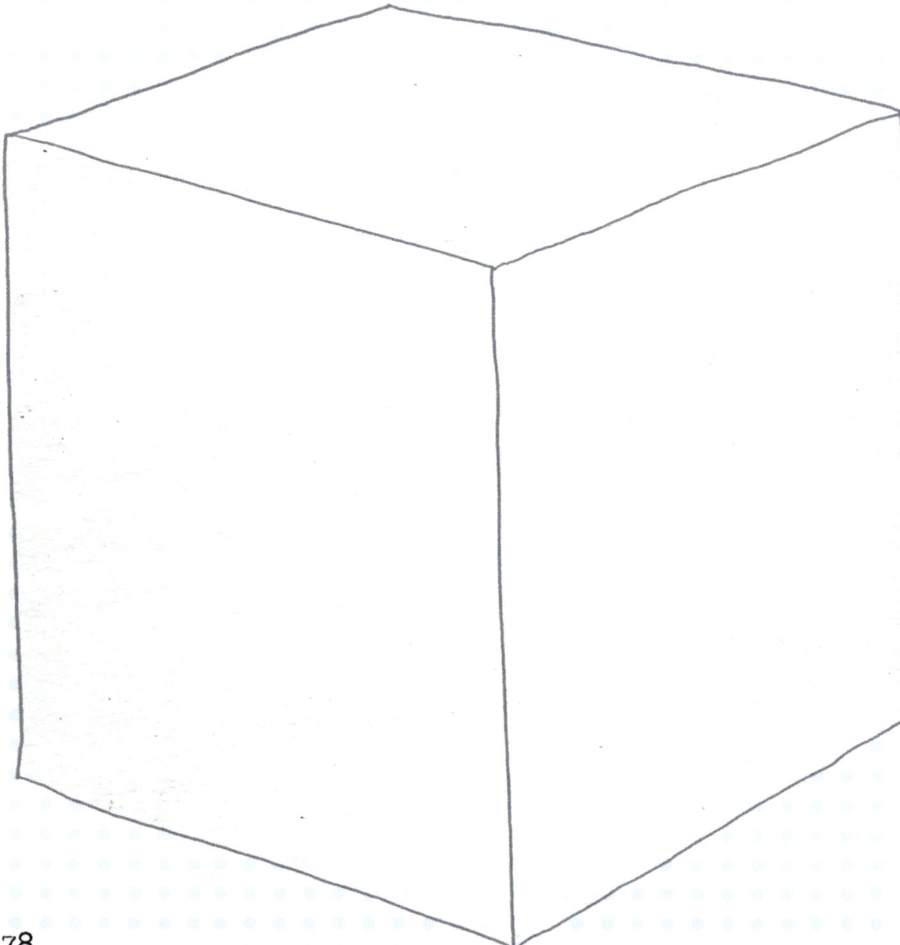

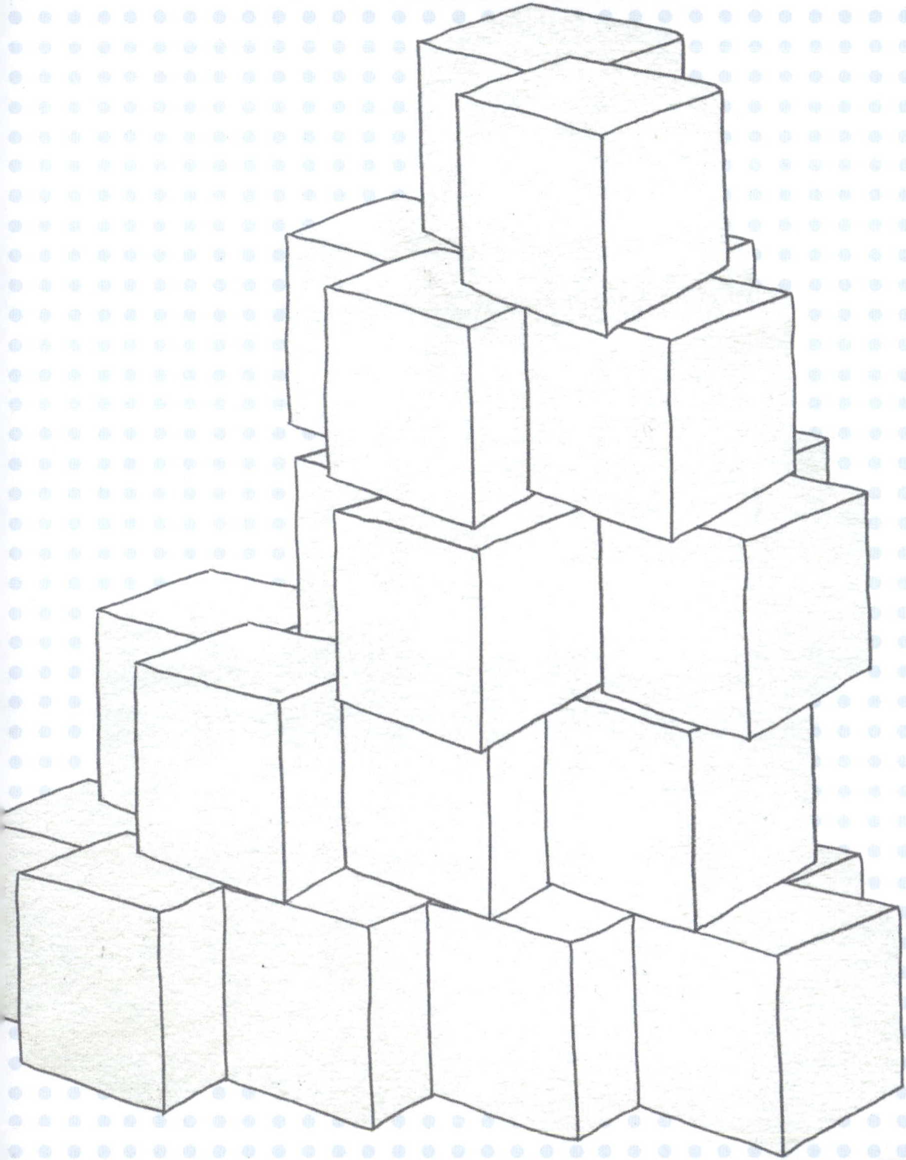

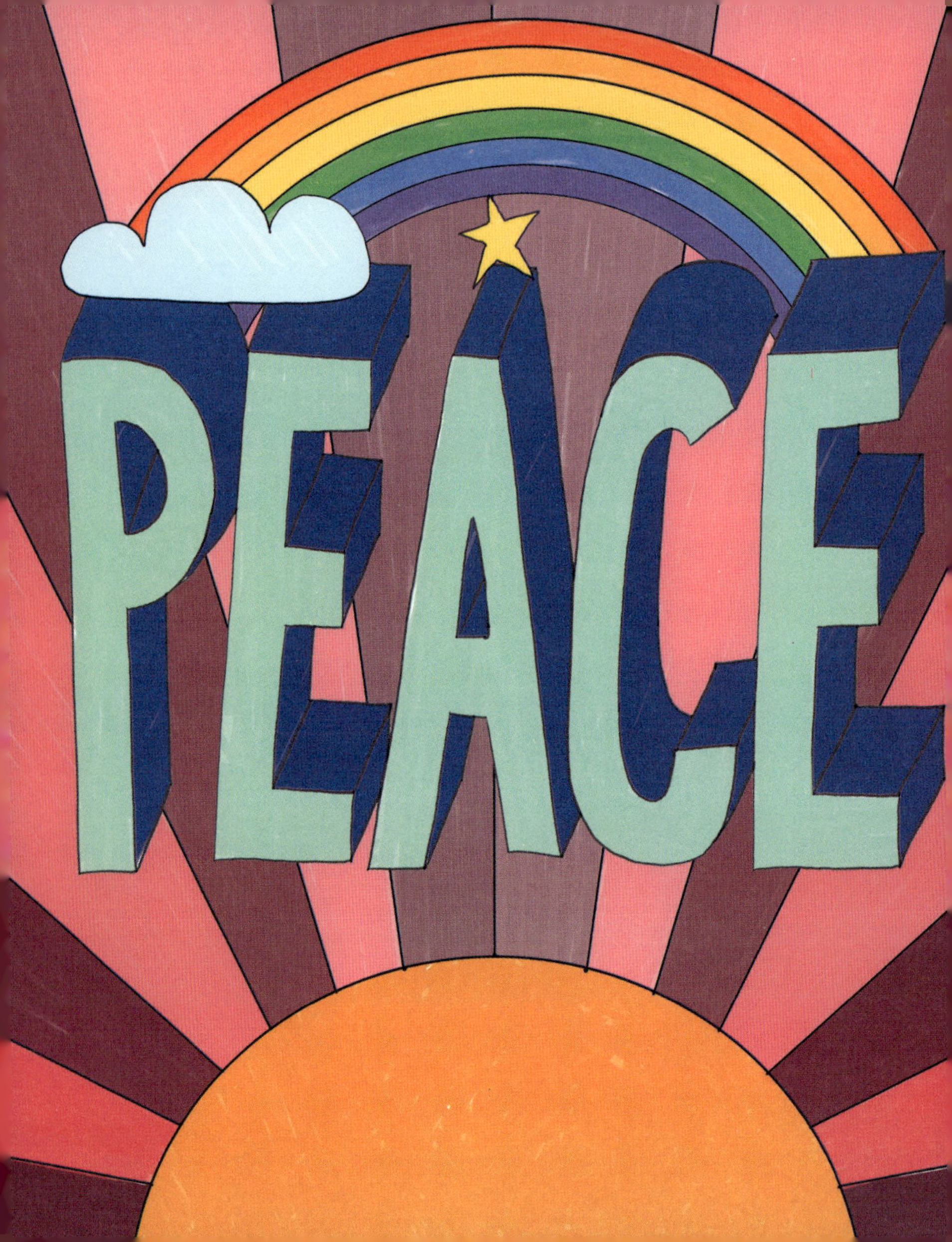
PEACE

Colour me in!

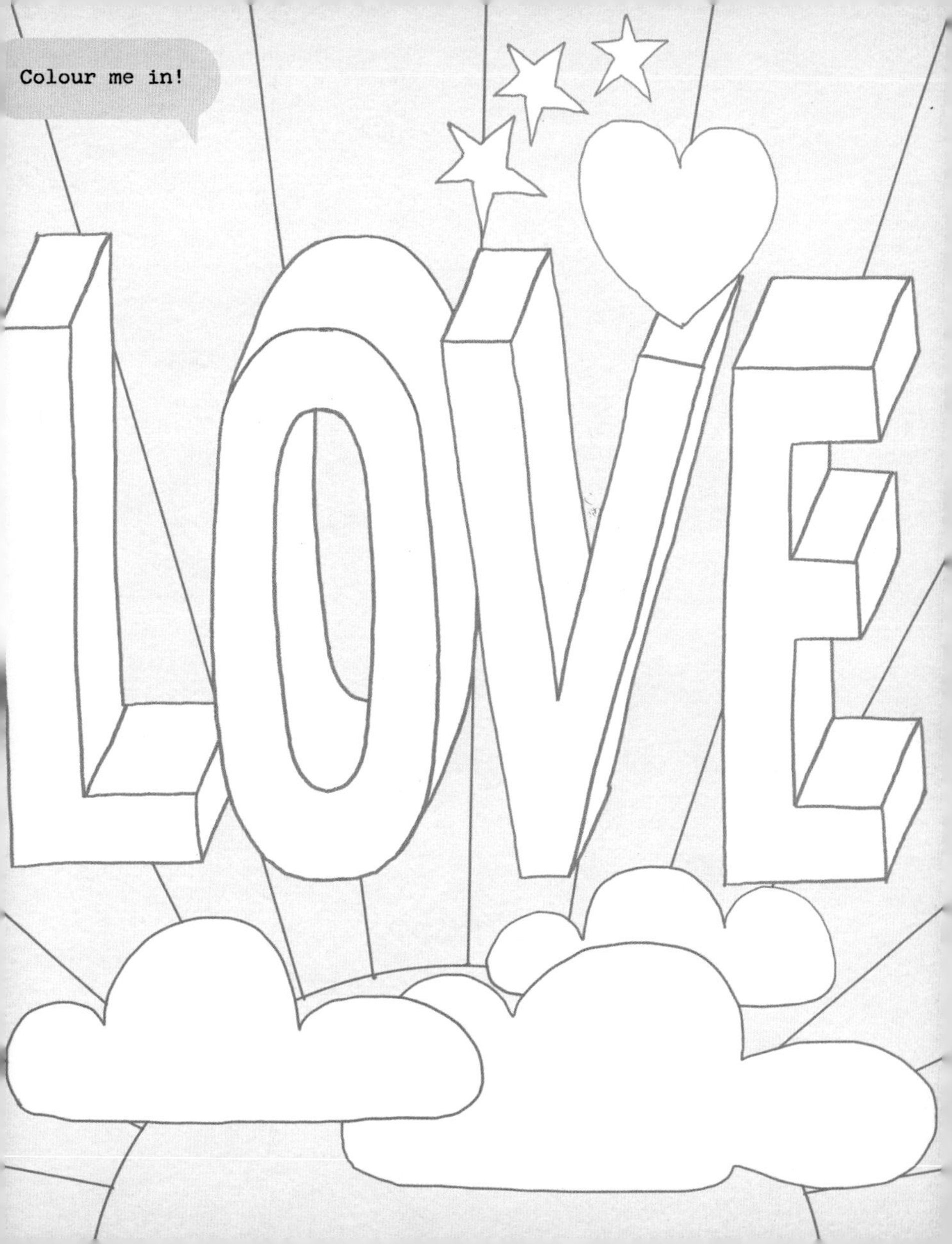

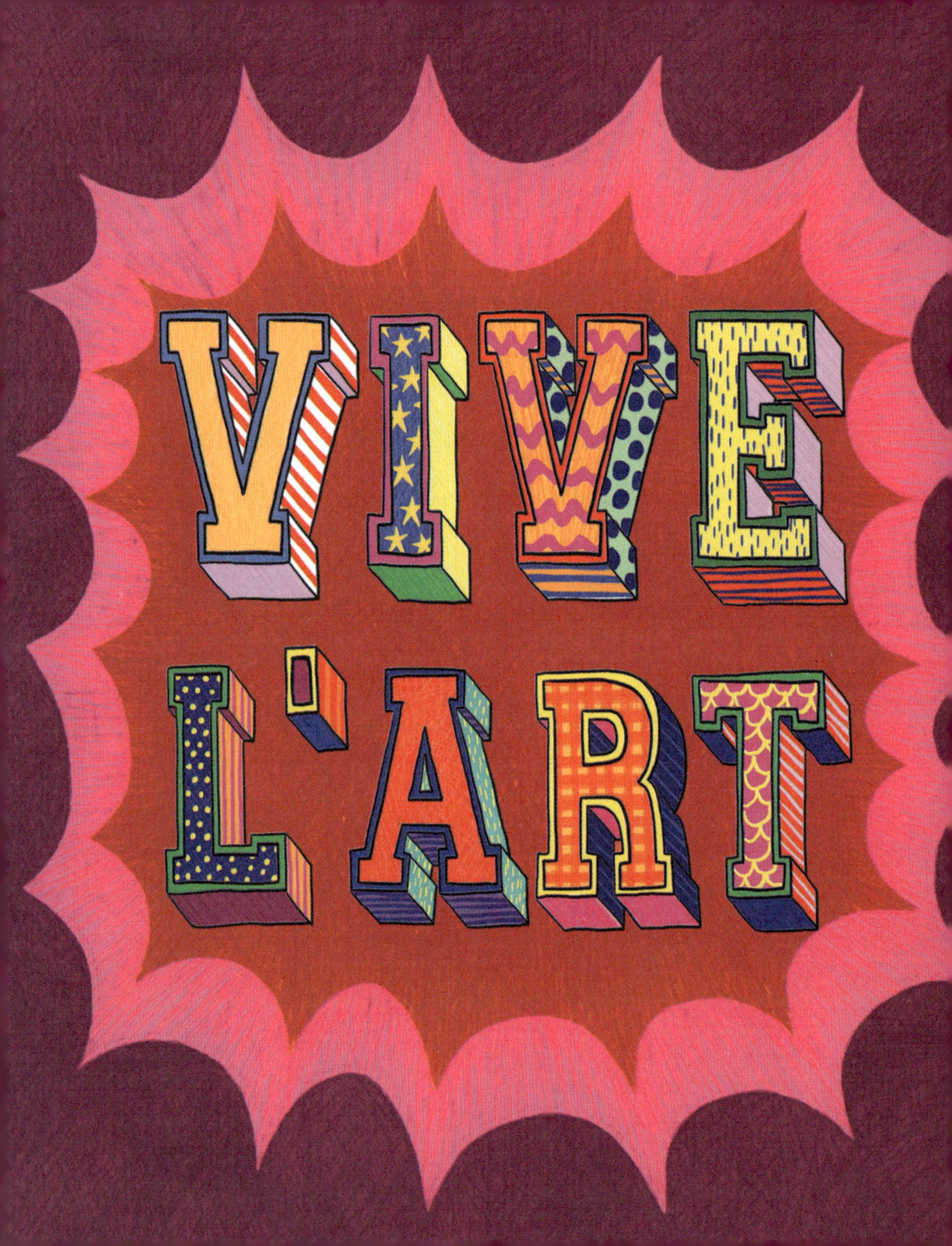
VIVE
L'ART

A page for patterns

Practise your patterns here.

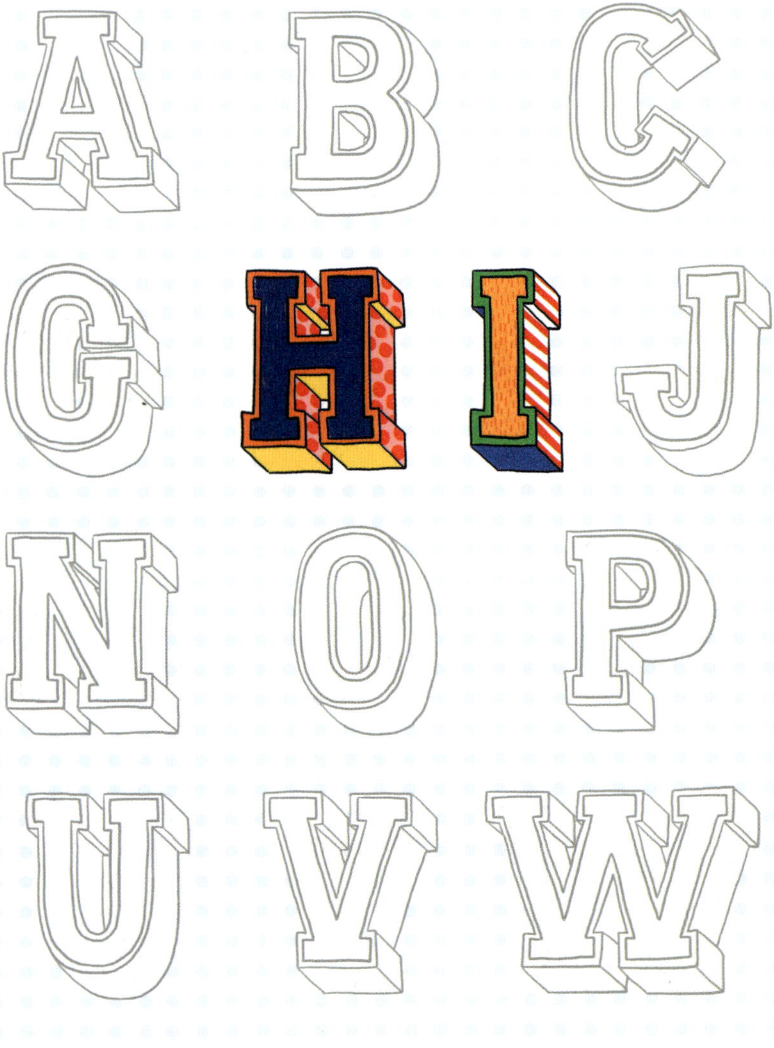
A B C
G H I J
N O P
U V W

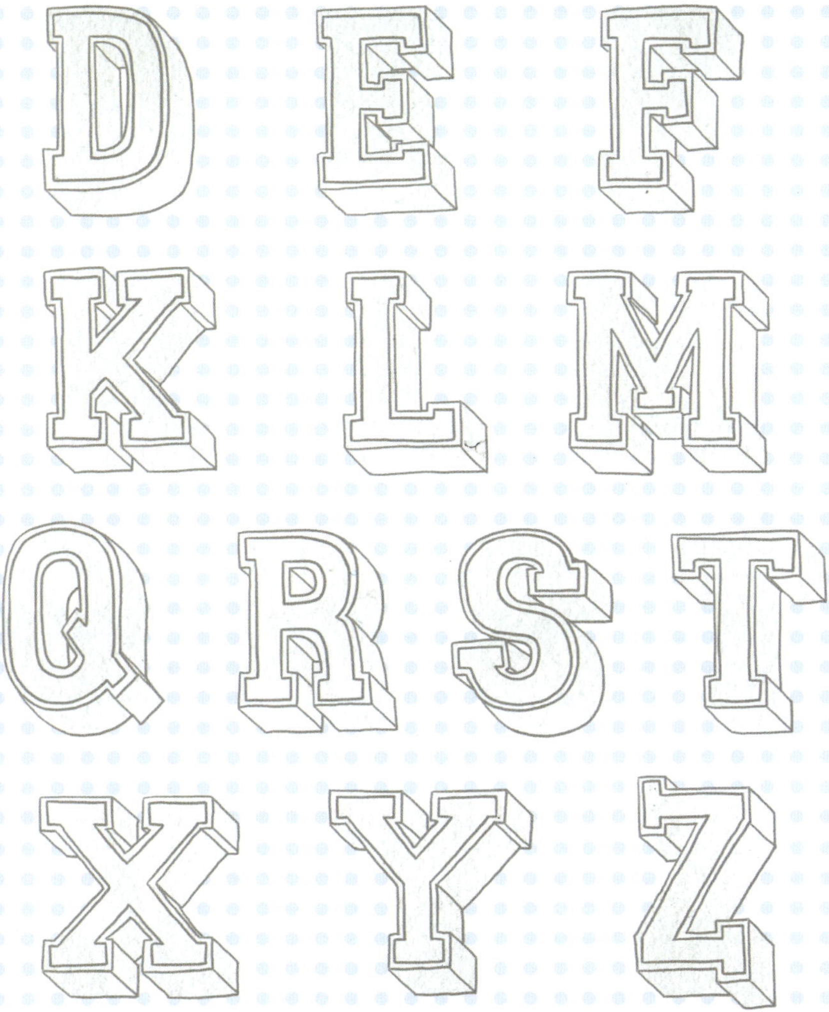

Go crazy for colour and pattern. Fill in the blanks and make each letter unique.

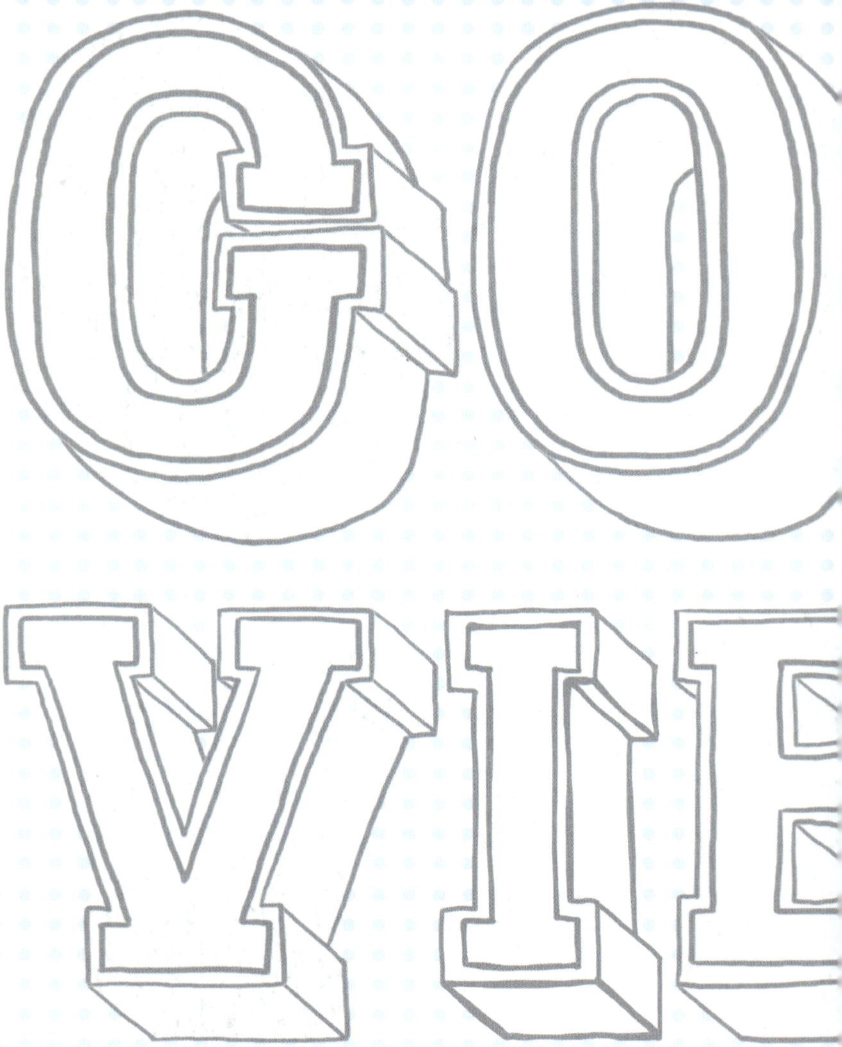

Scale up your pattern prowess and
showcase your favourite fills.

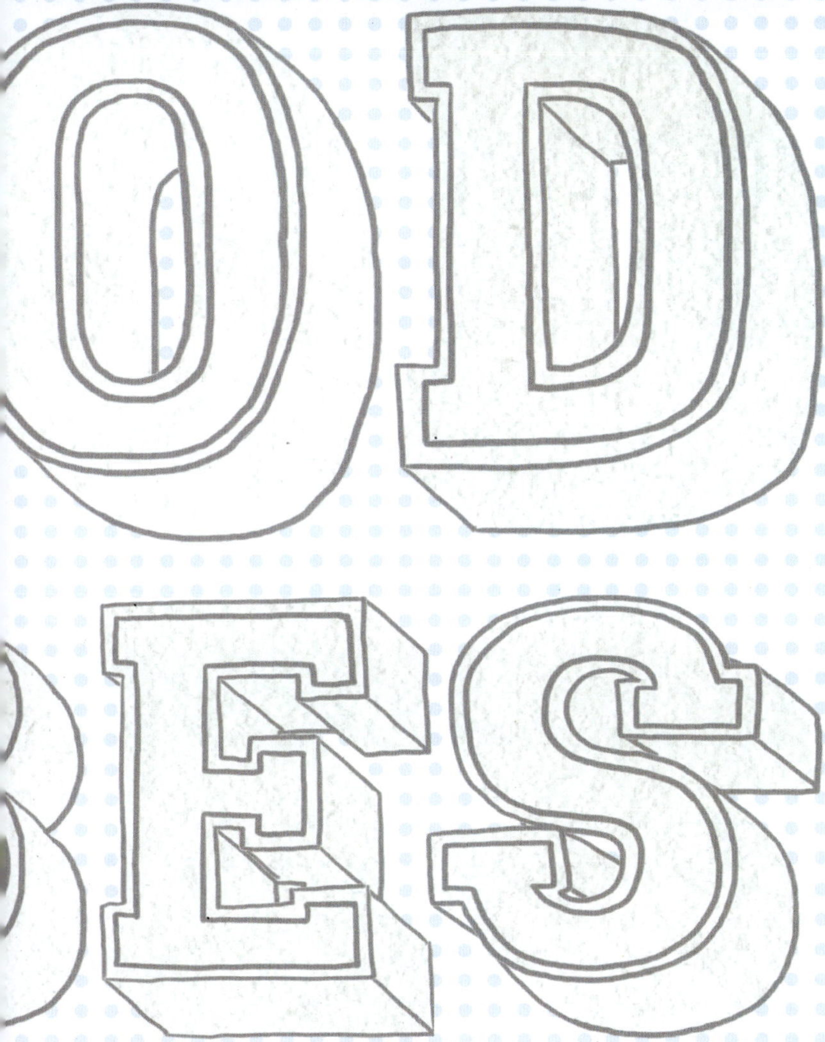
OD
ES

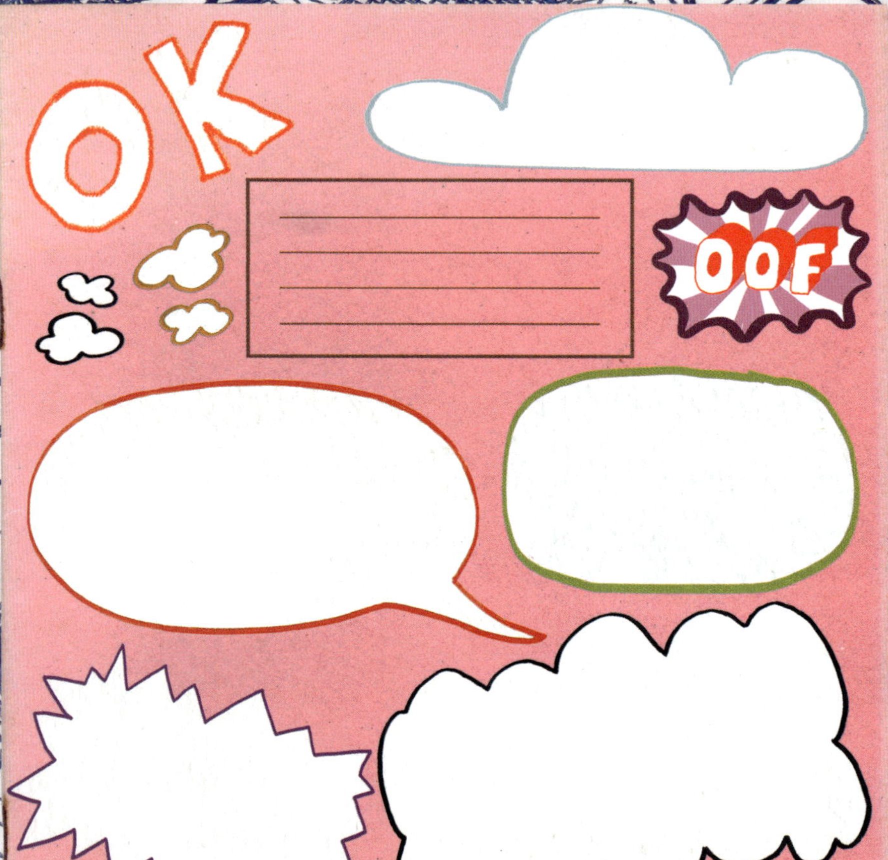

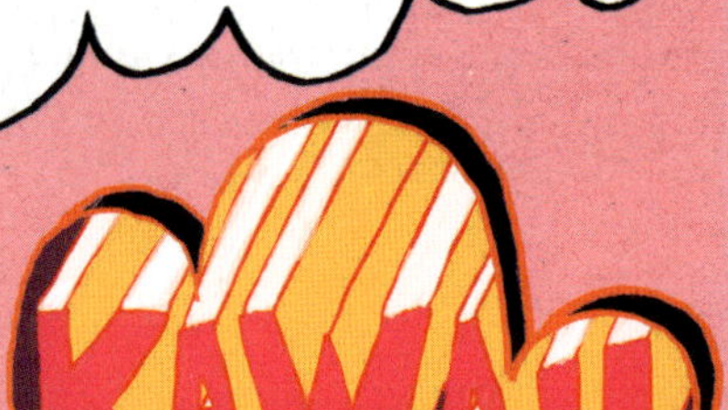

It's doodle time! Add some words of your own to these blank stickers and try using chalk pens if you have them.

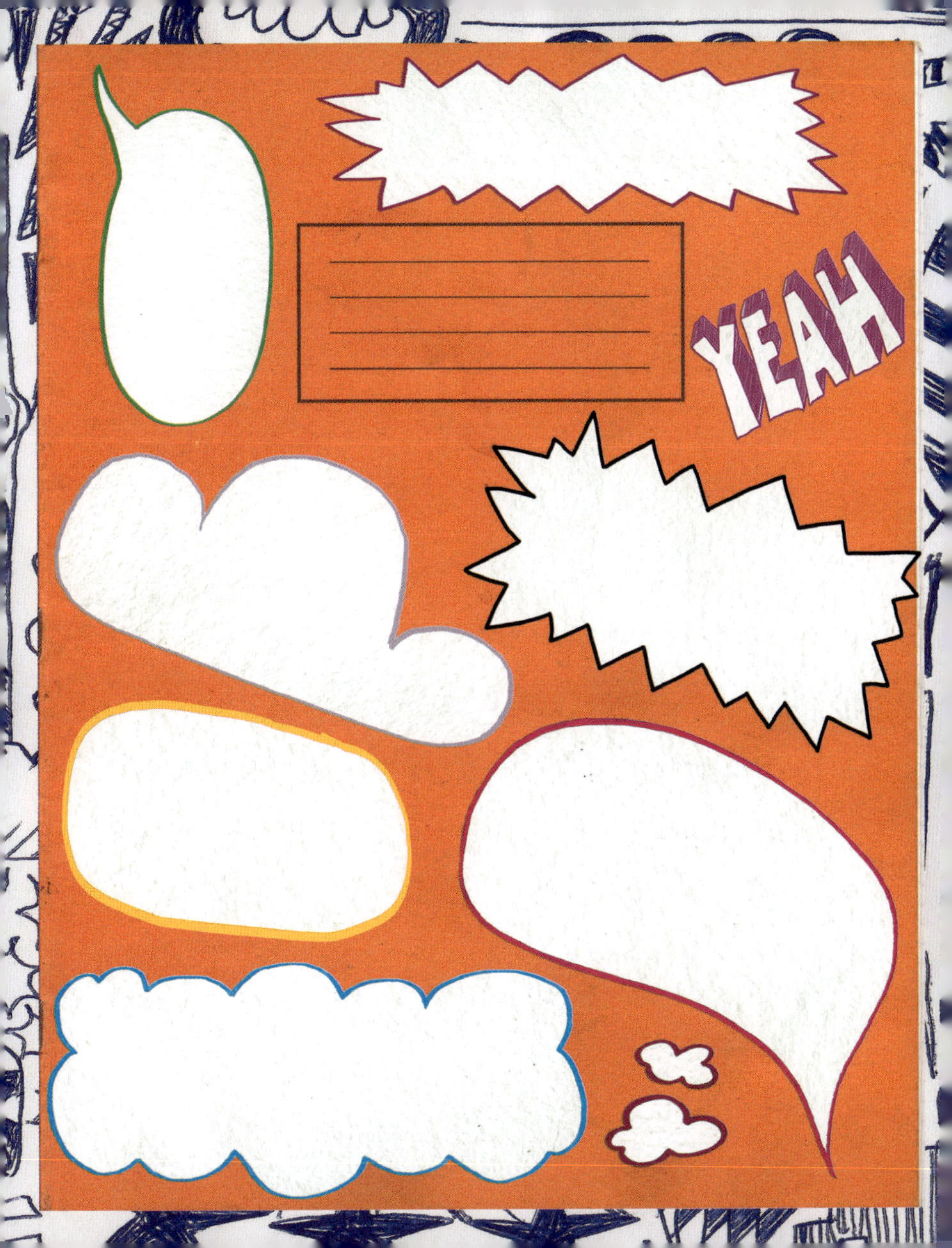
YEAH

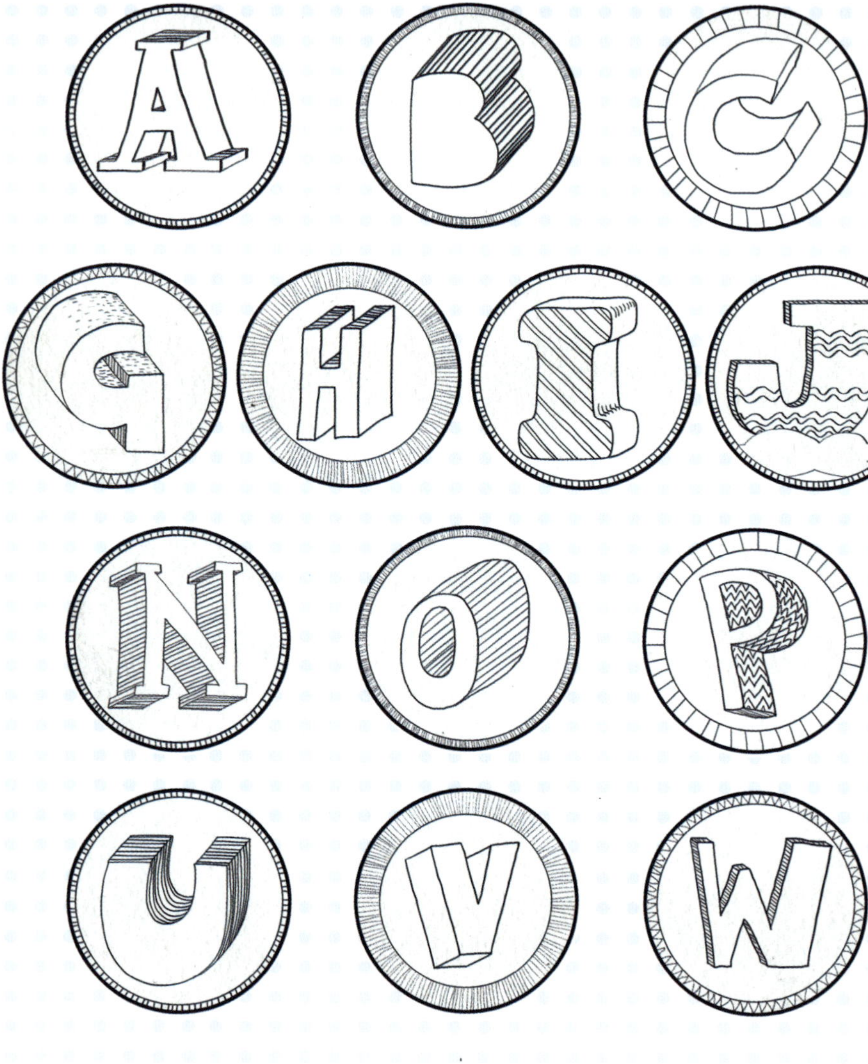
A
B
C
G
H
I
J
N
O
P
U
V
W

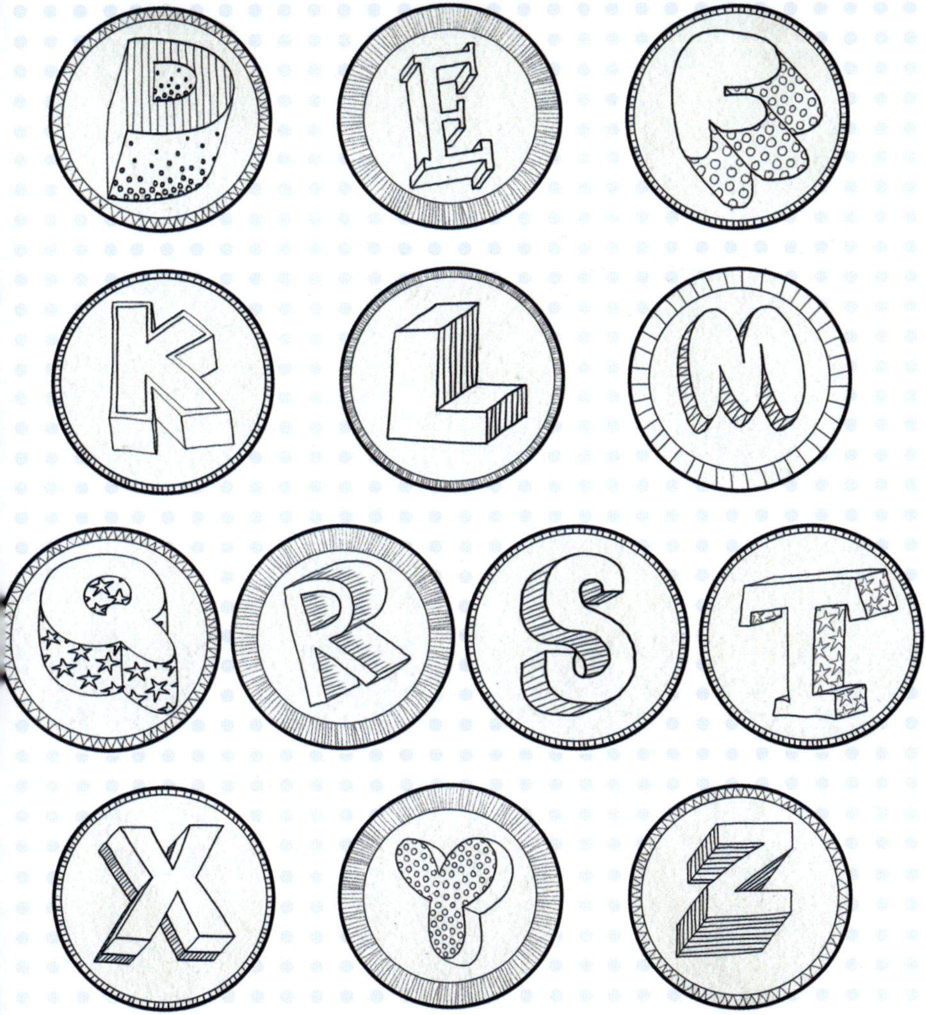

3D letters make great embroidered patches. Colour in this page of intricate initials.

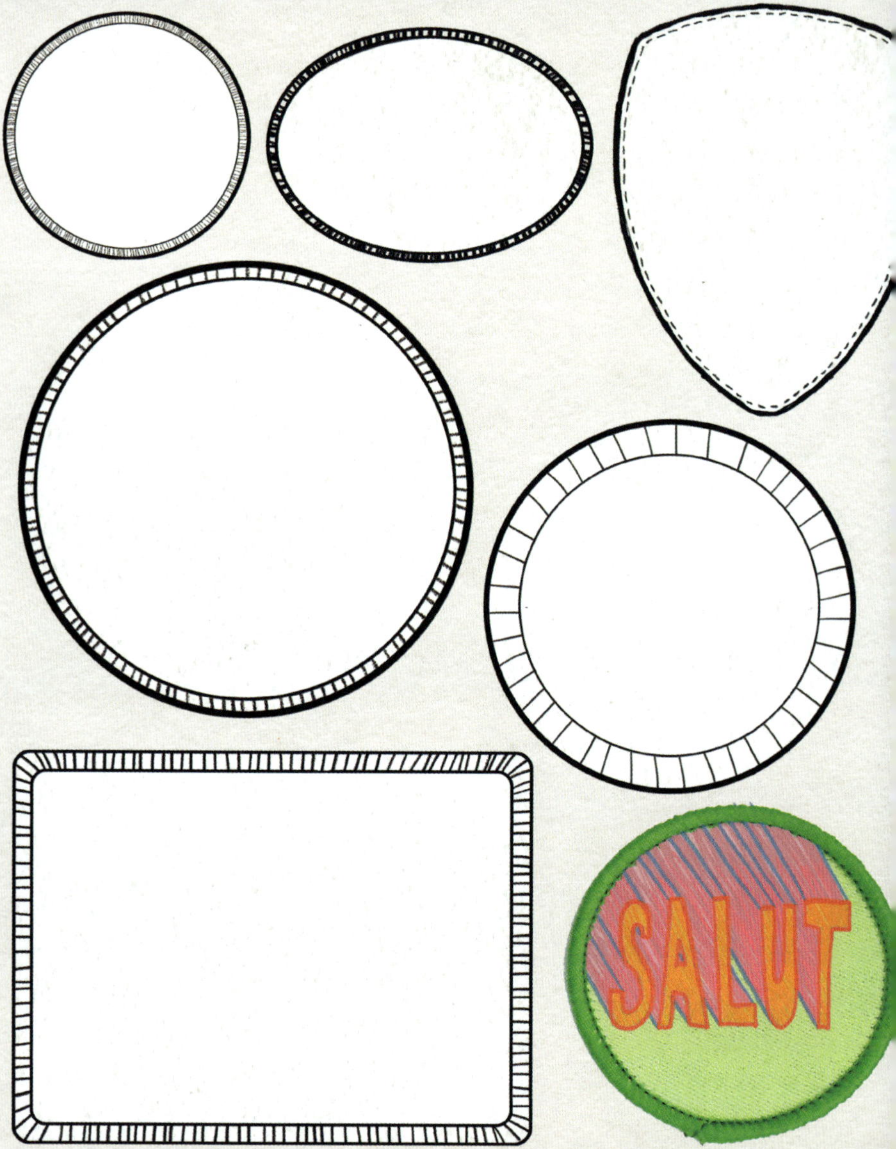
SALUT

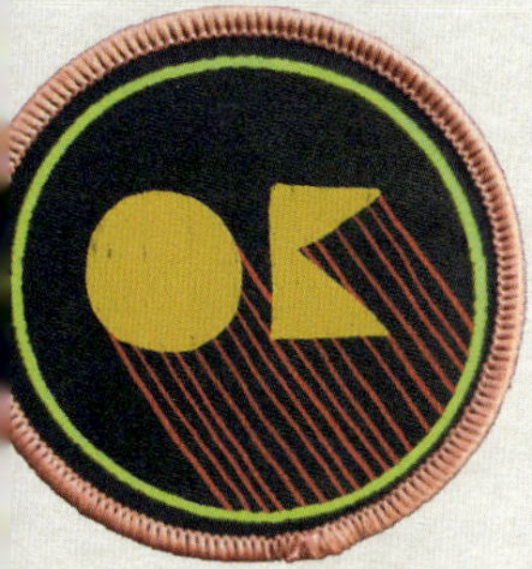

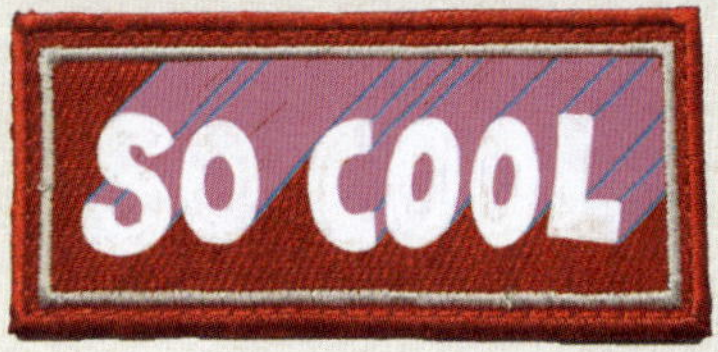

Develop your designs into some perfect patches of your own.

Grab a ballpoint pen and let the doodles and words spread.

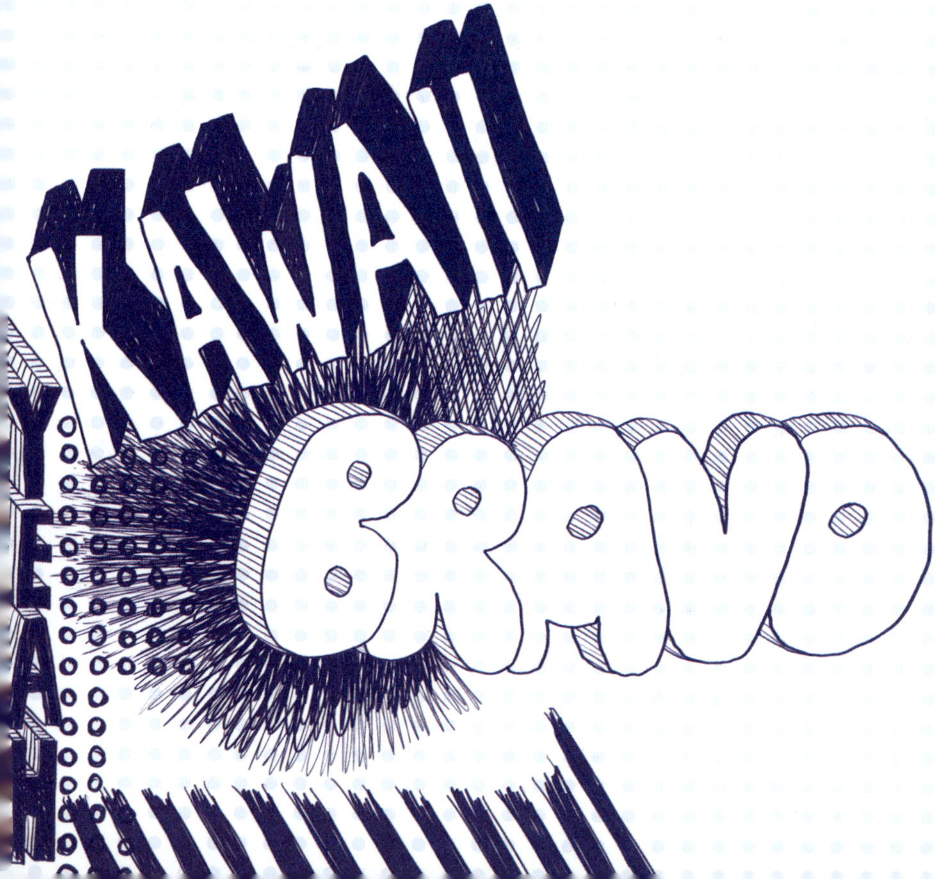

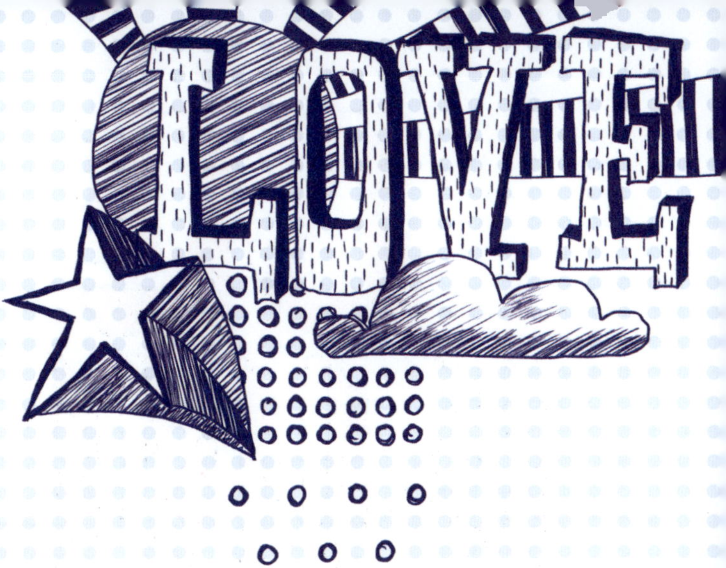
LOVE

These 3D words need some groovy decoration.

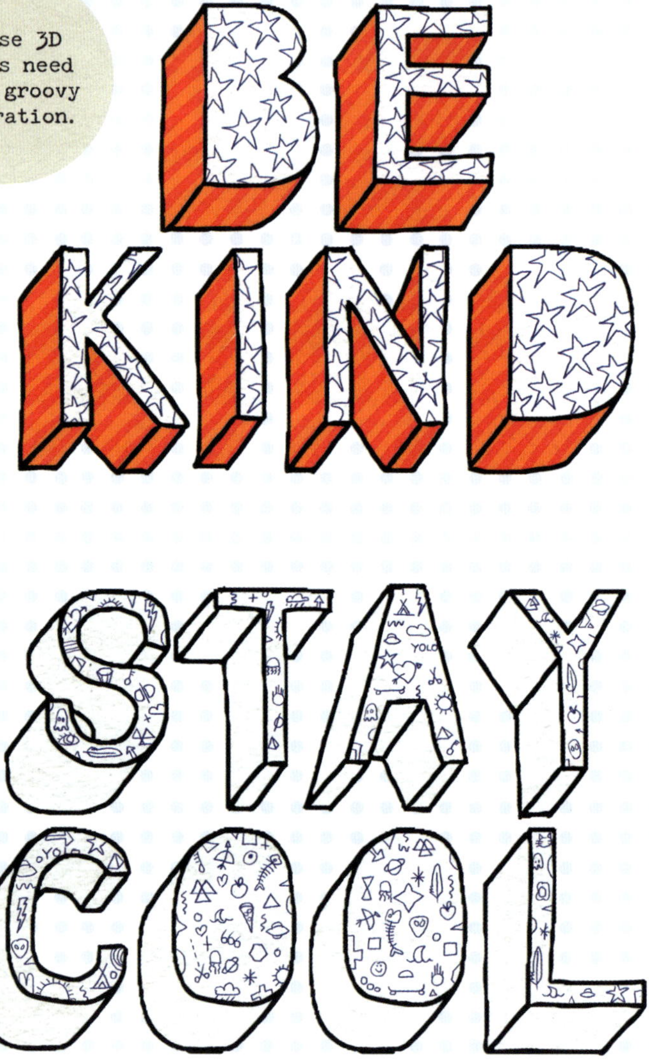

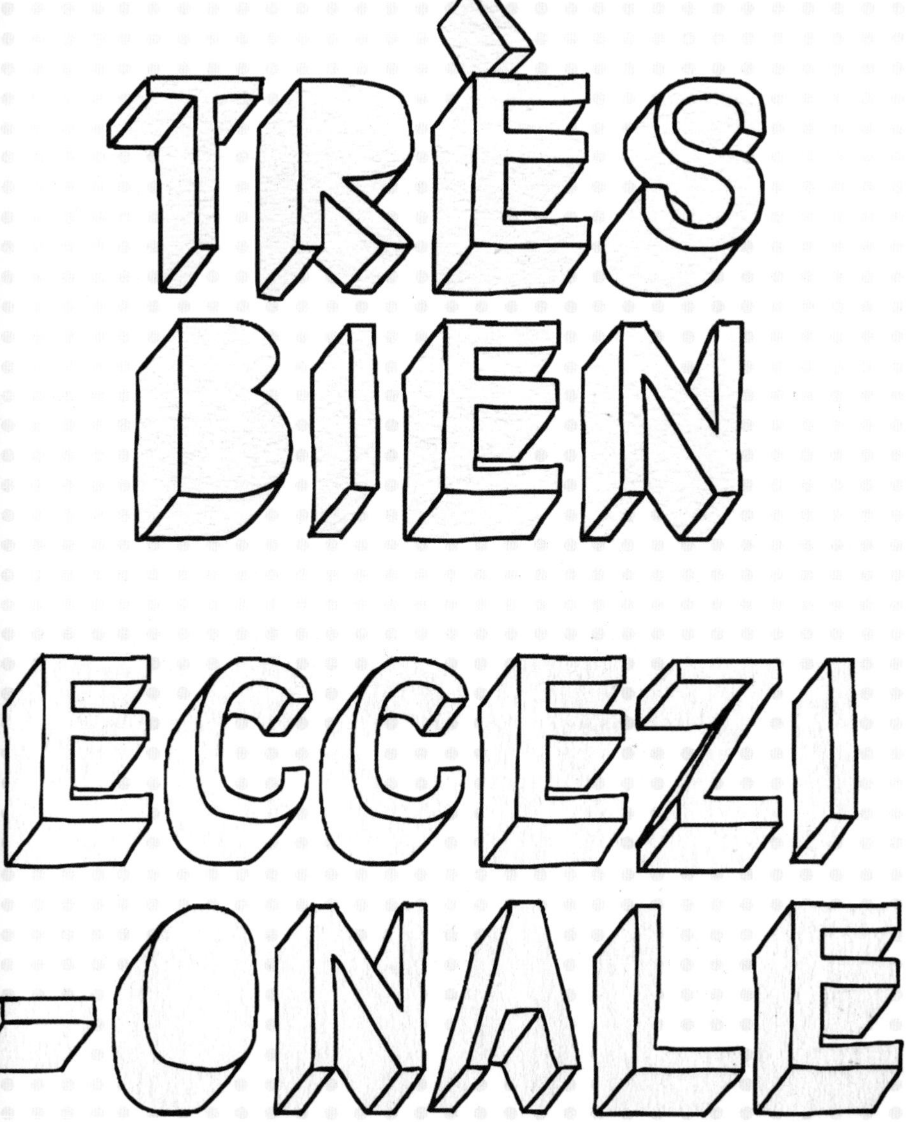
TRÈS
BIEN
ECCEZI
-ONALE

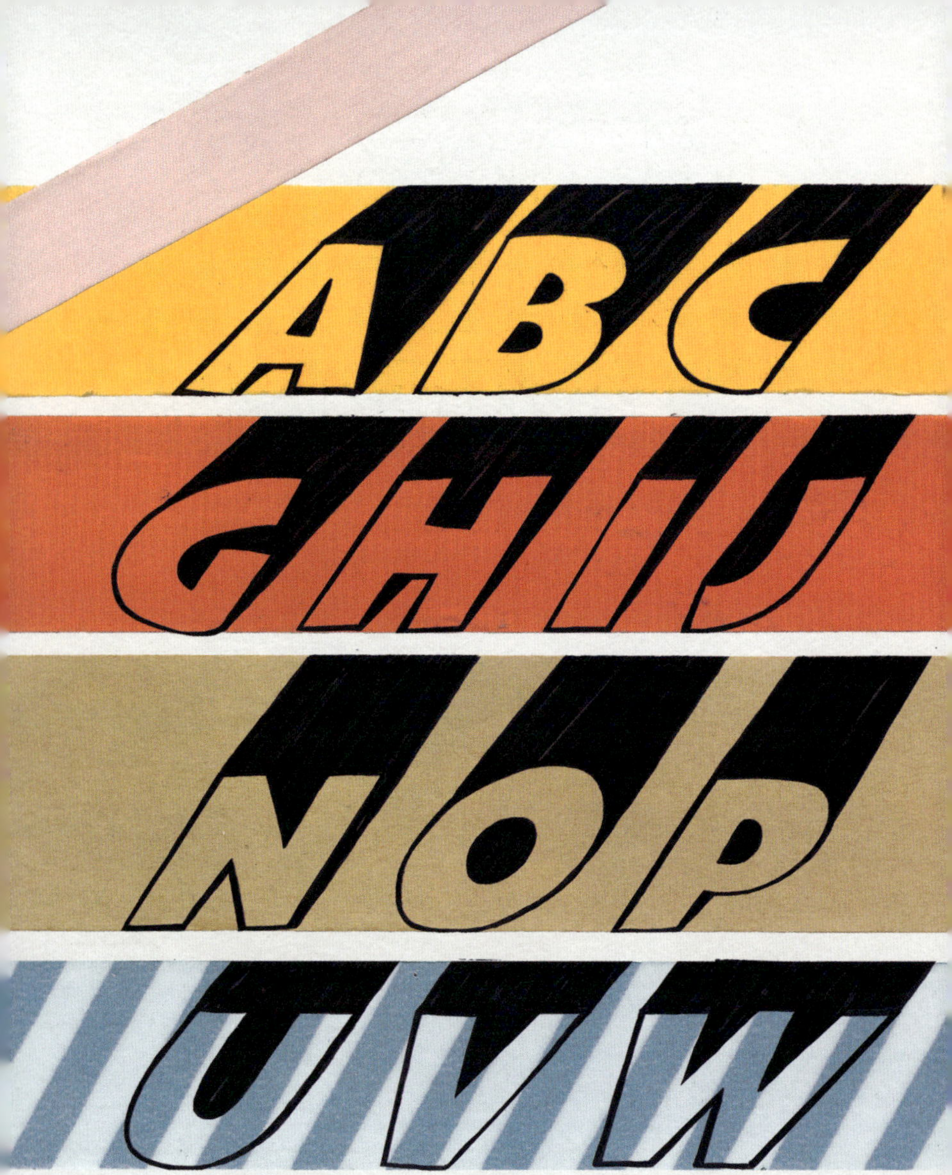
ABC
GHIJ
NOP
UVW

Play around with
3D letter tapes...

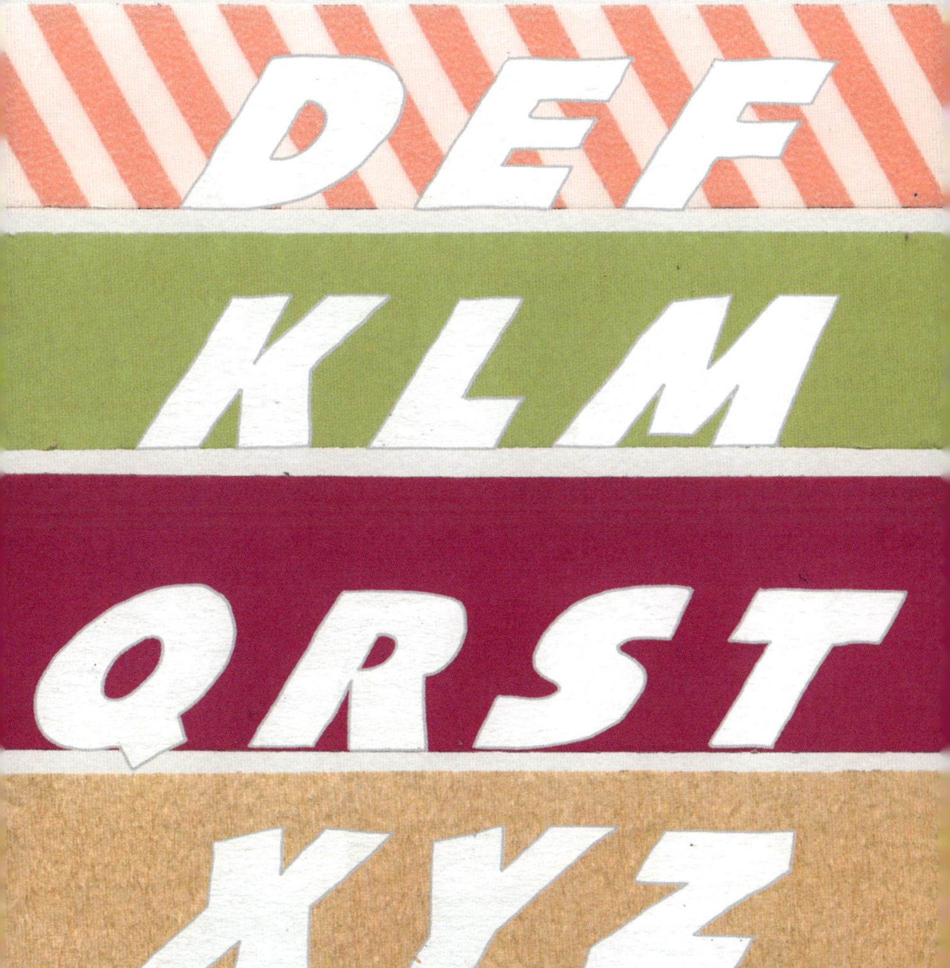

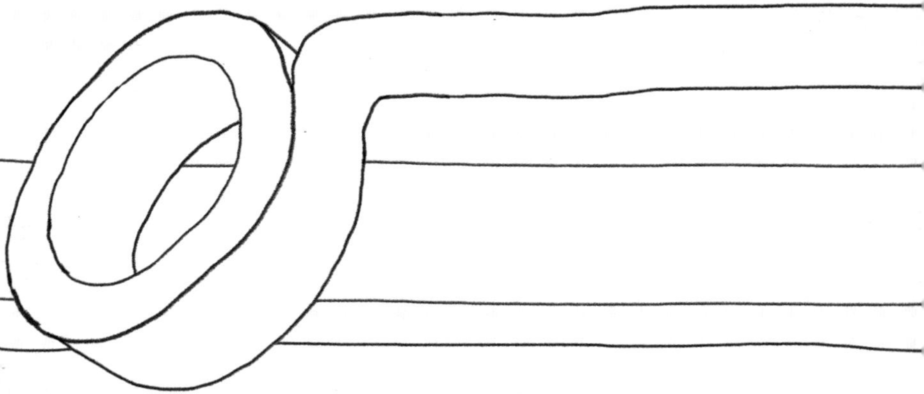

...What do you feel
like saying here?

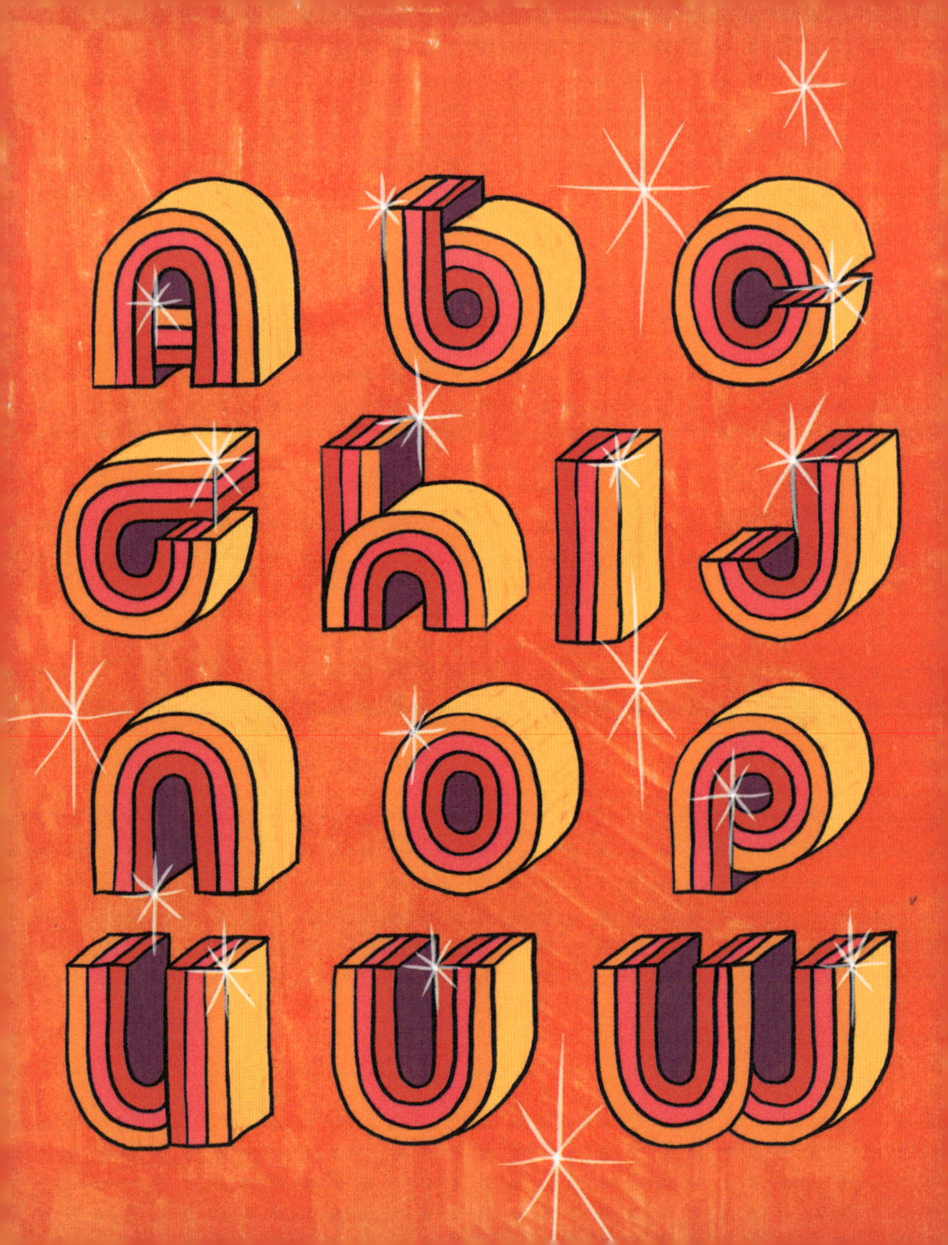

Bring some joy to these sunny disco letters by adding colour to the outlines below.

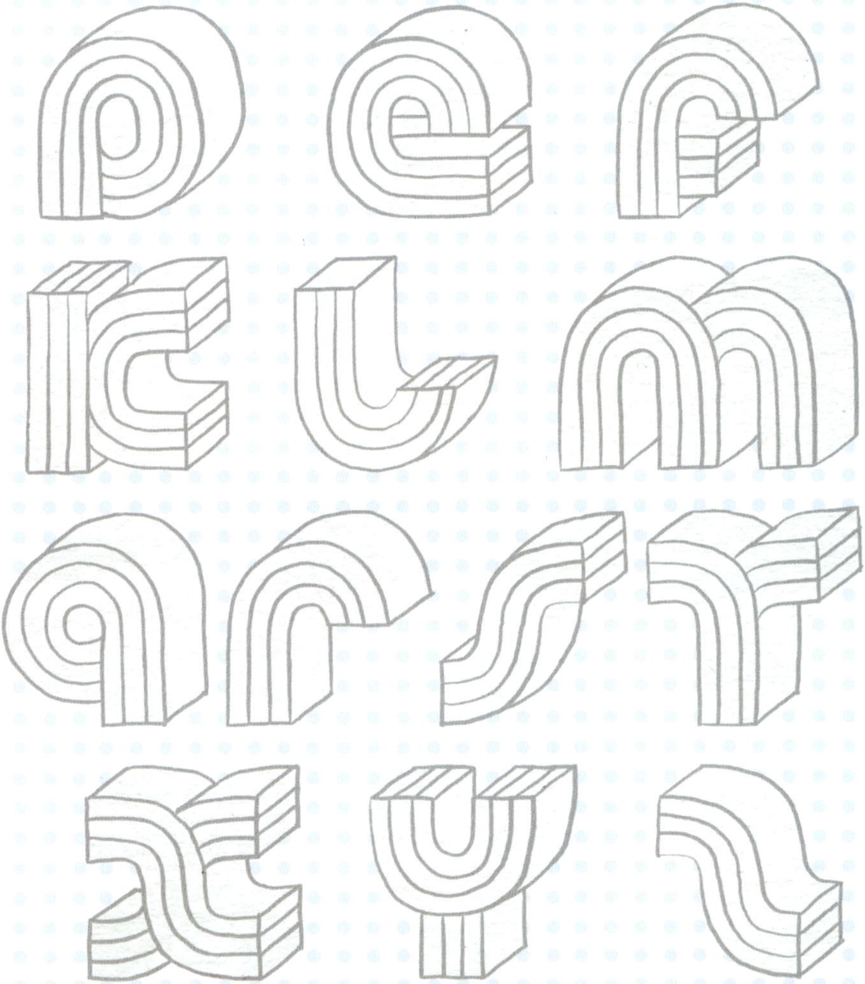

The disco letters are formed using simple arc shapes. Add deep lines to make them 3D and then some inner 'rainbow' lines.

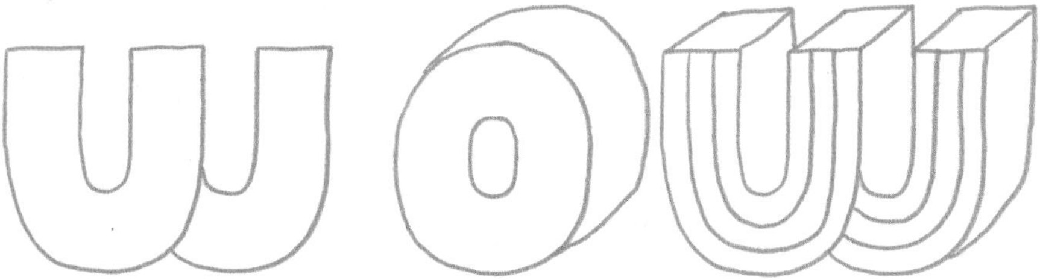

Bright, clashing colours are perfect for this style.

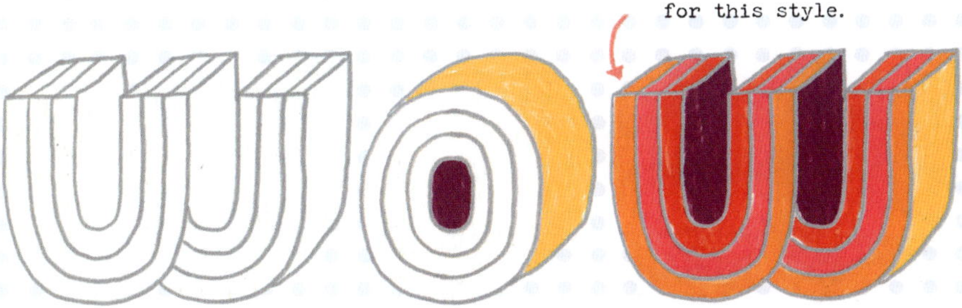

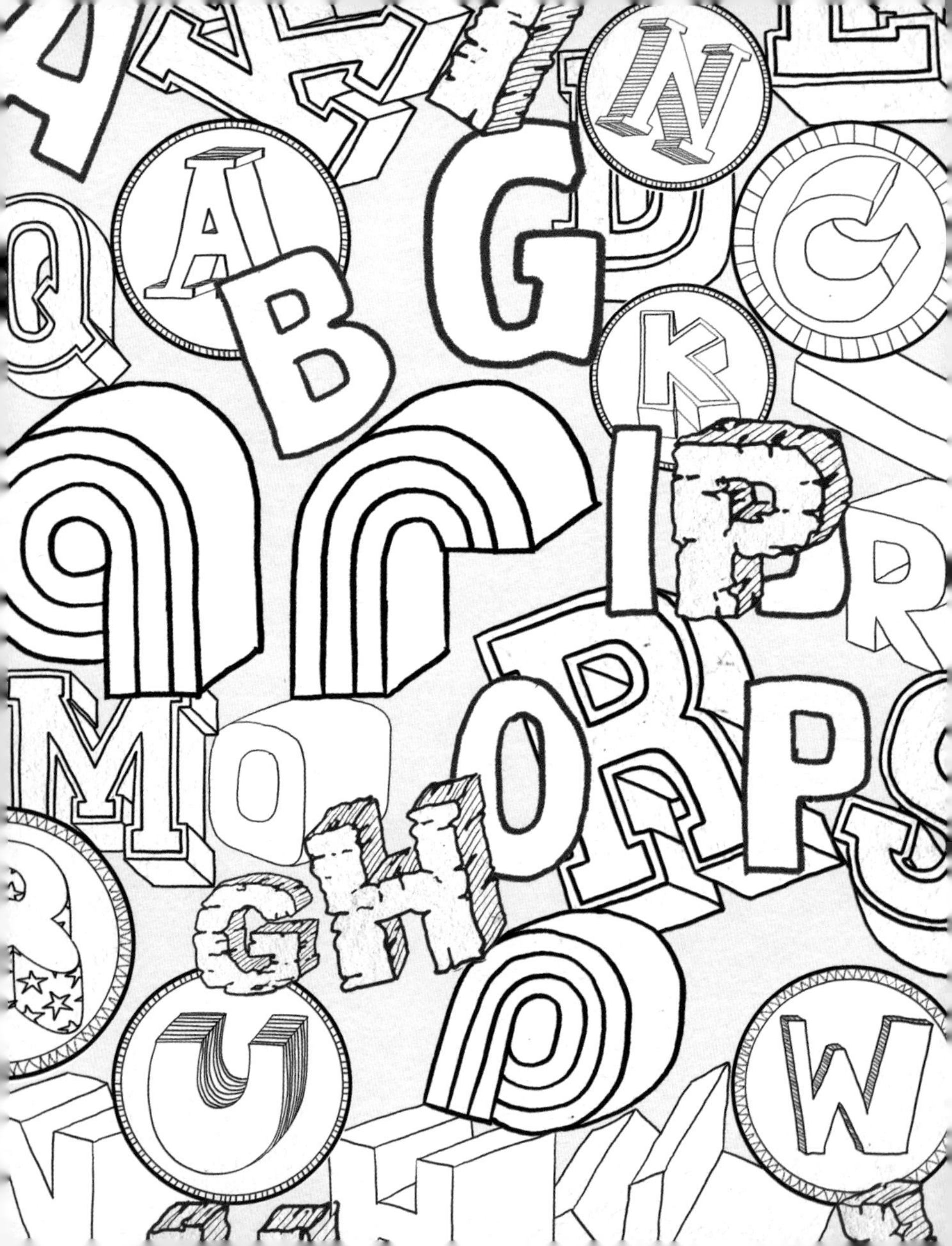

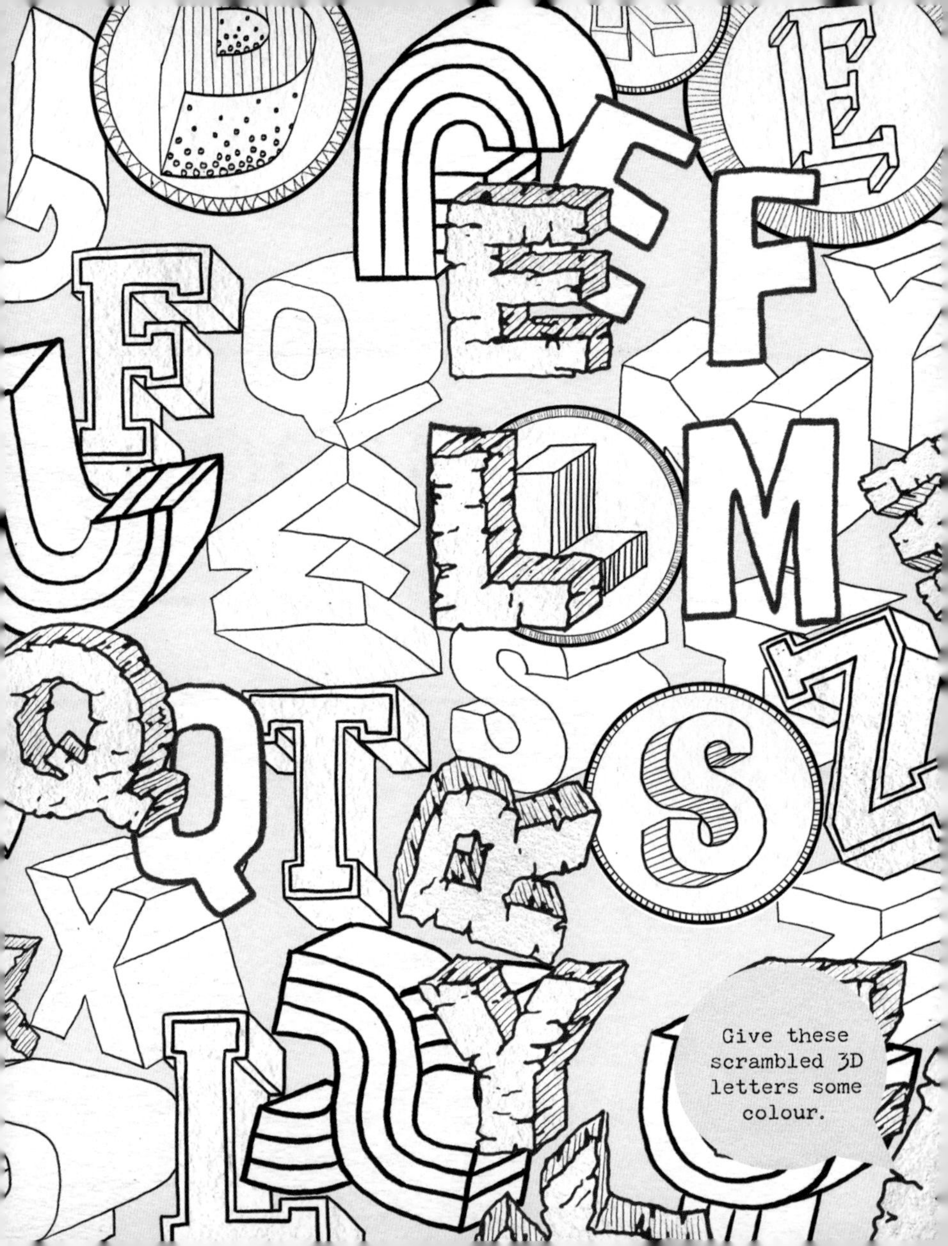
Give these scrambled 3D letters some colour.

BUBBLE

RITING

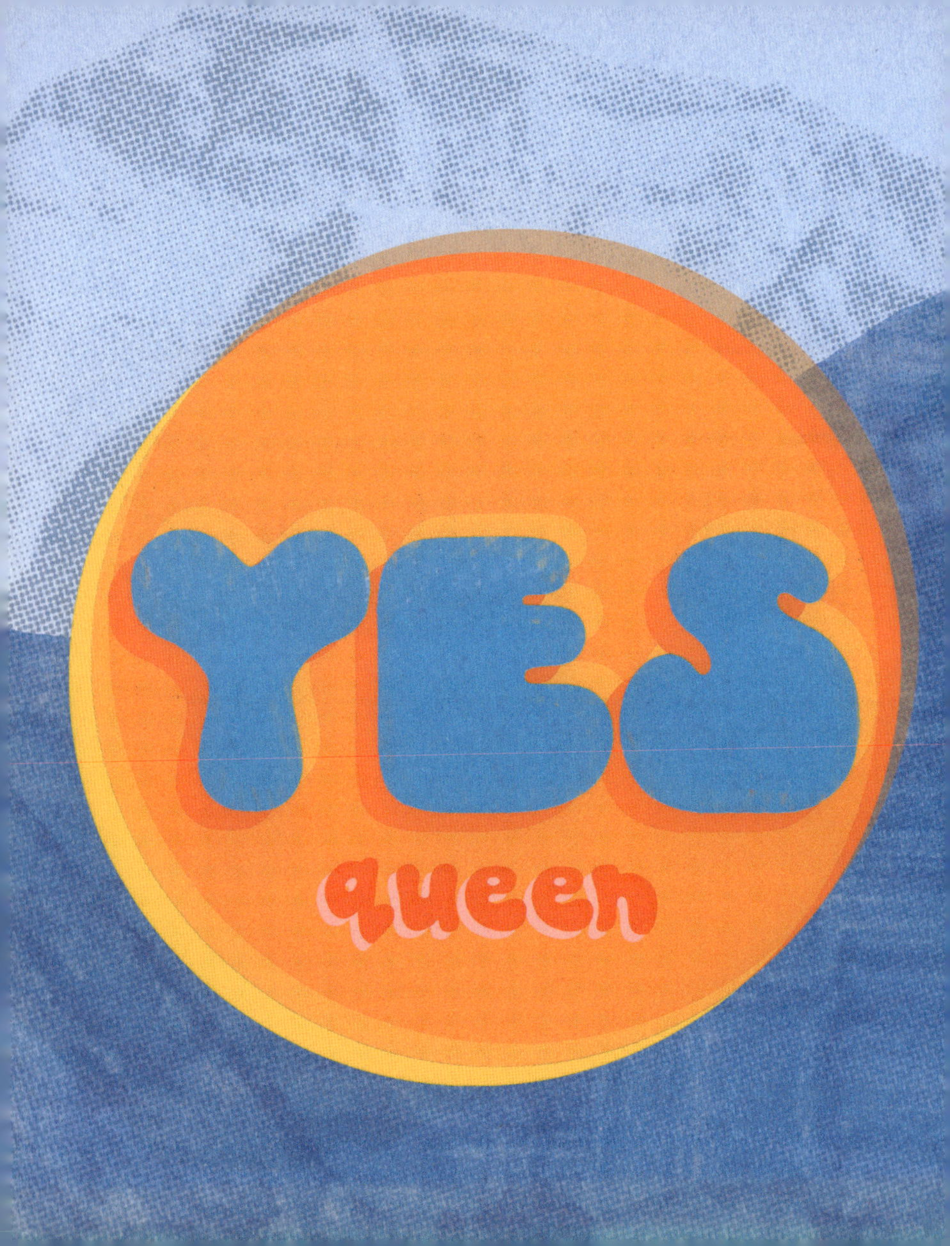
YES
queen

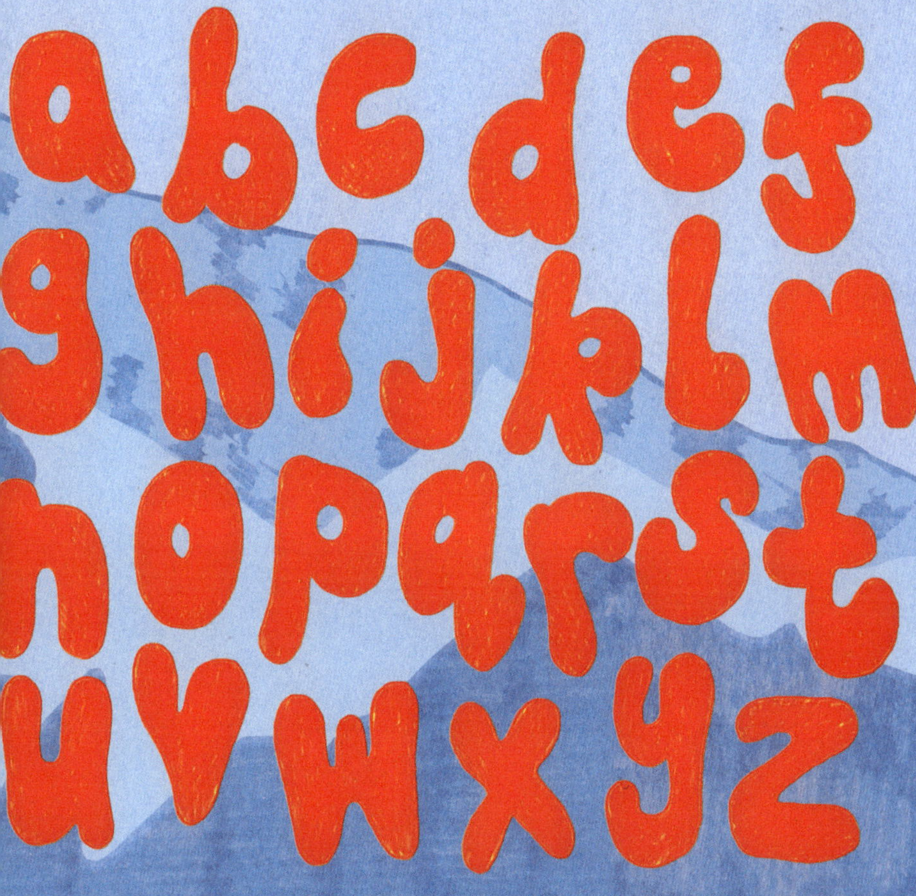

Time to conquer bubble writing! Learn this basic bubble alphabet to get started. Turn over to find out how...

Use your own handwriting and draw around each letter. Erase the pencil lines and then colour them in.

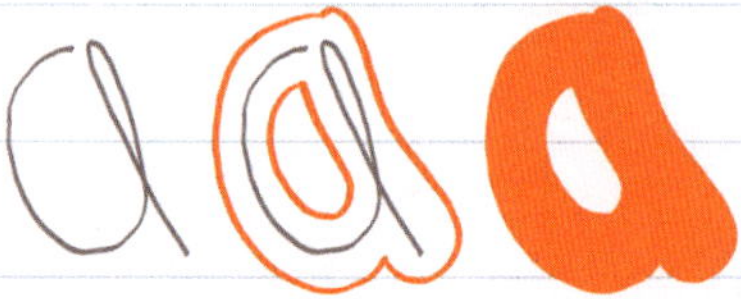

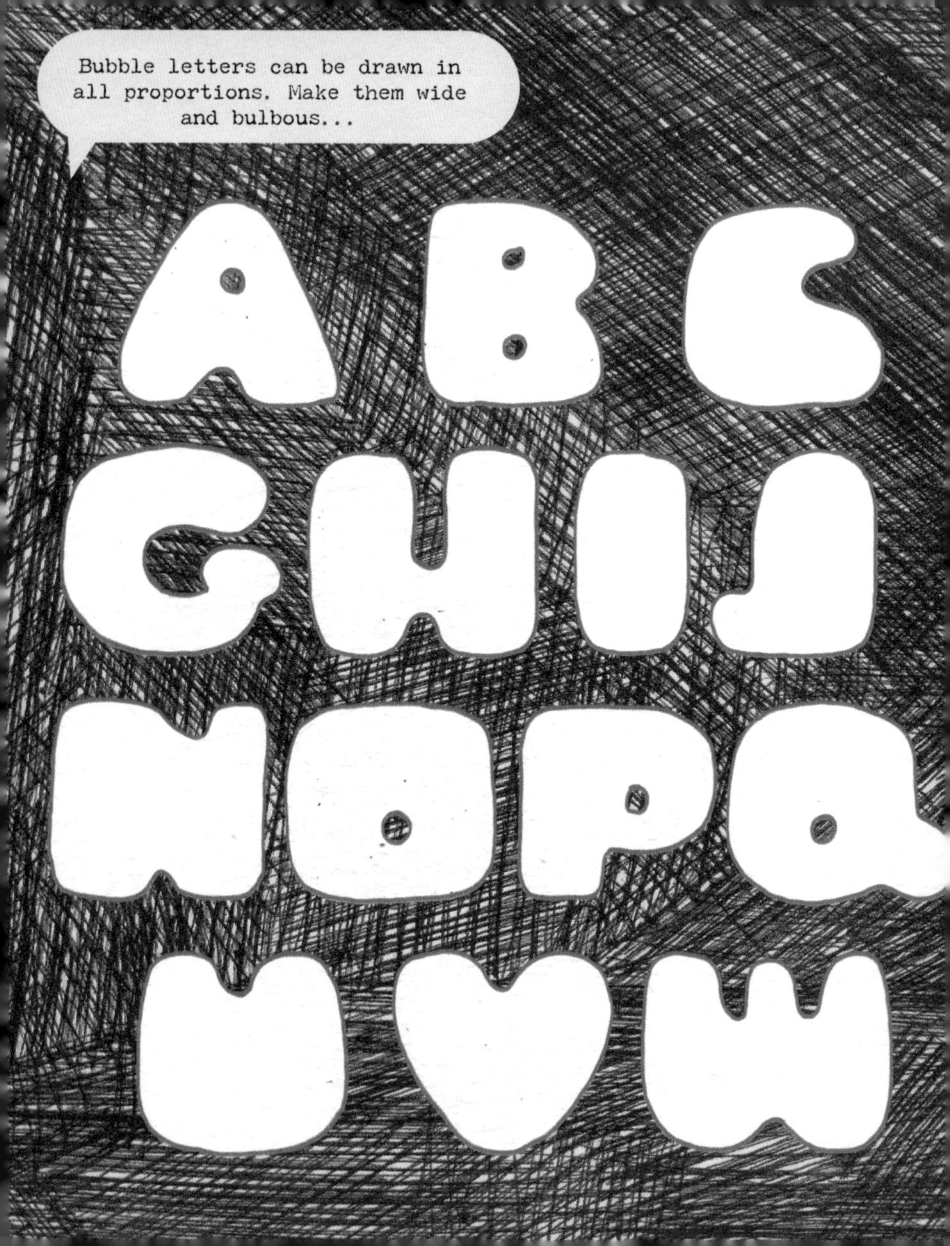
Bubble letters can be drawn in all proportions. Make them wide and bulbous...
ABC
GHIJ
NOPQ
UVW

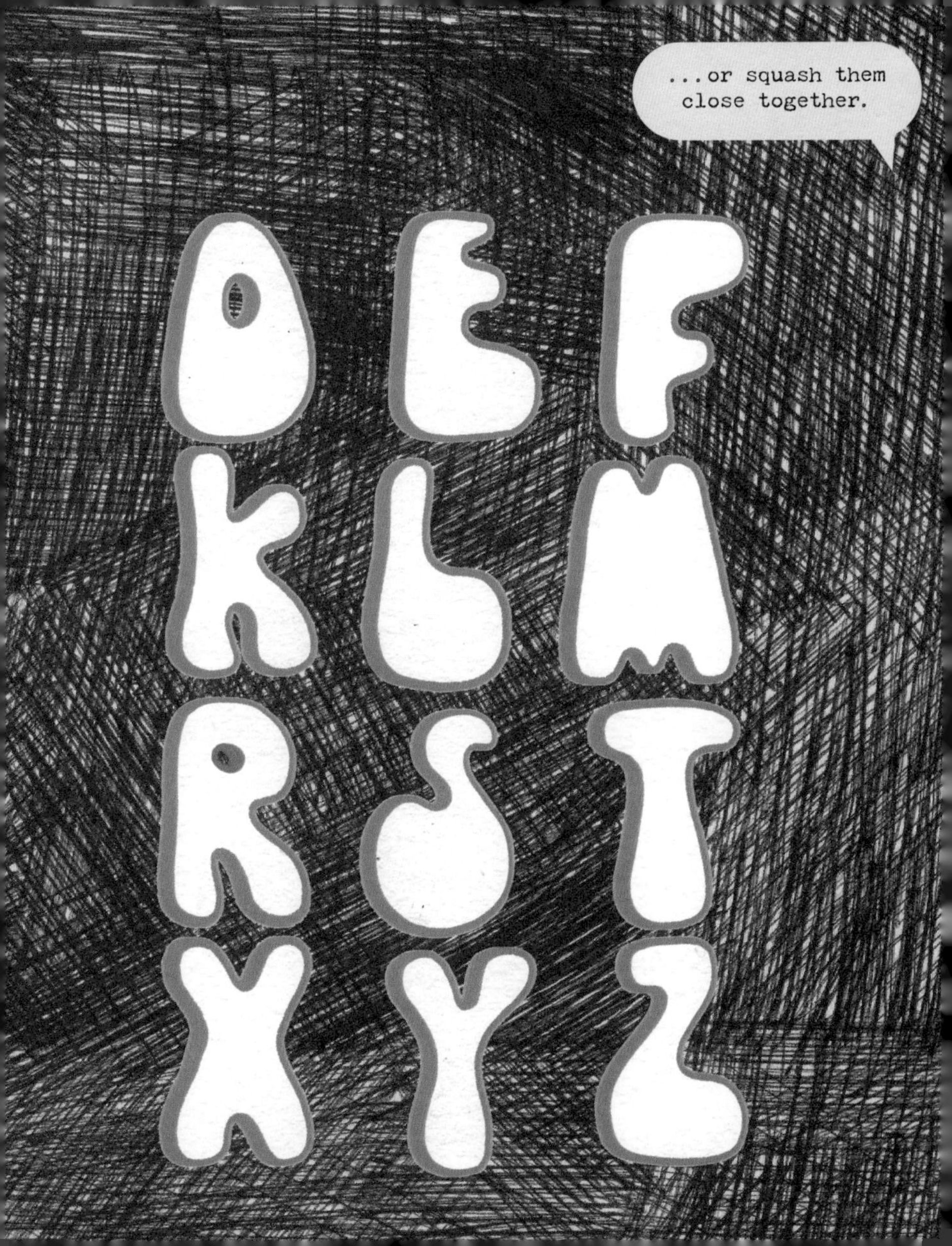
...or squash them
close together.

Fill these pages with bubble letters in all shapes and sizes.

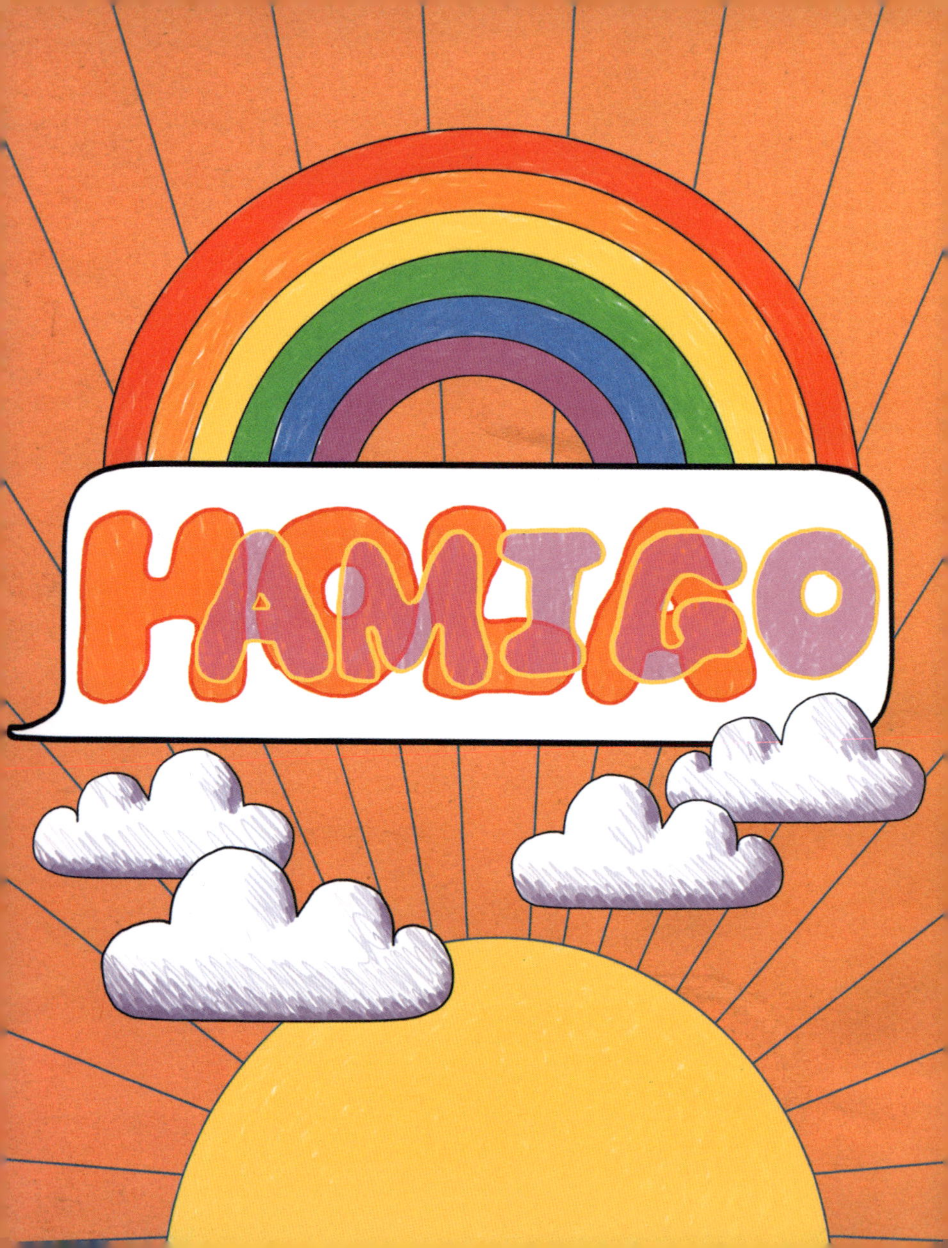
HAMIGO

WHY USE ONE WORD WHEN YOU CAN USE

TWO DEUX KAKSI

ZWEI DOS TWEE DUE

Try doubling up your letters and words. Play around with colour combos and different media.

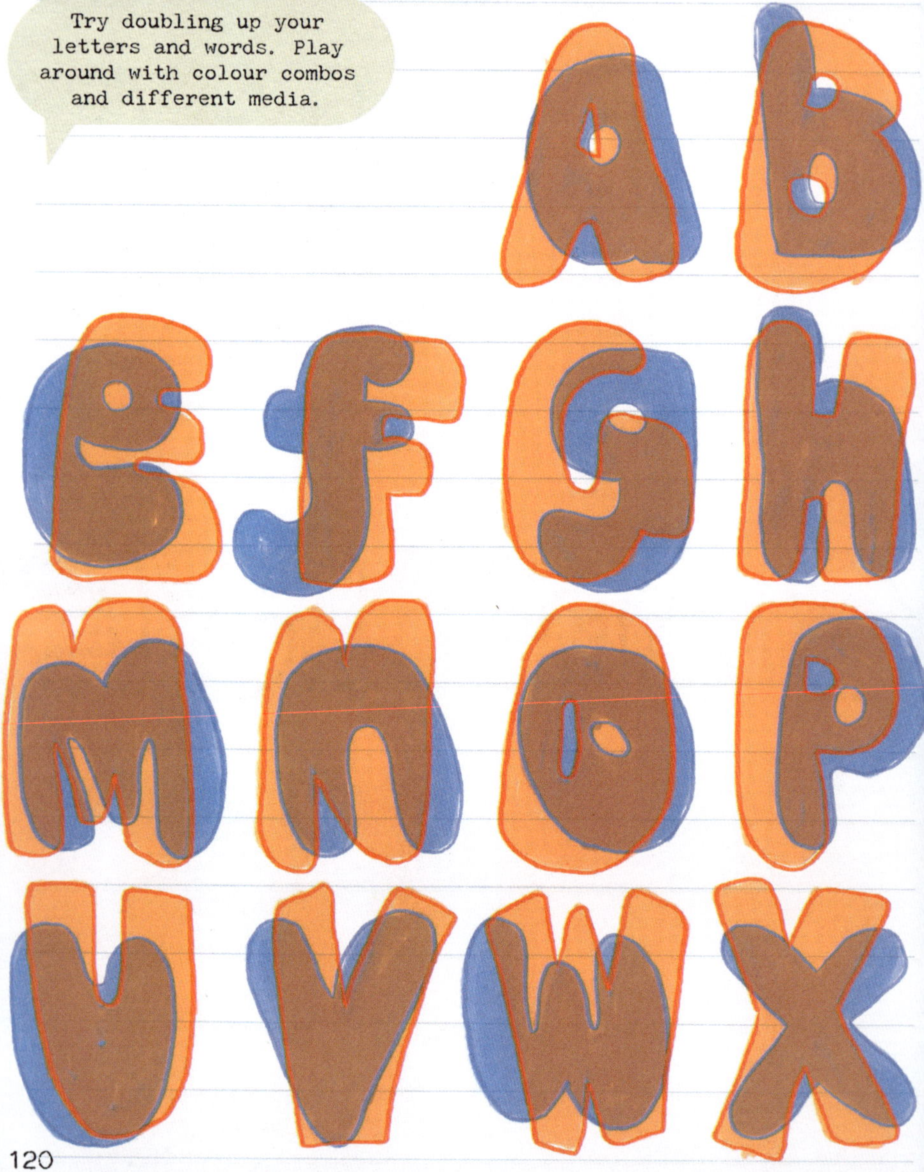

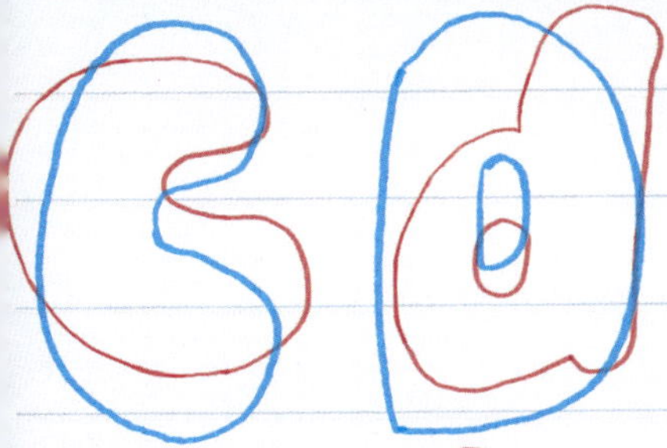

Layer up capital and
lower case letters.

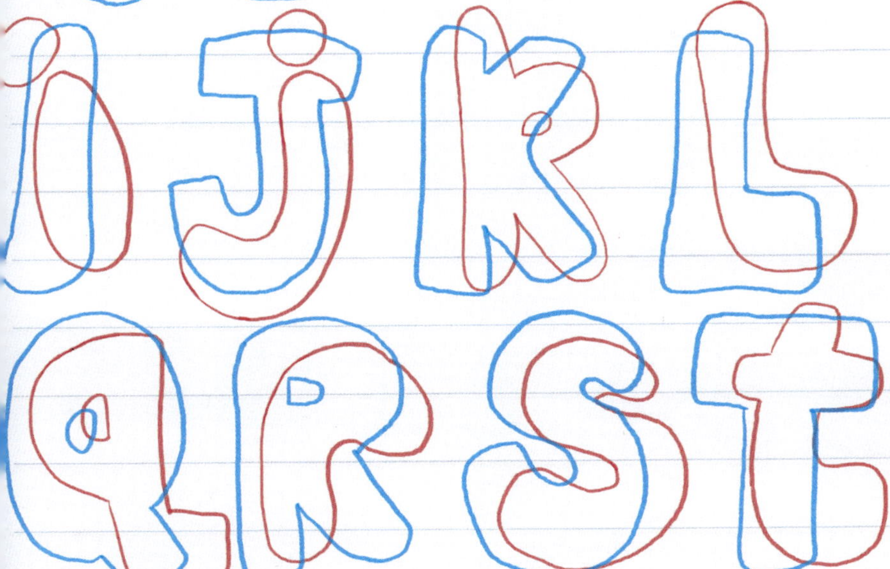

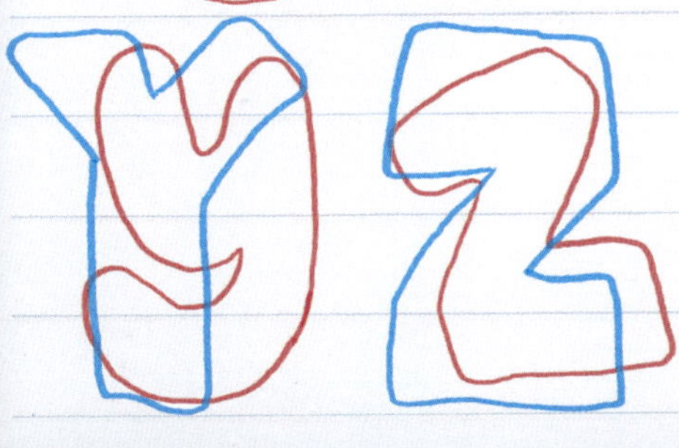

No need
to be neat and
tidy – none of
that matters
here!

Create your own double letters and words. What will they be?

NOW PRACTISE SOME YOURSELF

Greetings cards are a great way to show off your groovy lettering skills.

Who doesn't love rainbows? This colourful lettering style is full of feel-good vibes.

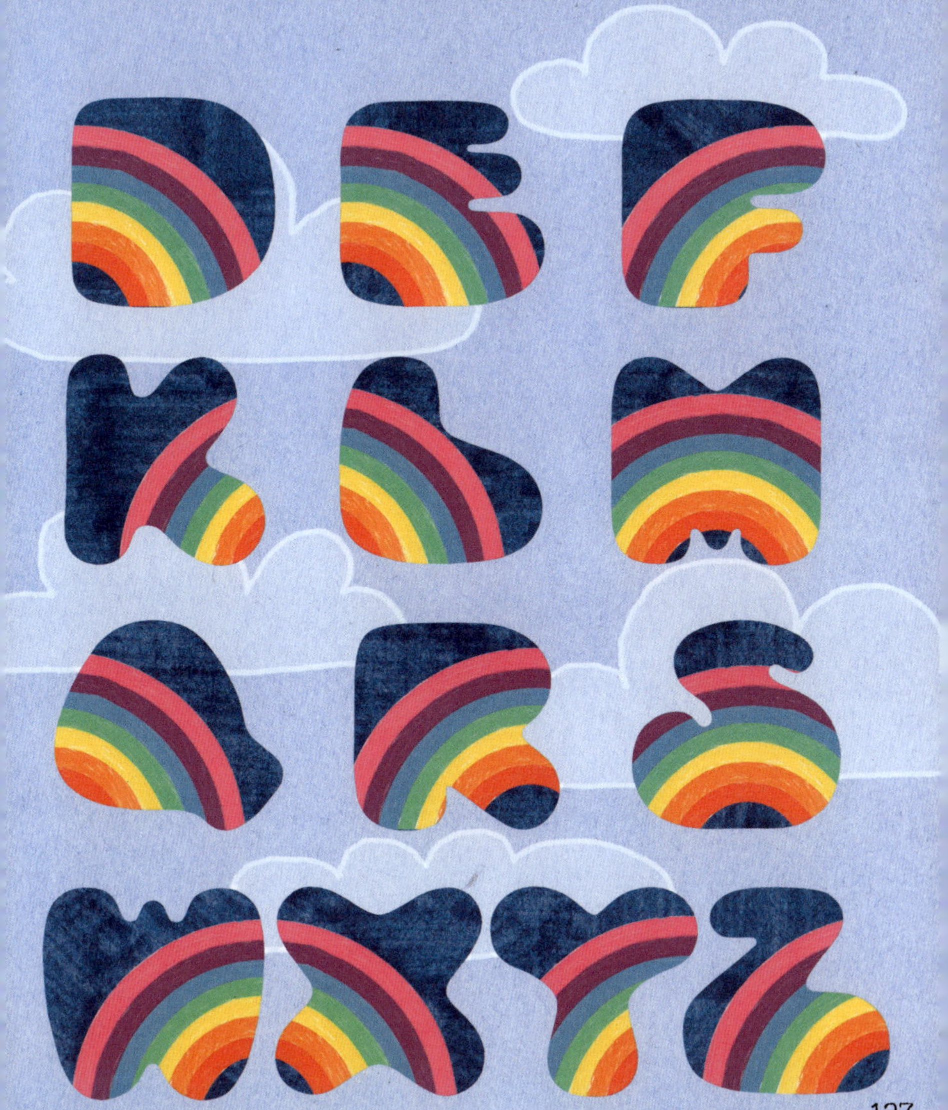
DEF
KLM
QRS
WXYZ

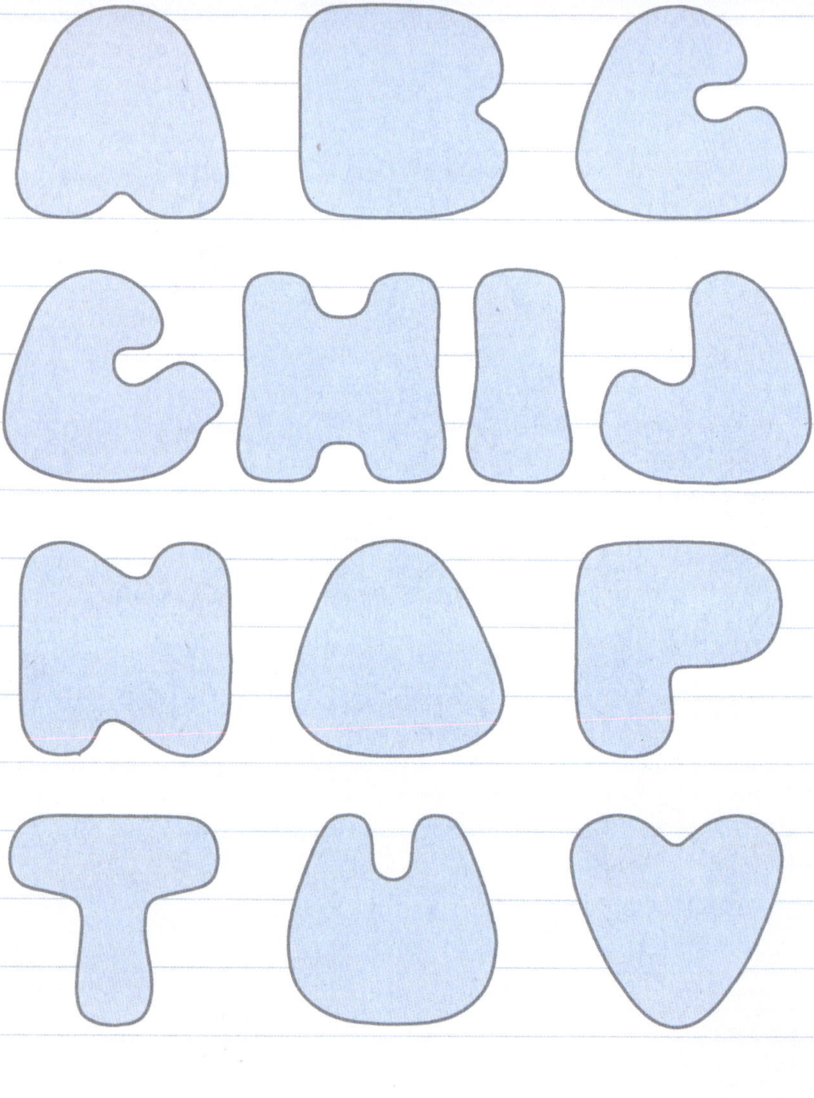

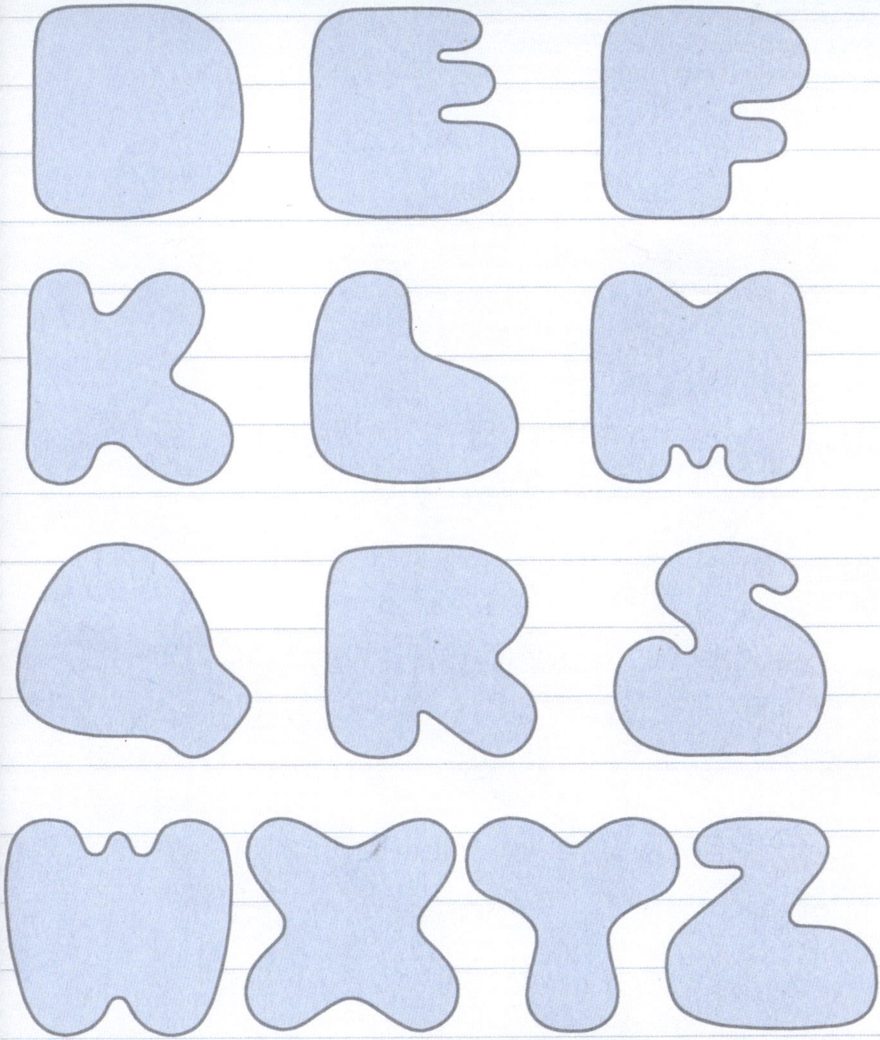

Add your own rainbows to these empty bubble letters.

Turn your bubble letters into clouds...but will you make them stormy, or fluffy and white?

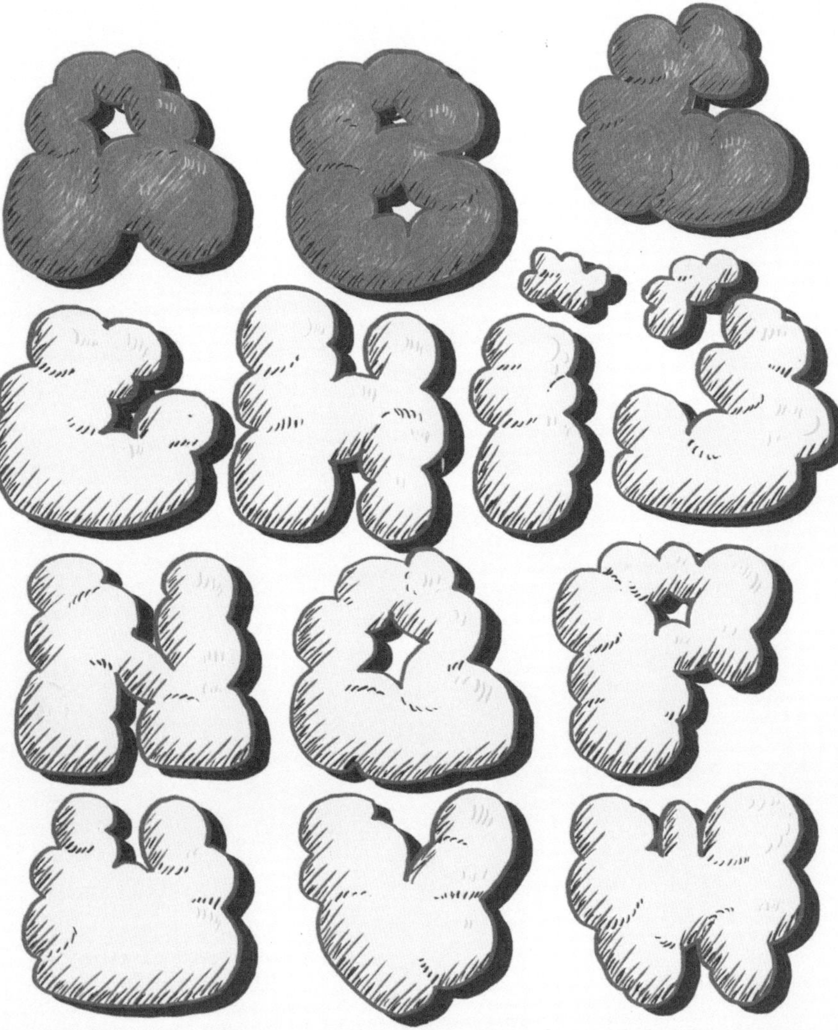

Add lines, shading and drop shadows to these empty letters.

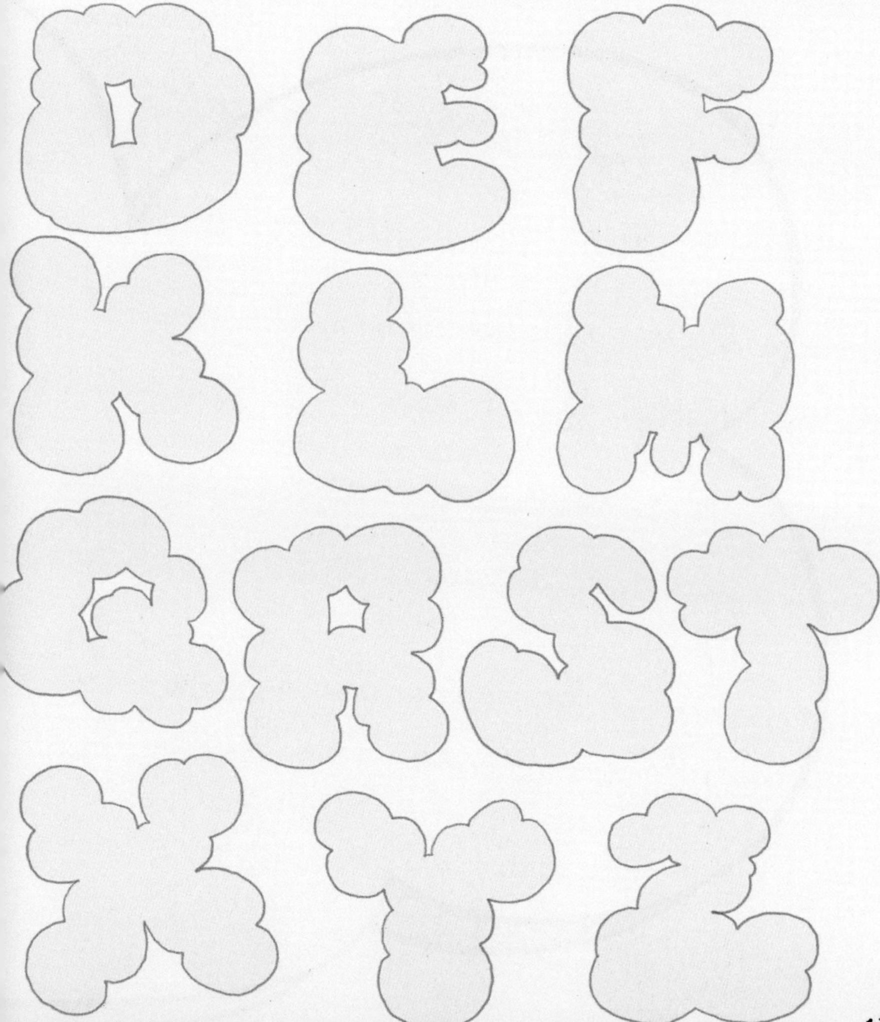

Write something here. Always be charming, clever and kind with your words.

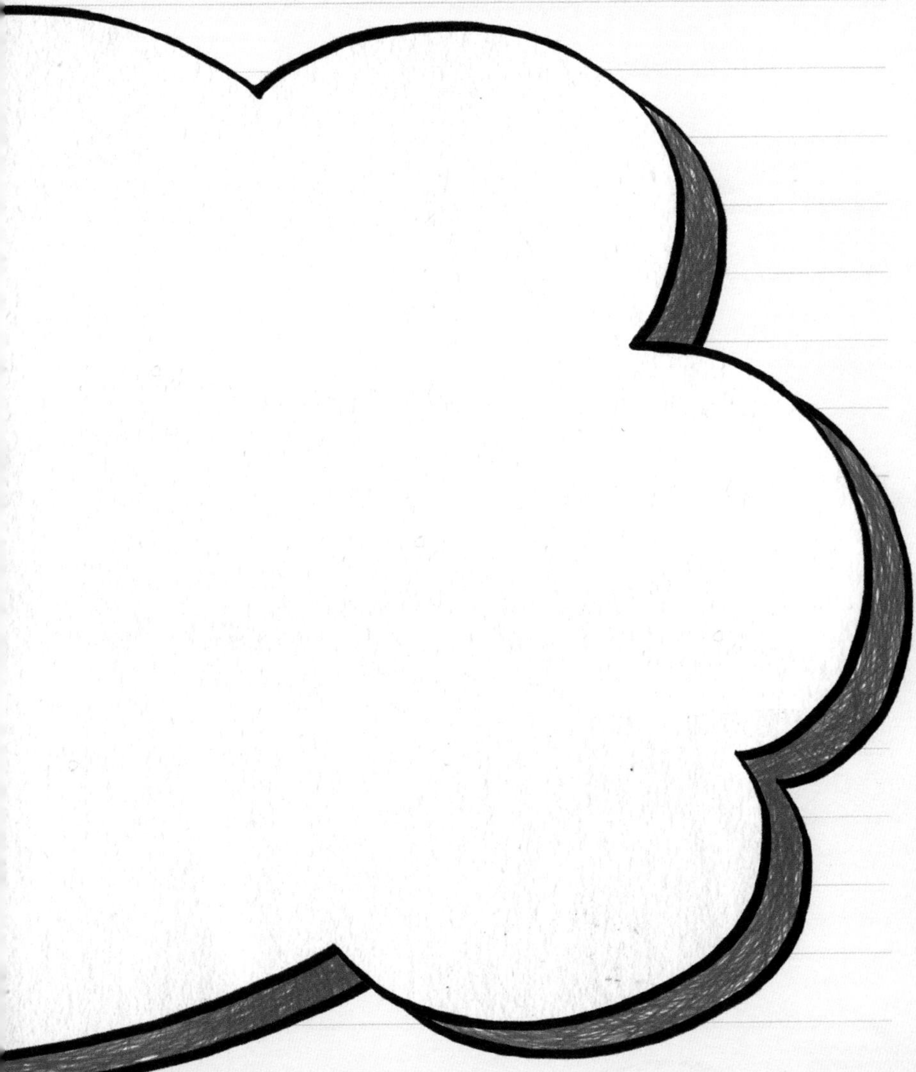

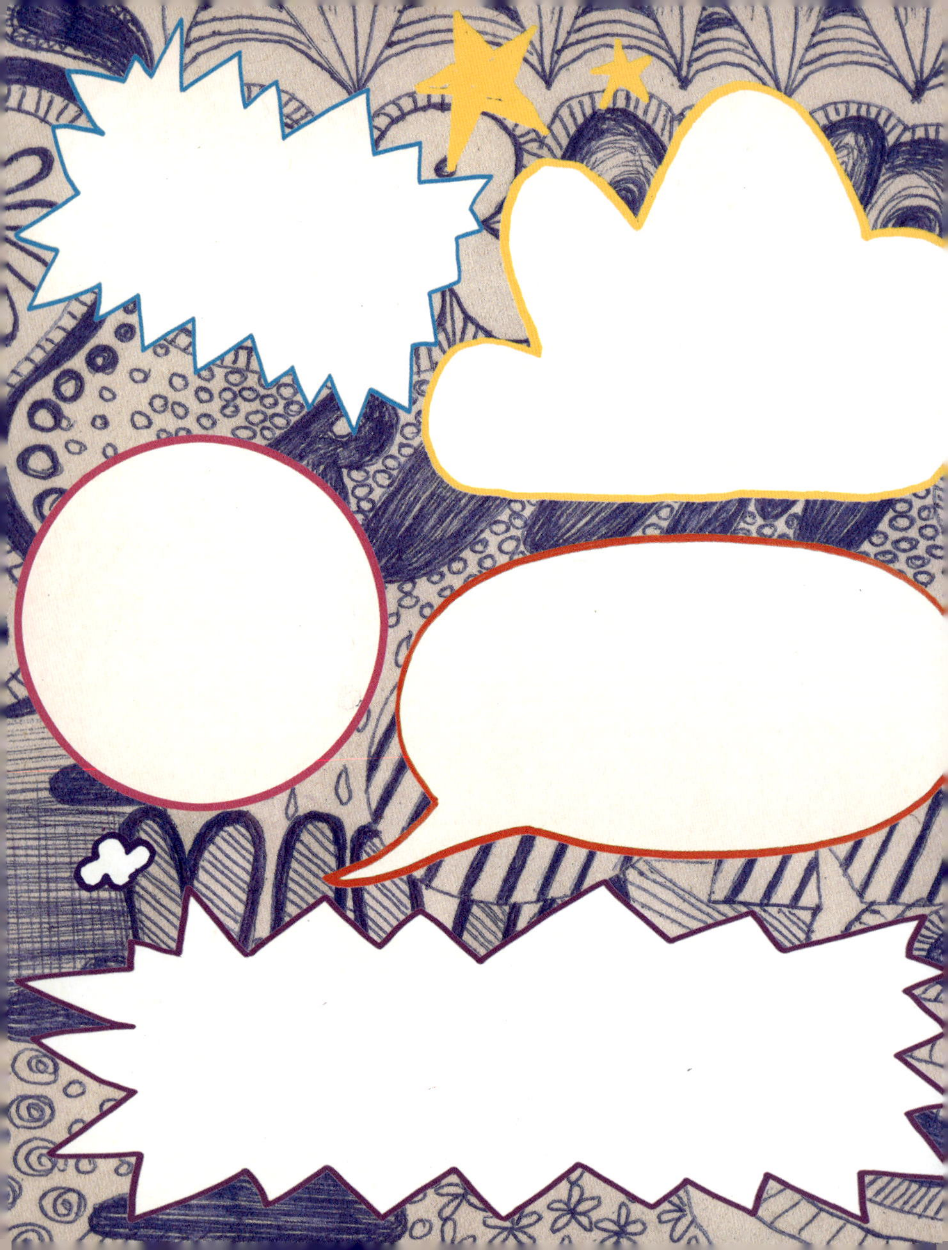

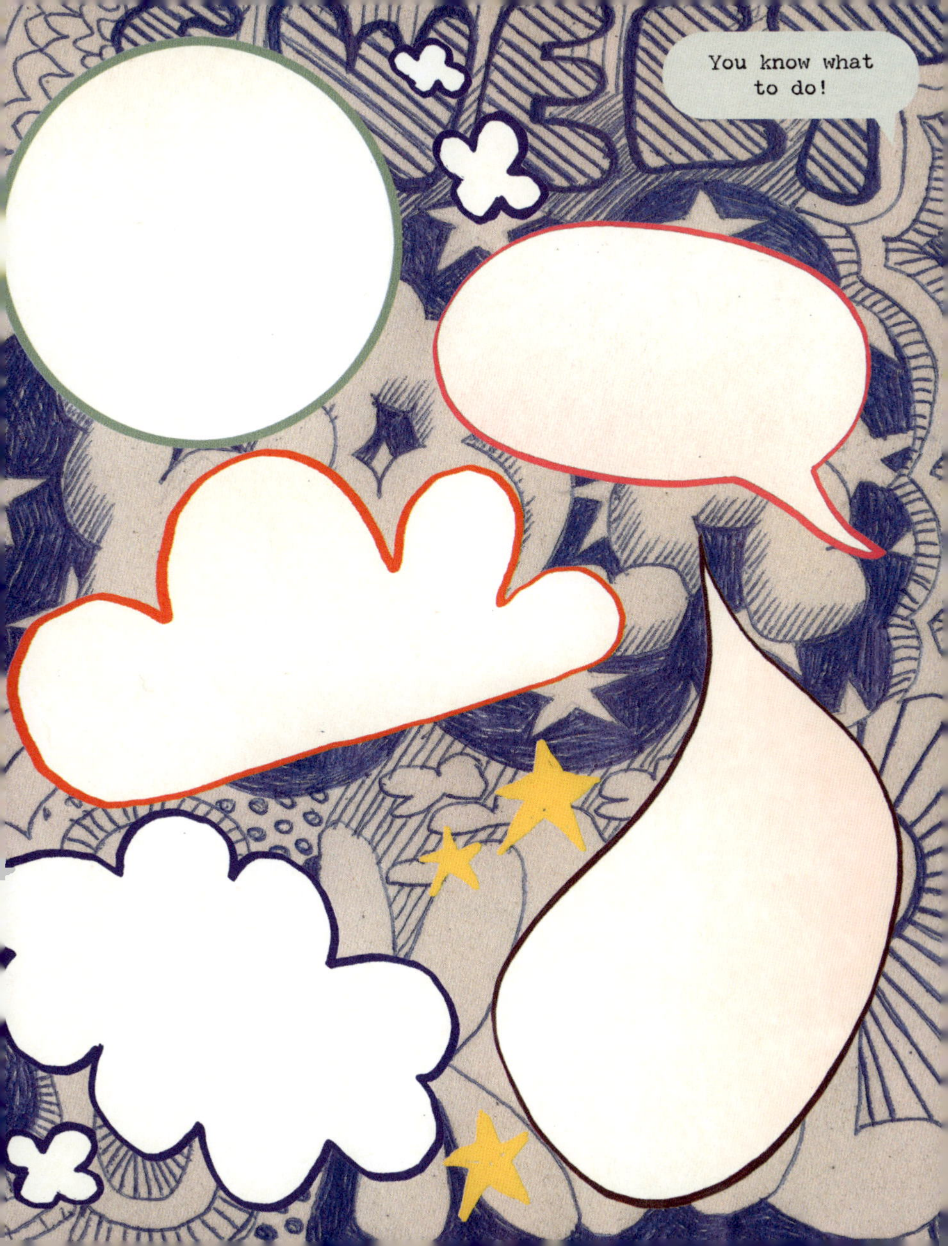
You know what to do!

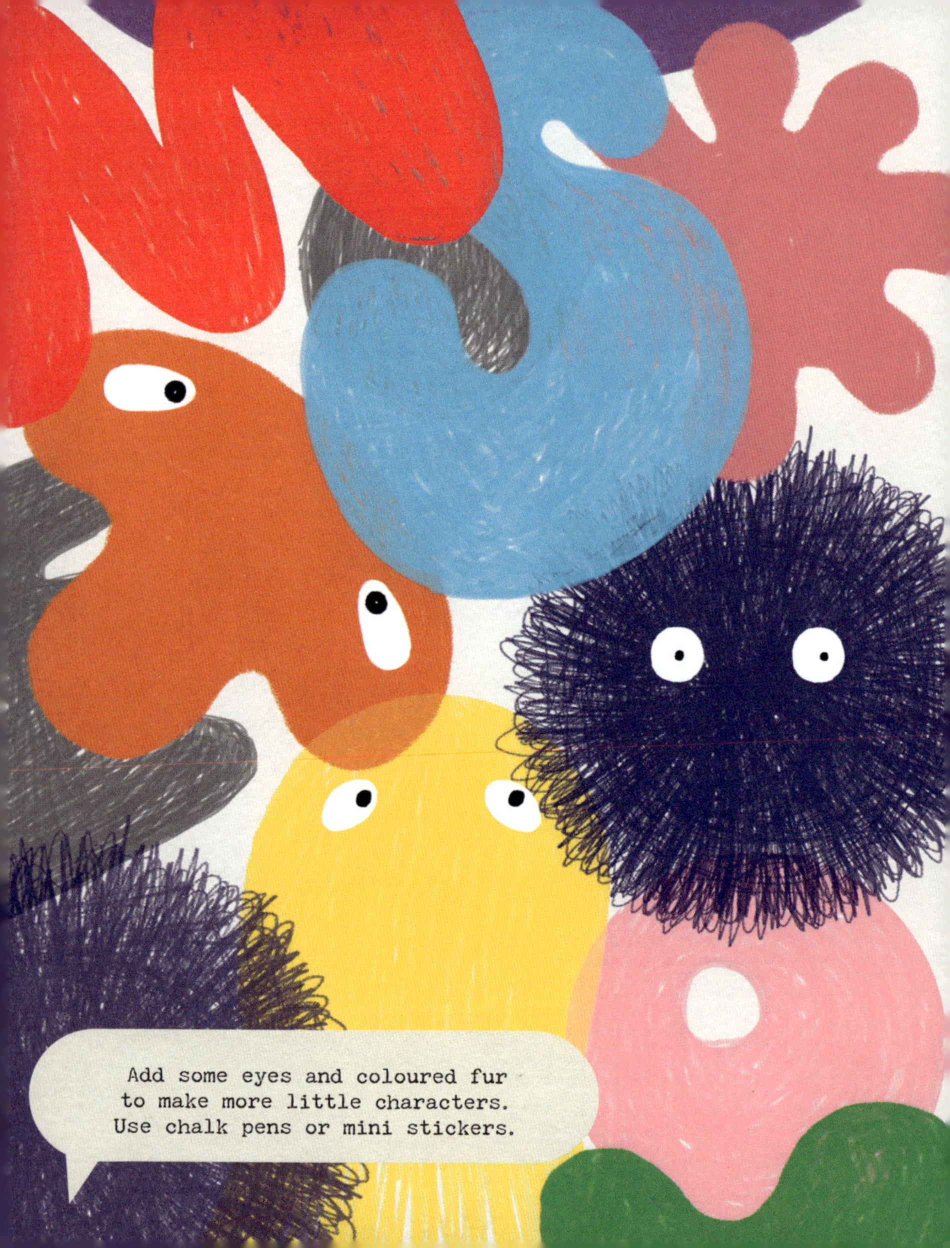
Add some eyes and coloured fur to make more little characters. Use chalk pens or mini stickers.

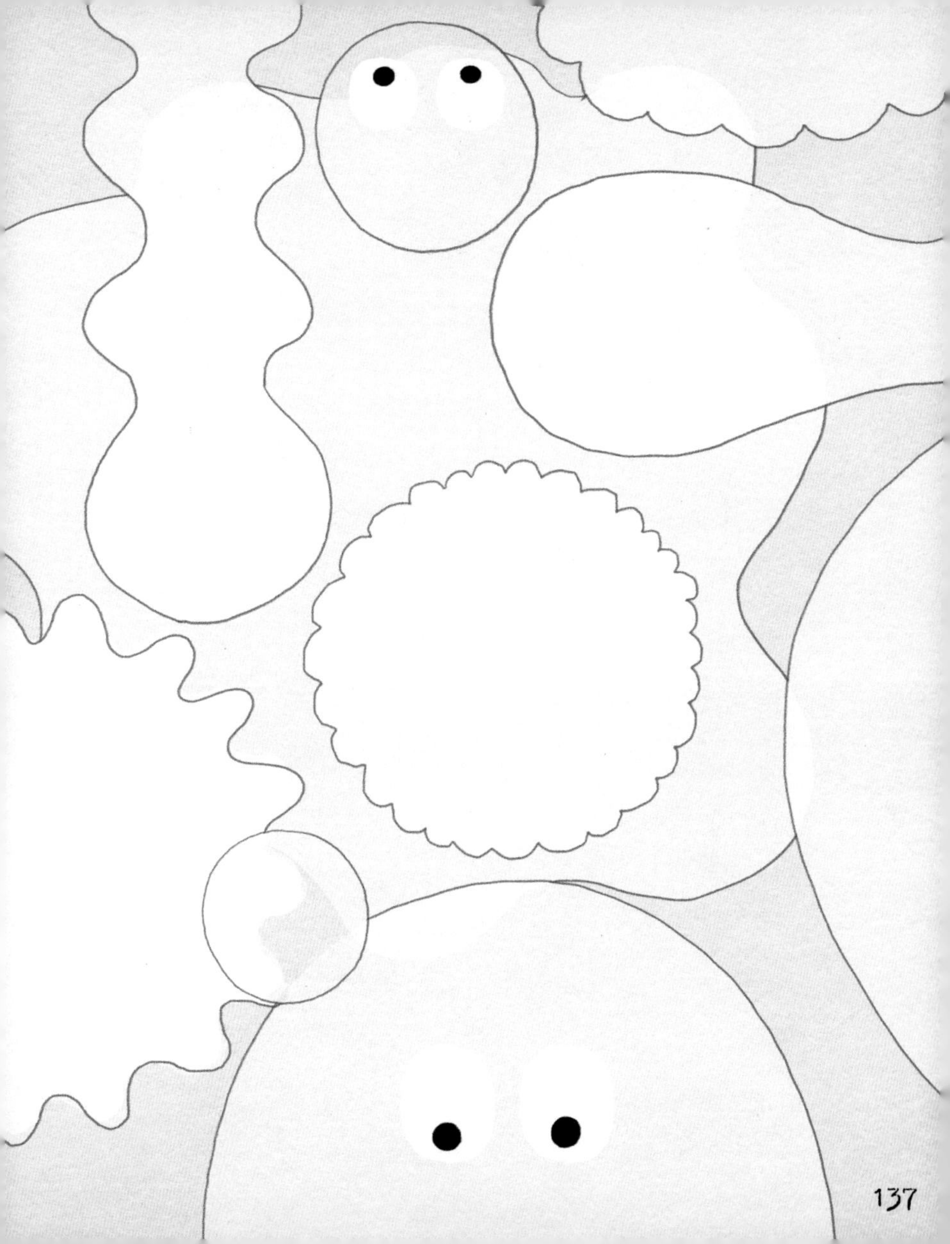

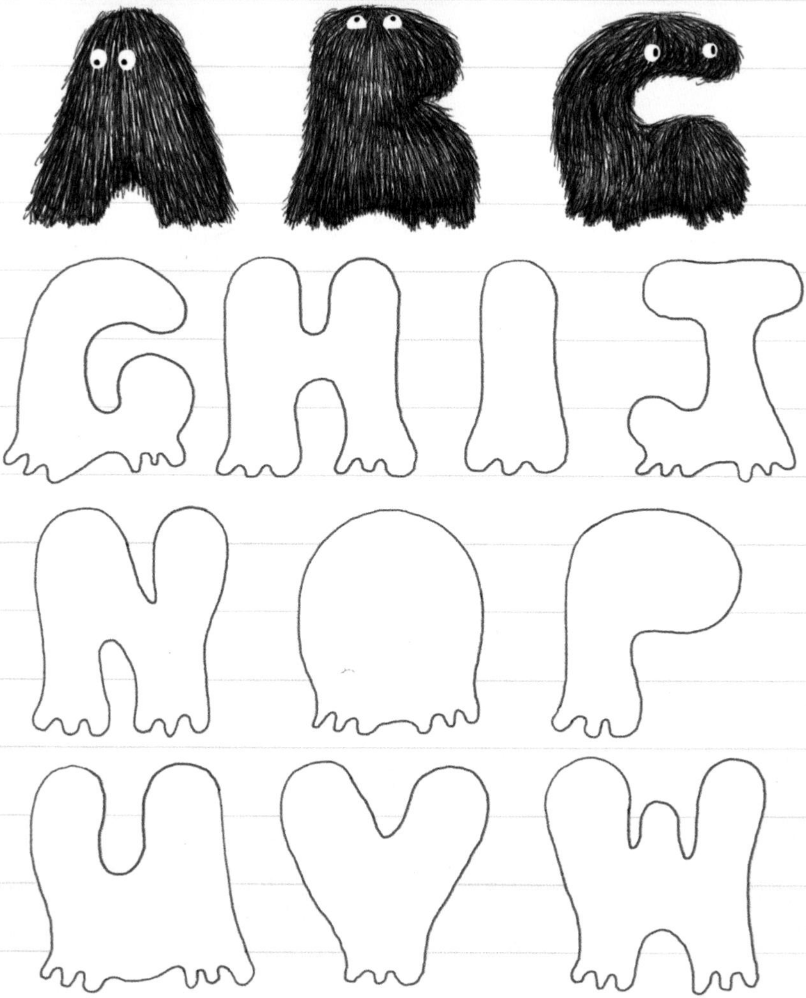

Finish off these little monsters by adding some fur and eyes. Turn over for some for tips.

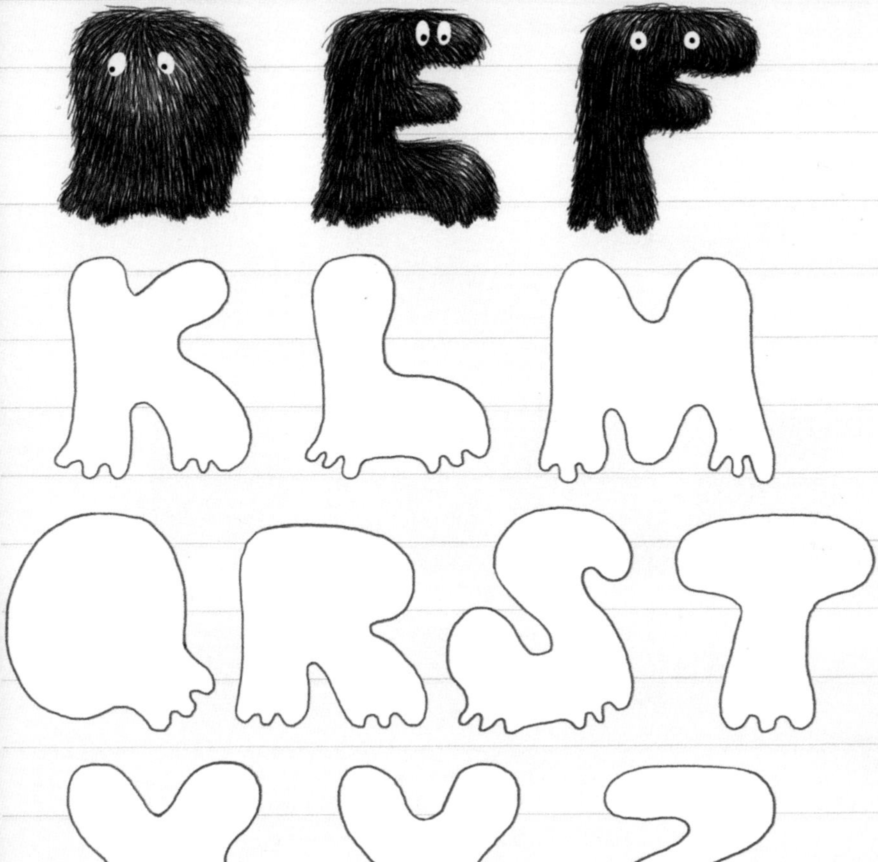
DEF
KLM
QRST
XYZ

Draw a letter shape and give it some feet. Add layers of tiny lines to make fur, making it darker at the bottom.

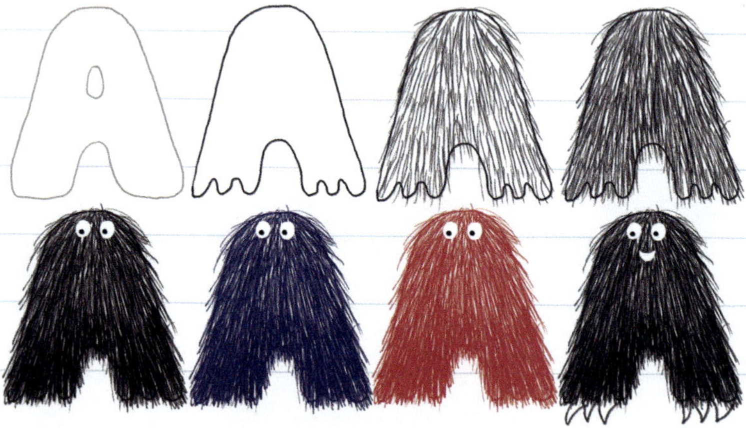

You can even add a mouth and claws!

Add some funny eyes with a chalk pen or stickers. Ballpoint pens work in any colour, but you can try pencils, markers, and anything else too!

Bubble letters don't have to be on a straight path: they can bend and stretch to fill wobbly shapes. Colour in these hills and add some words of your own.

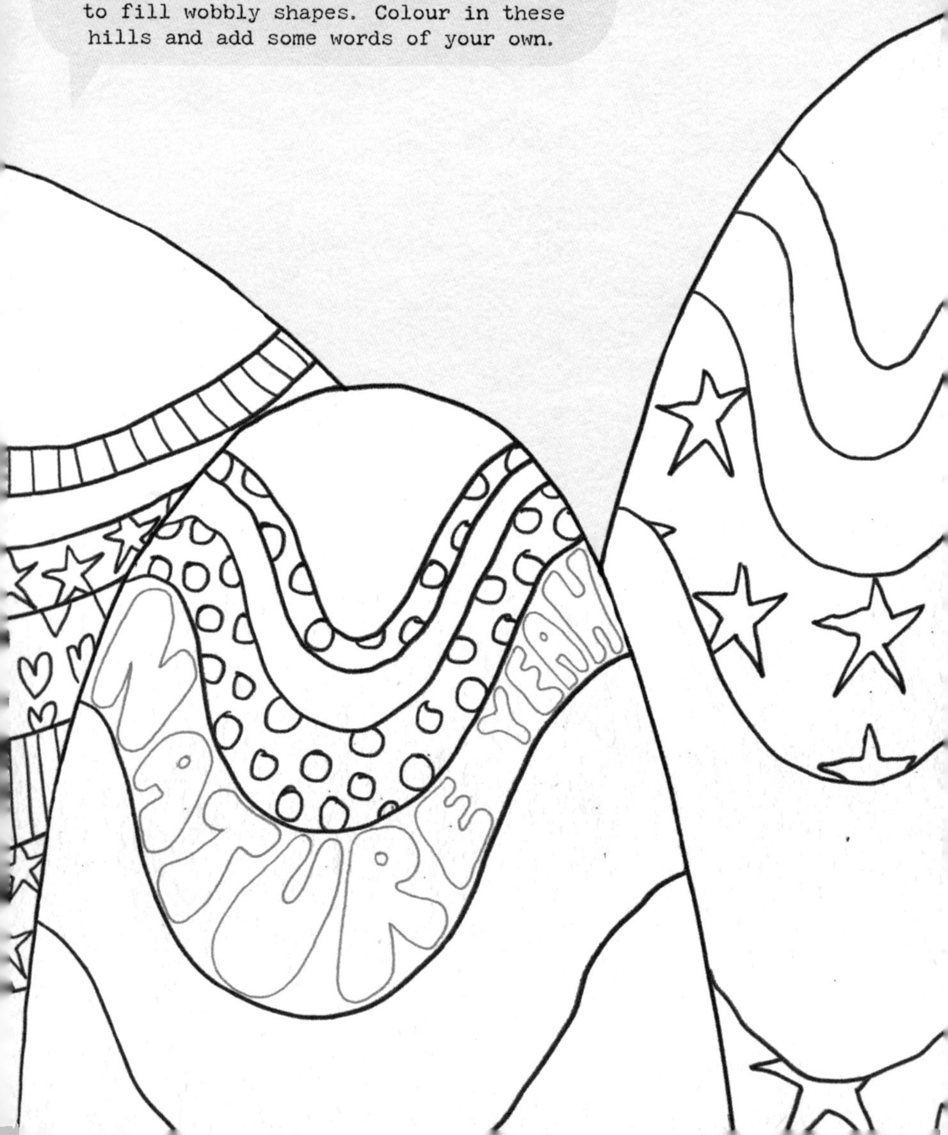

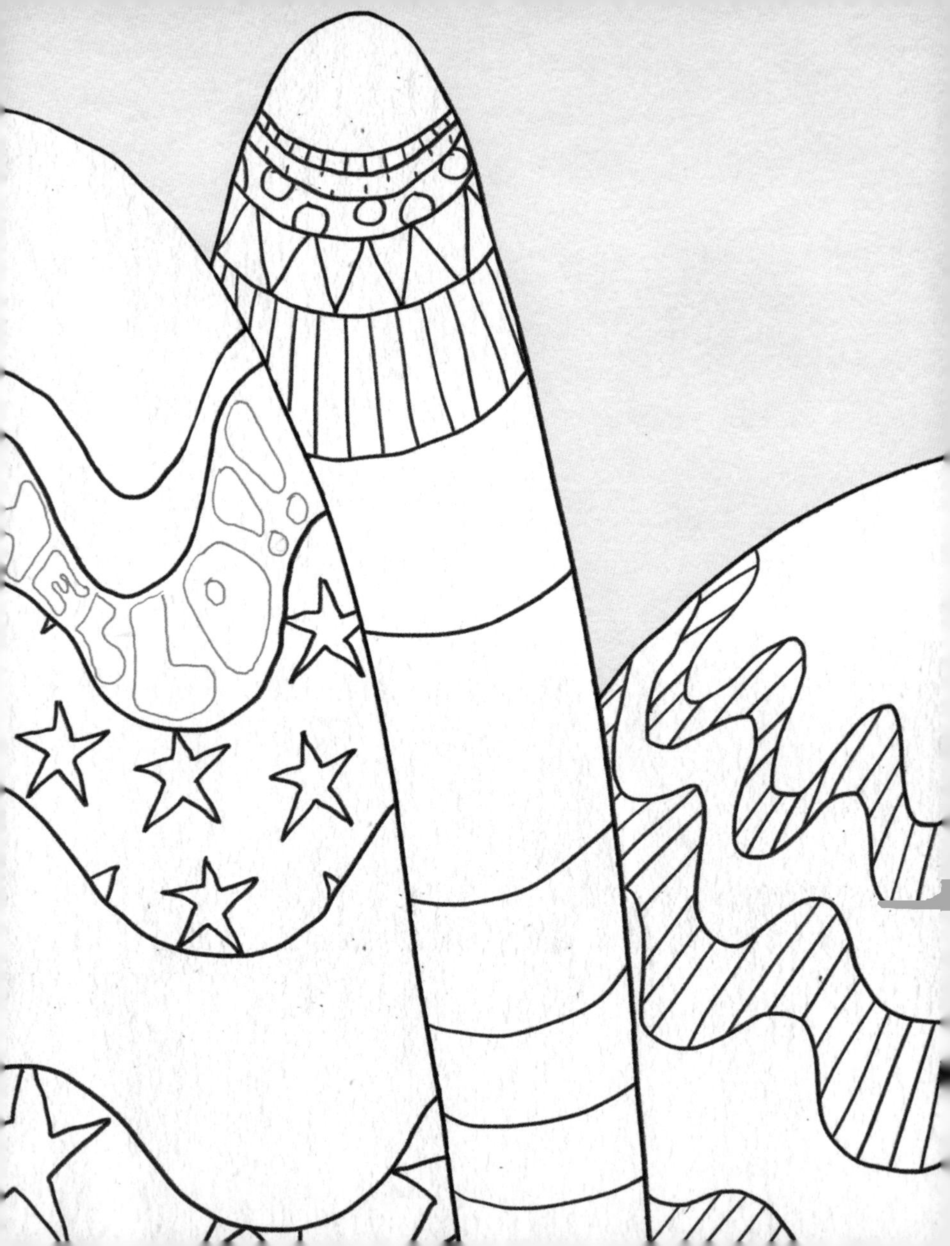

Colour in the contour lines and practise drawing your own. You can stick to gradients of the same colour or mix them up!

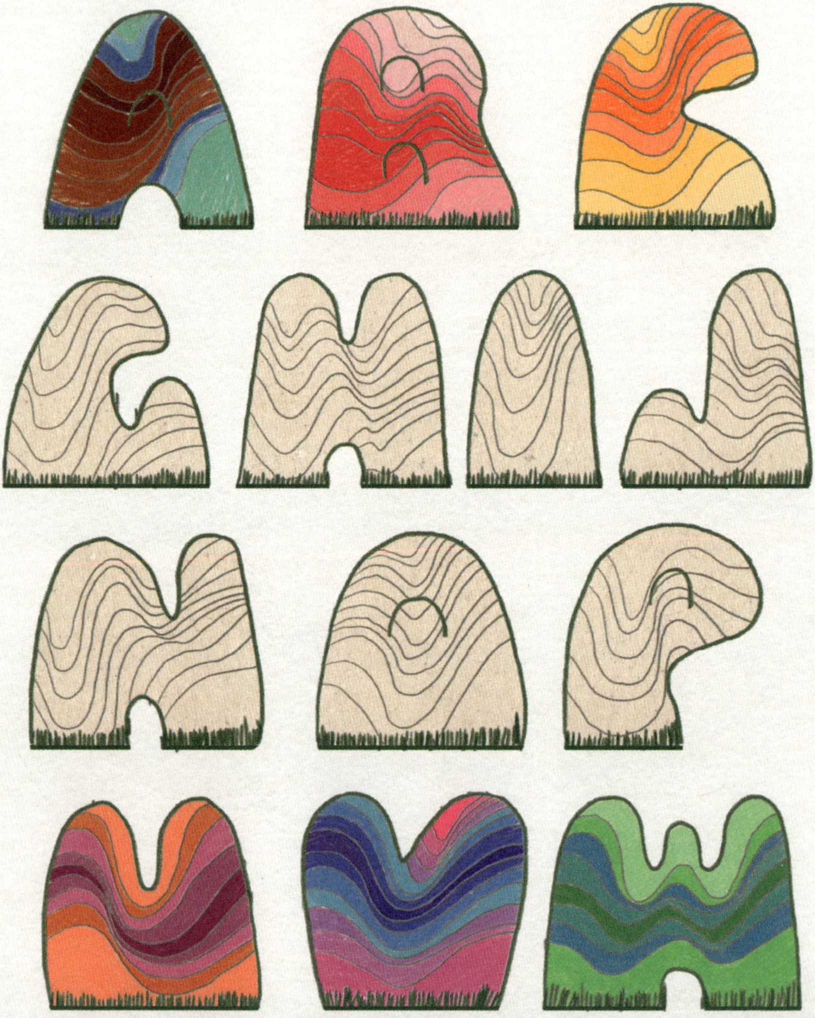

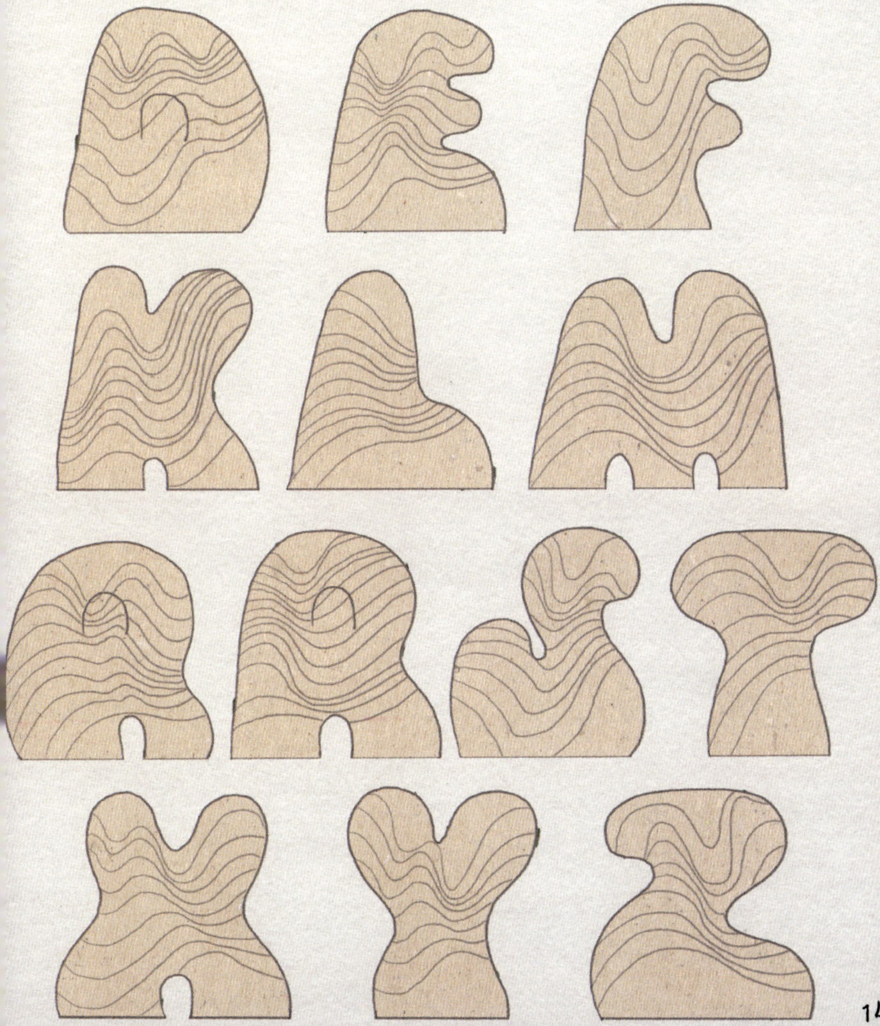

It's time to talk about tote bags. Finish colouring these ones in to get in the mood.

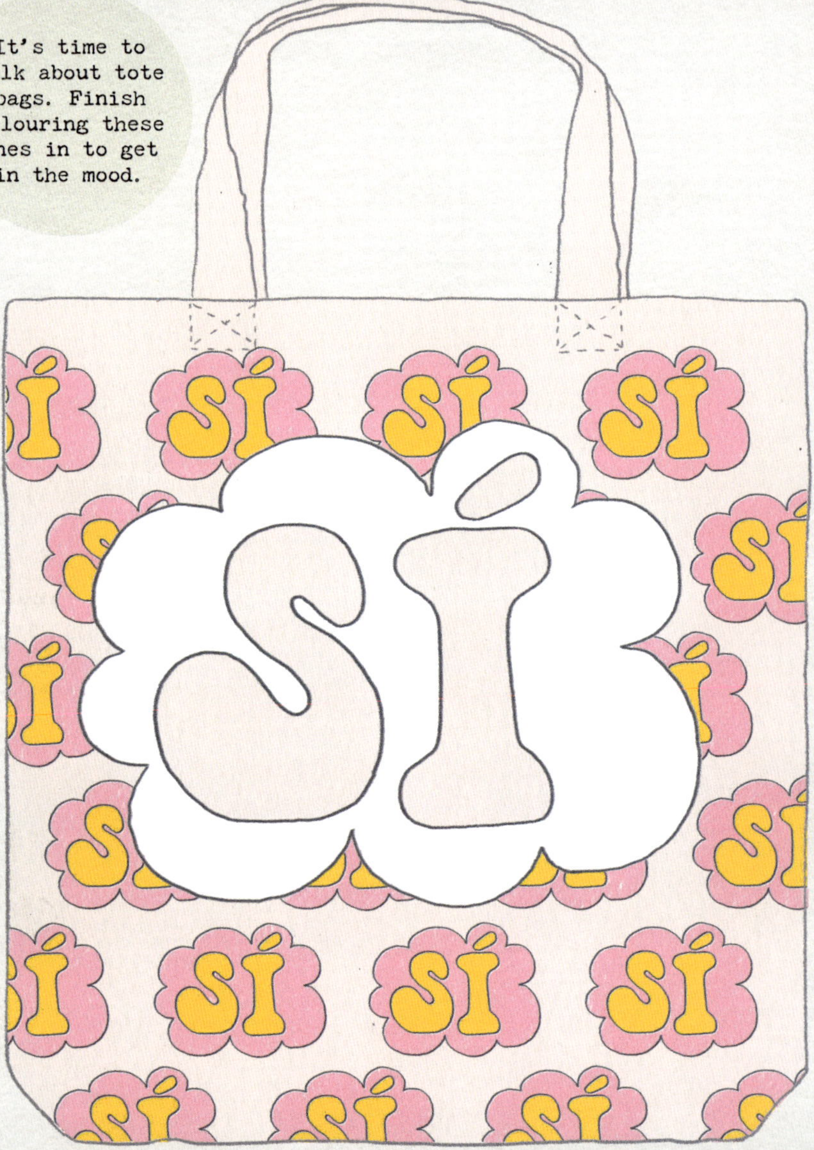

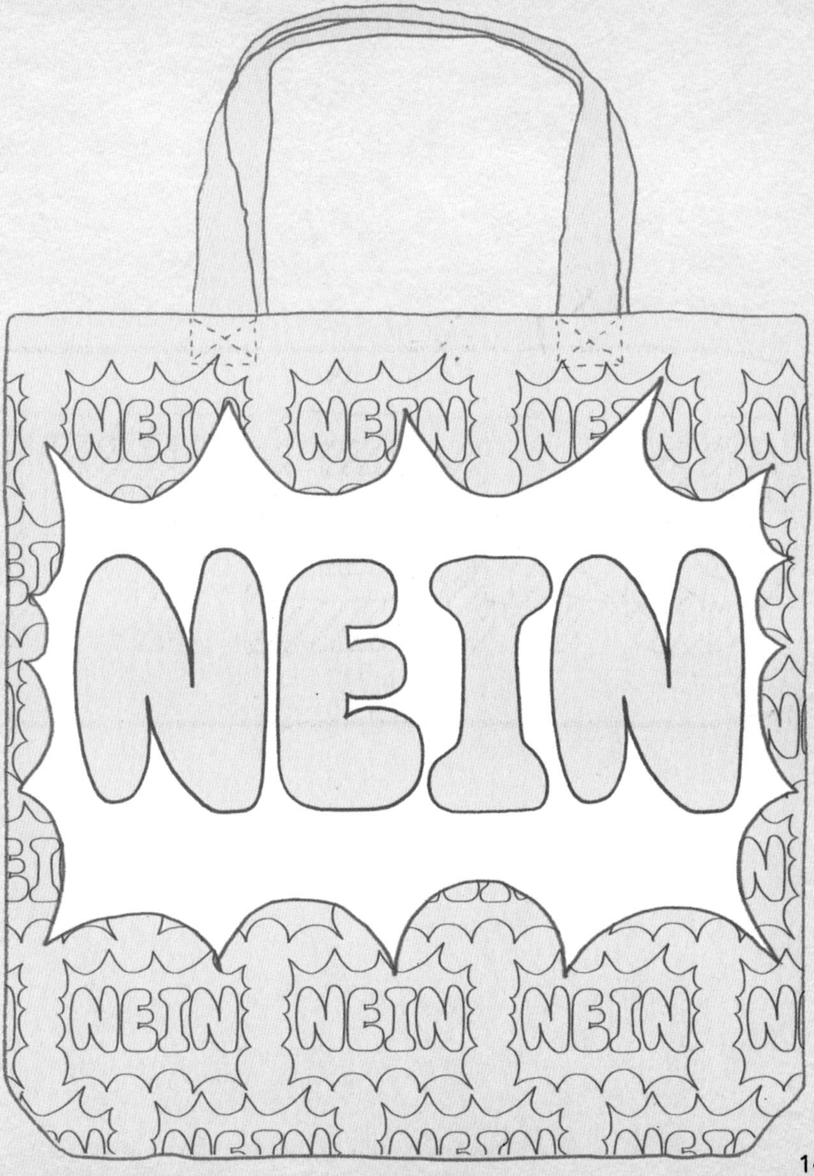
NEIN

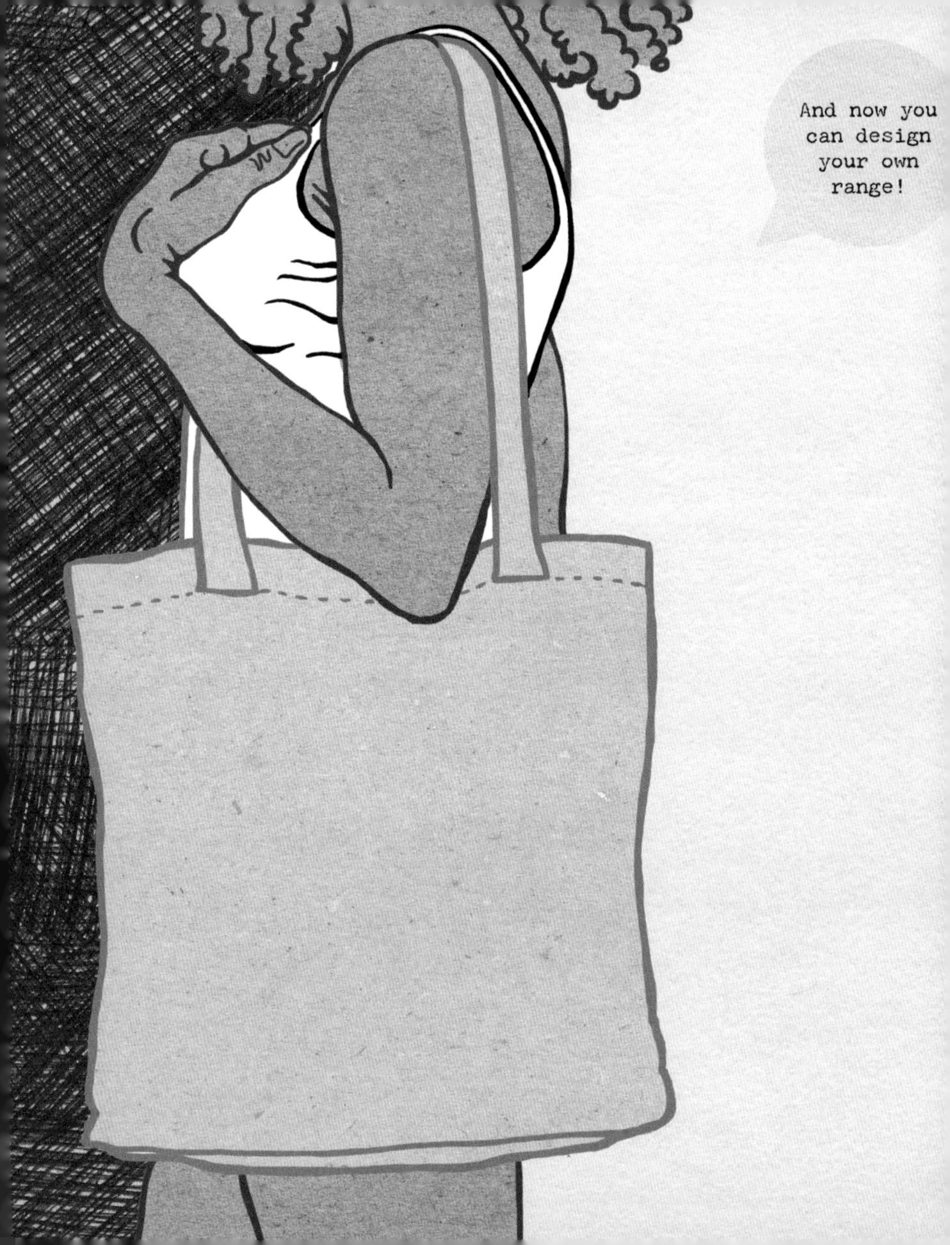
And now you can design your own range!

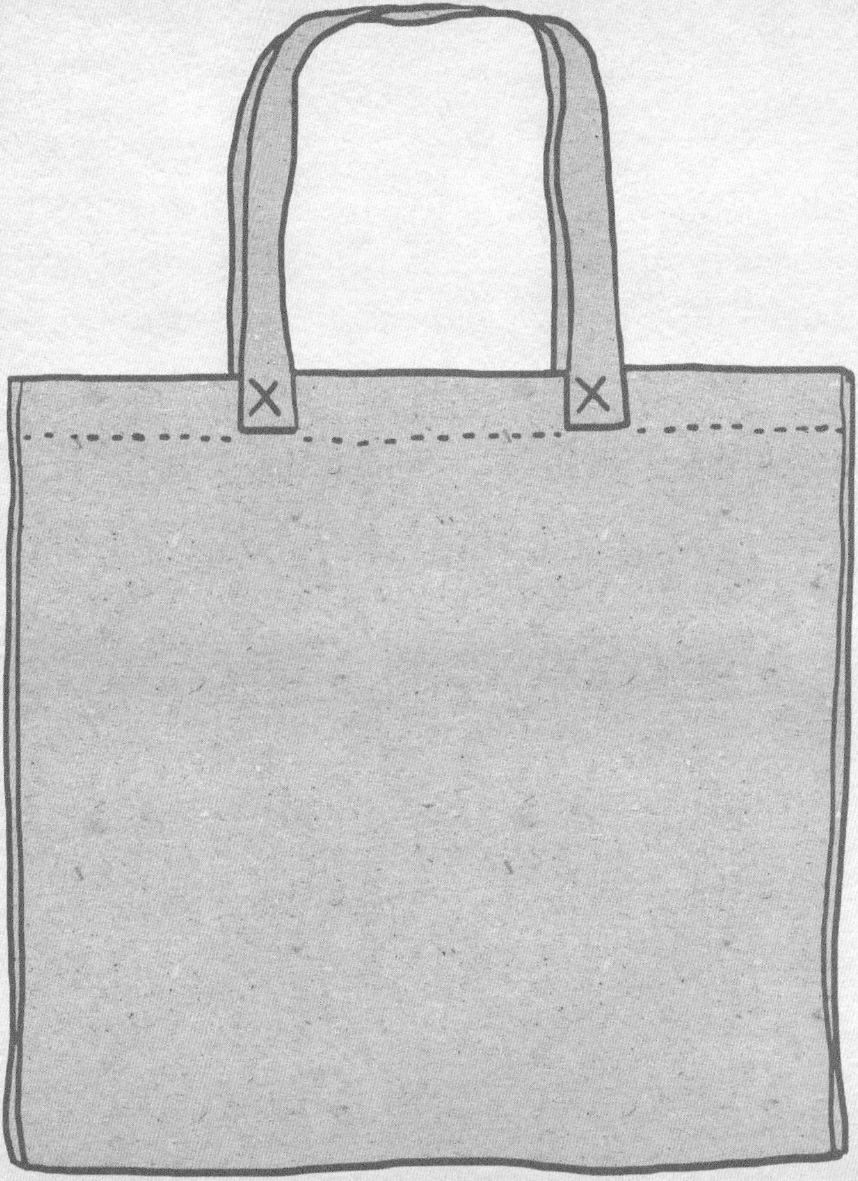

Draw the bubbliest letters that you can and add a little triangle and string at the bottom.

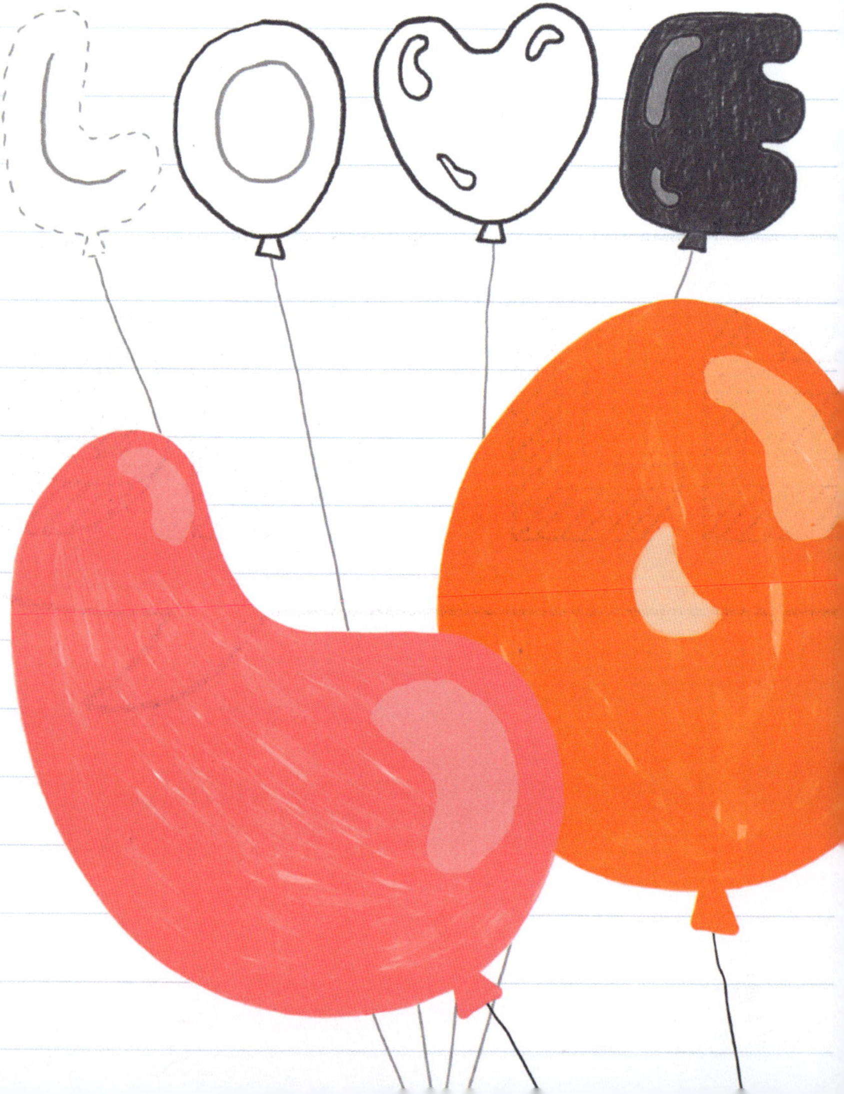

You can add the highlights last with a white pencil, or fill in the whole thing using a light colour. Go over in a darker shade afterwards, leaving them out.

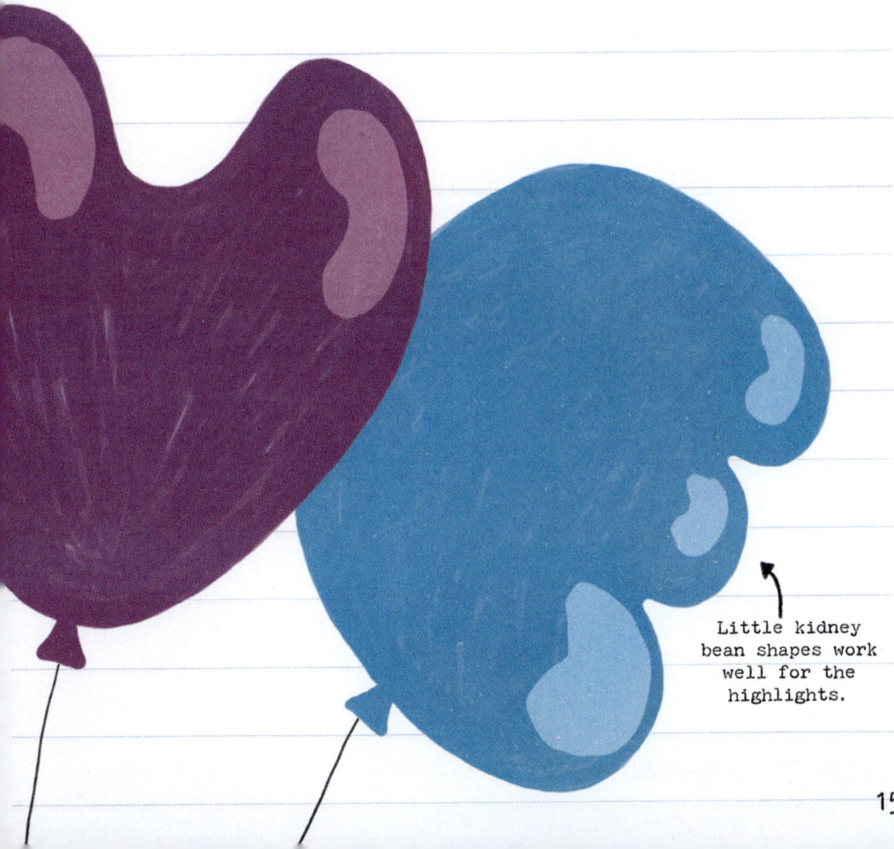

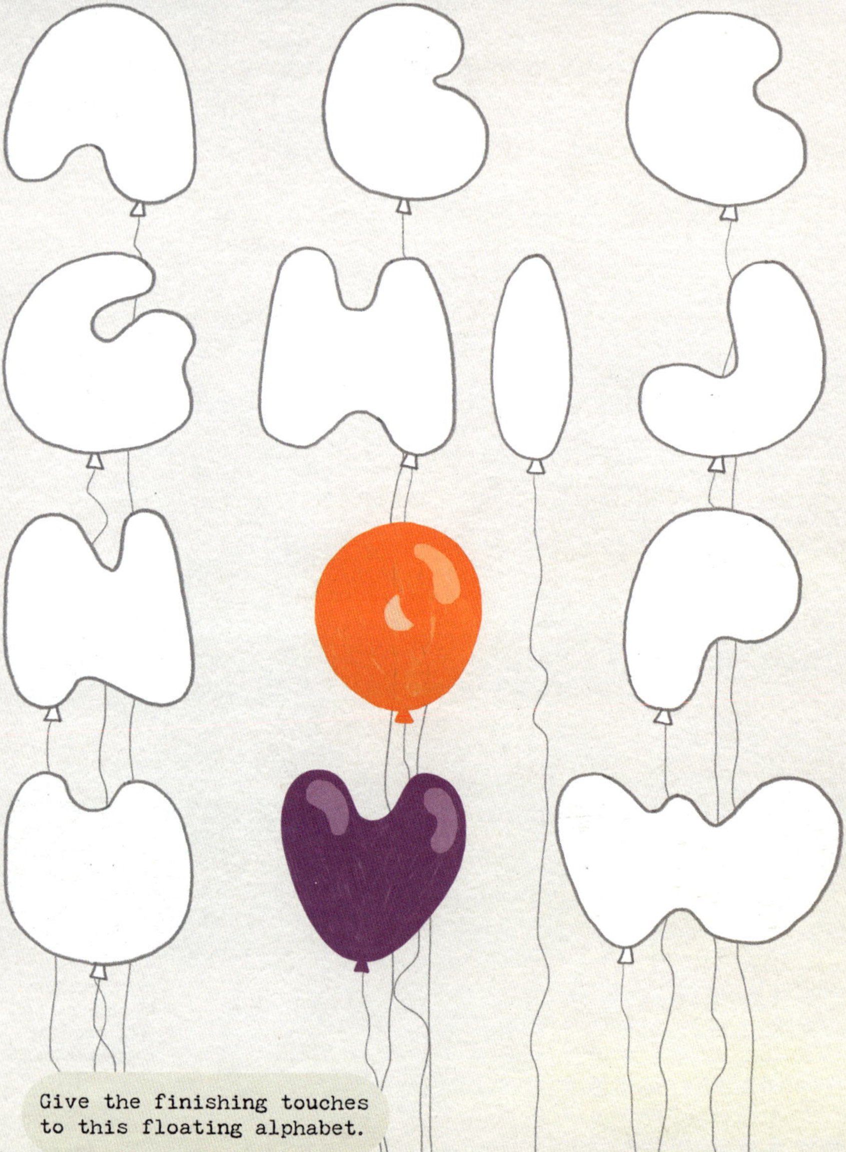

Give the finishing touches to this floating alphabet.

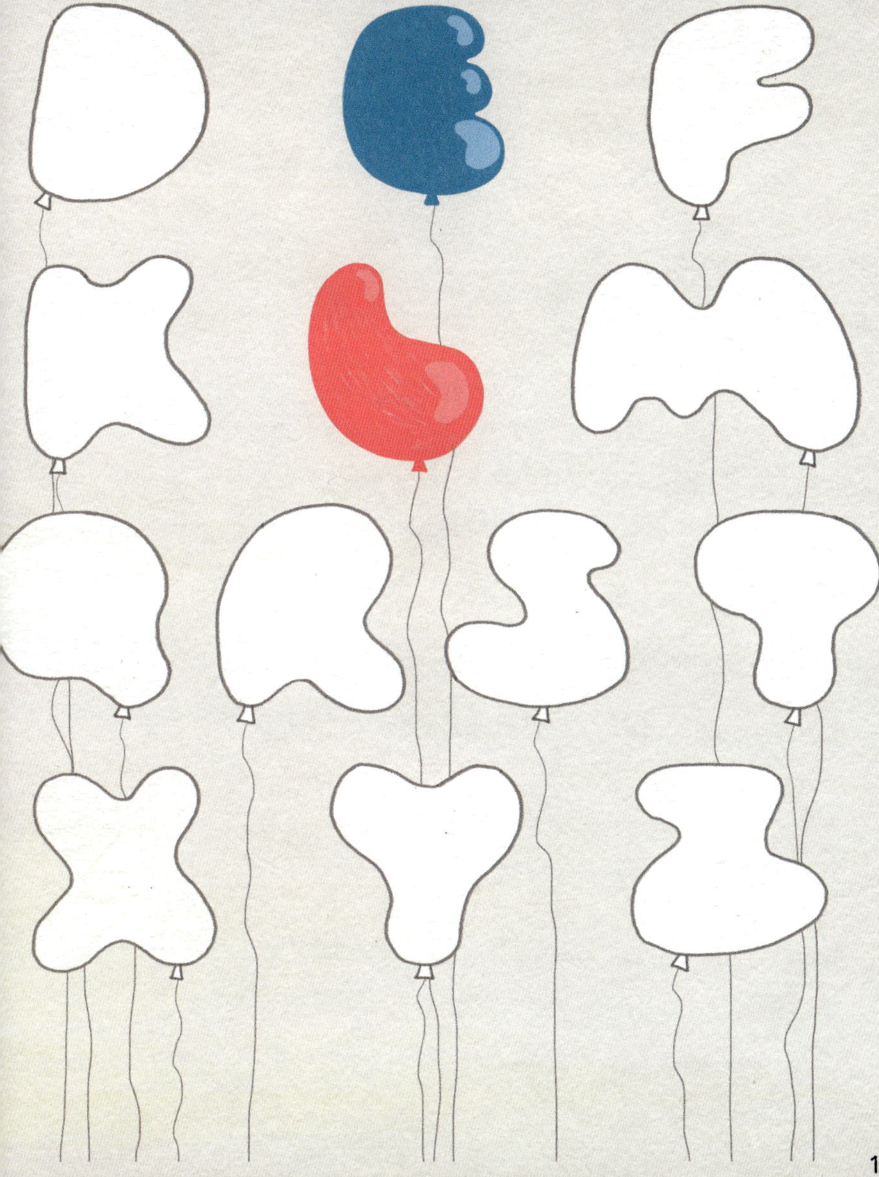
D E F
K L M
Q R S T
X Y Z

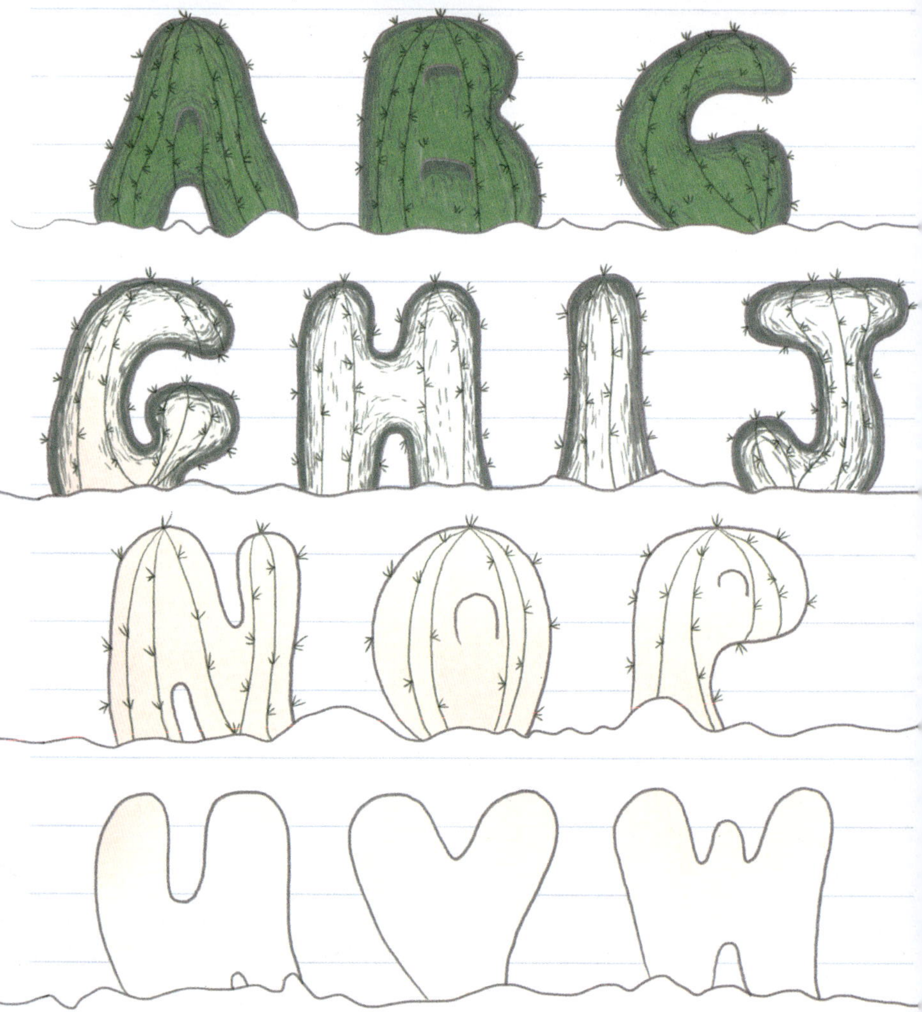
A B C
G H I J
N O P
U V W

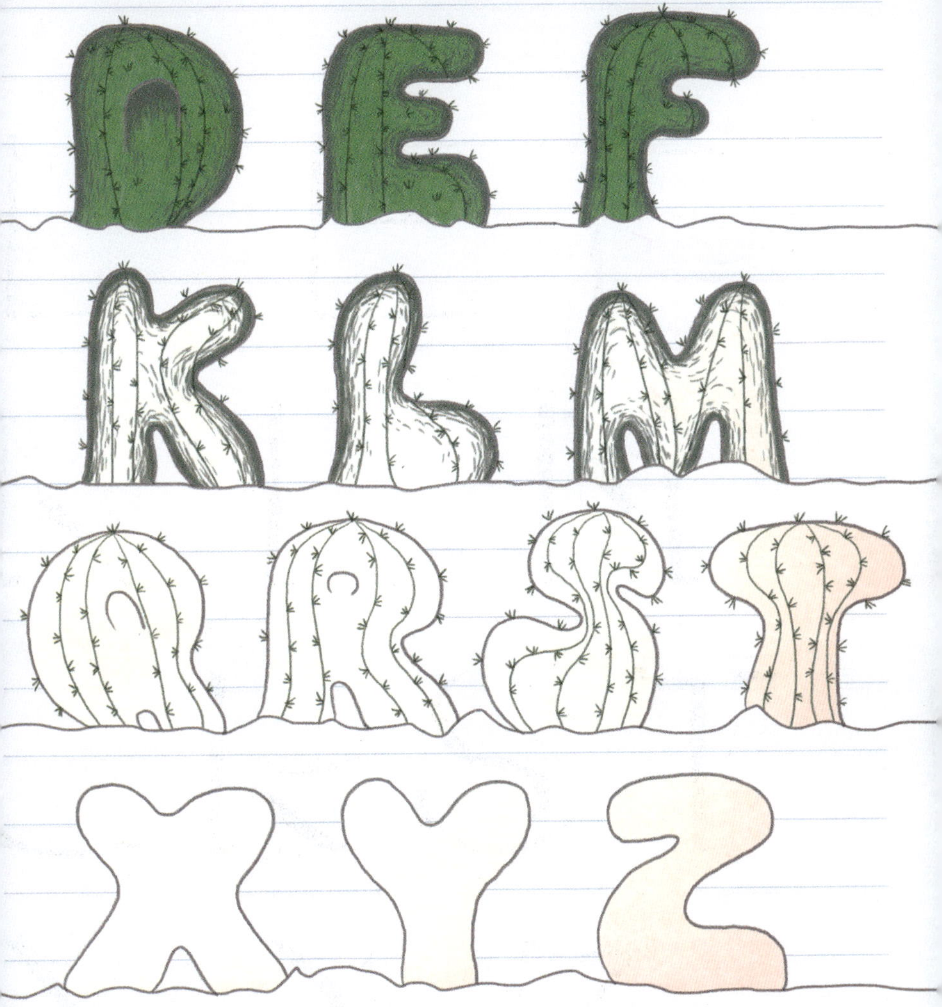

Watch out for the prickles! Be brave and finish off the cactus letters with lines and shading.

Perfecting a cactus takes some practice. Go for it here!

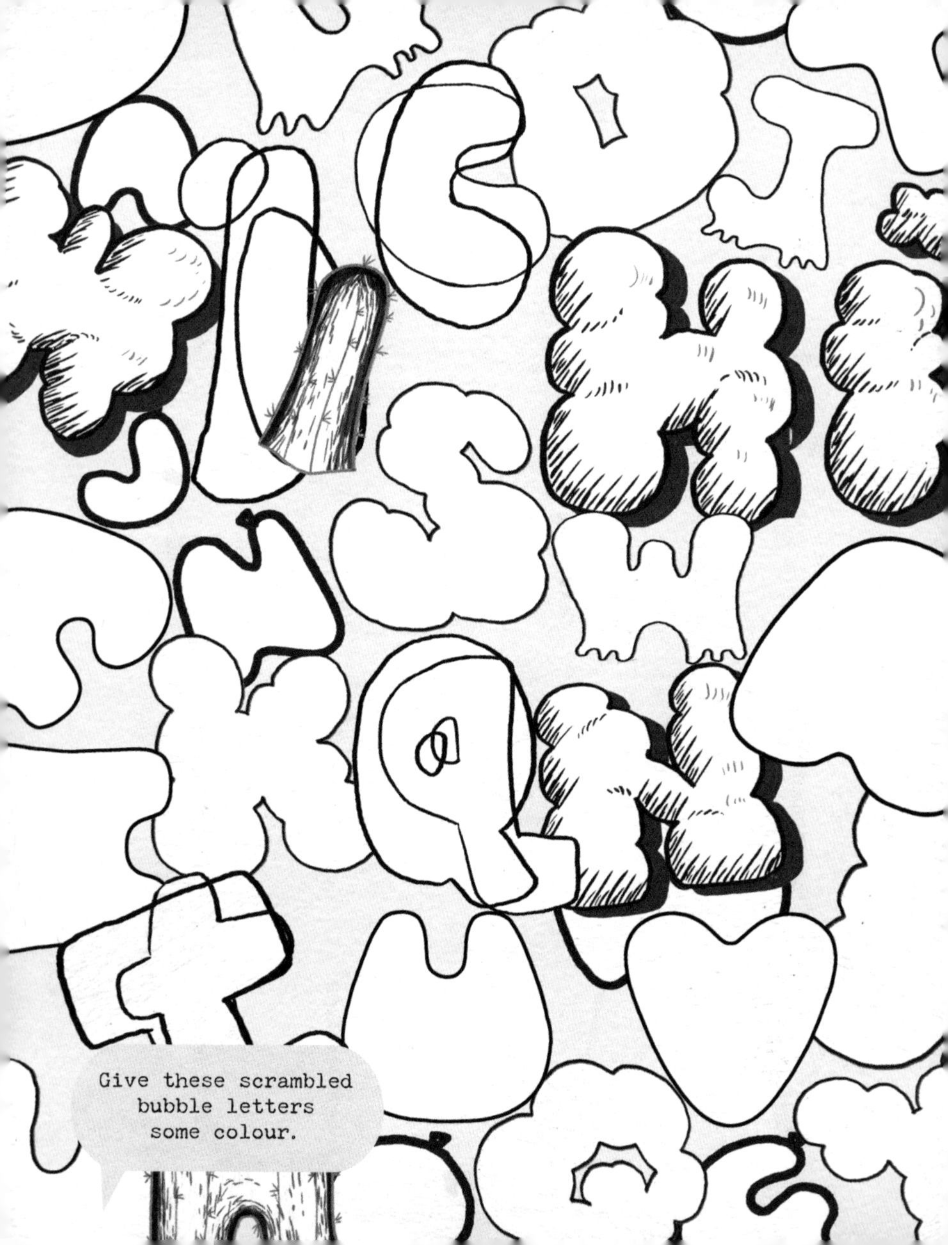

Give these scrambled bubble letters some colour.

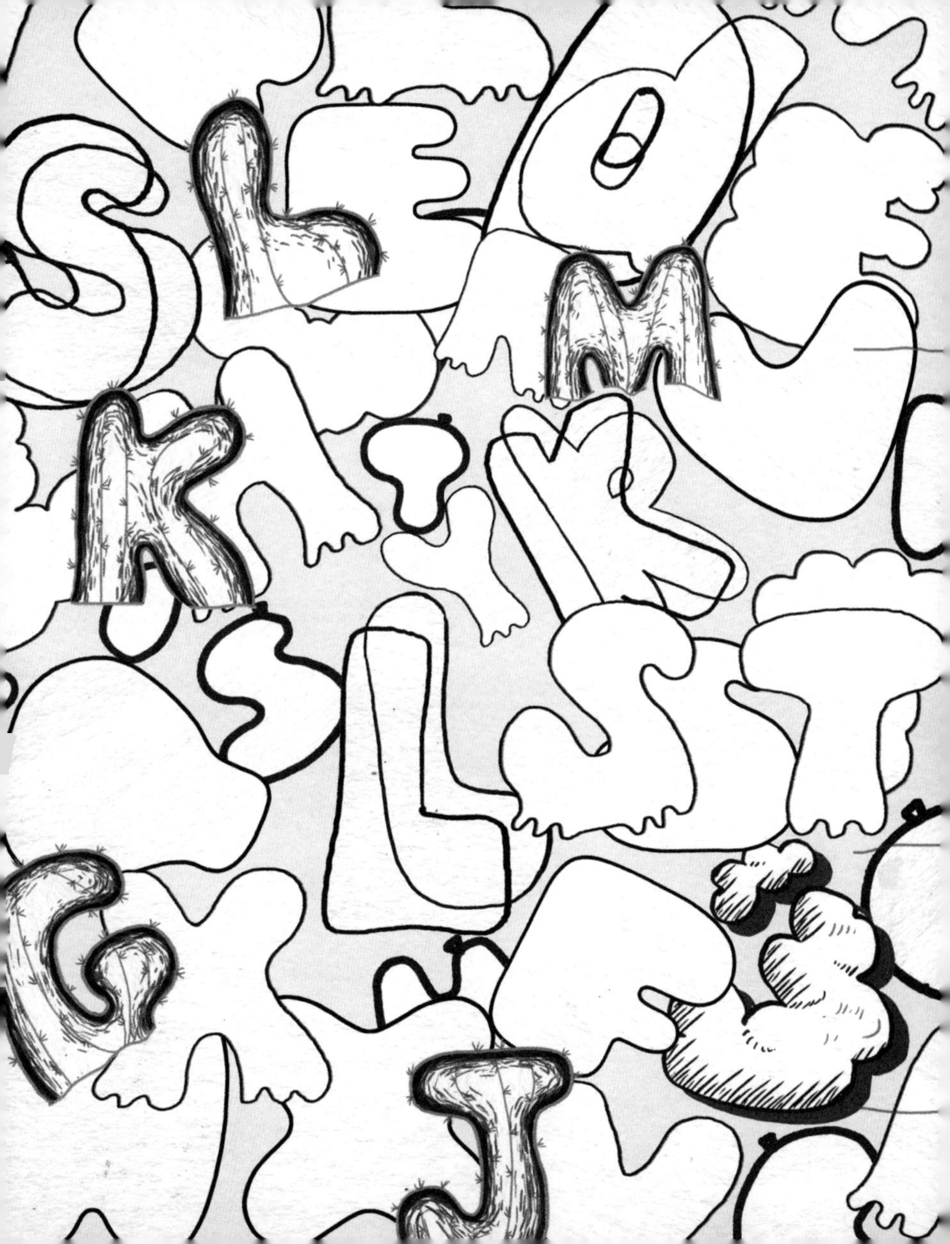

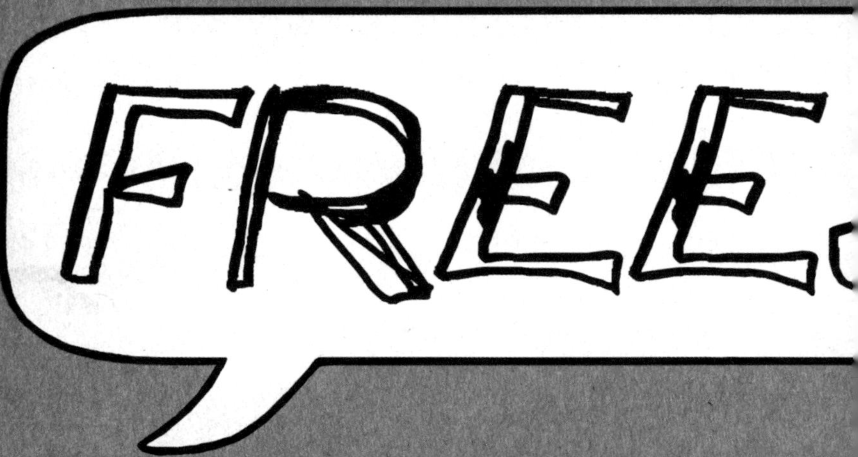
FREE

STYLE

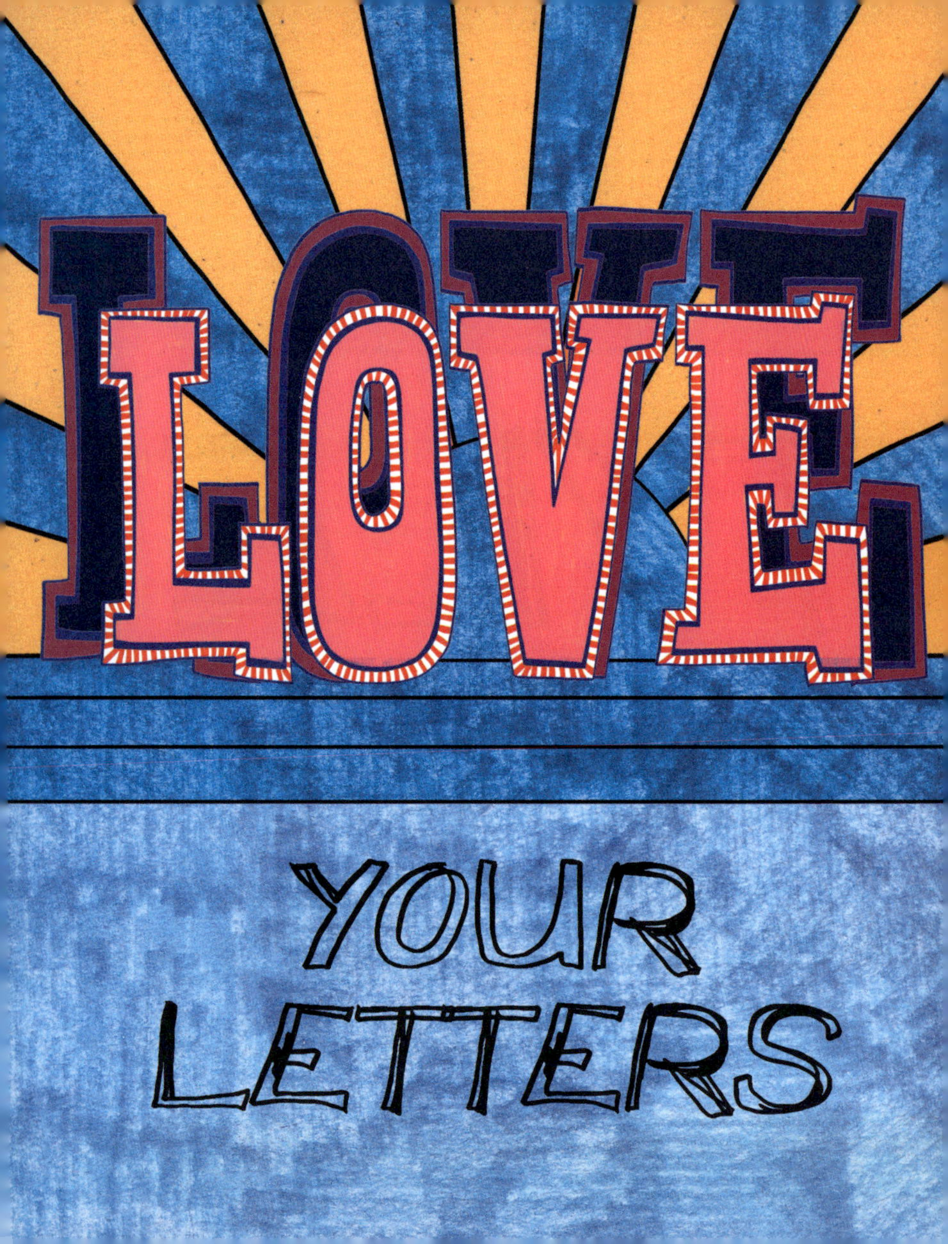
LOVE
YOUR
LETTERS

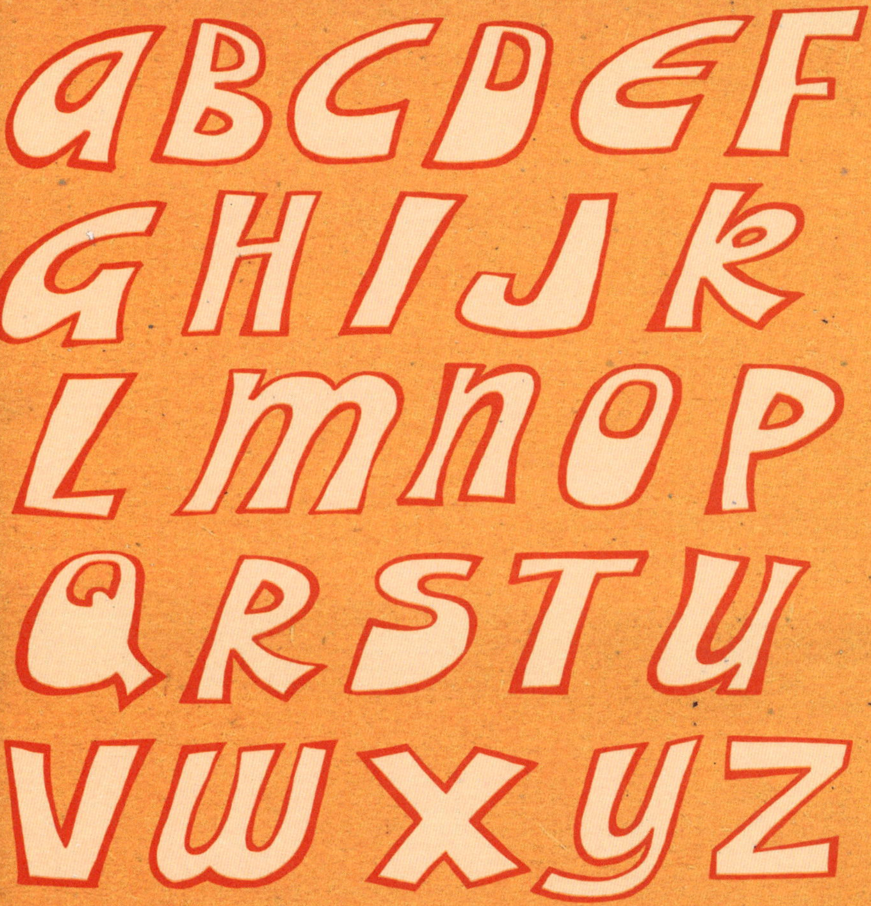

What's not to love? Learn this basic freestyle alphabet to get started. Turn over to find out how...

Going freestyle means you can create letters in any form you like, so don't overthink it. Neatness has no place here.

a b c d

j k l m

r s t u v

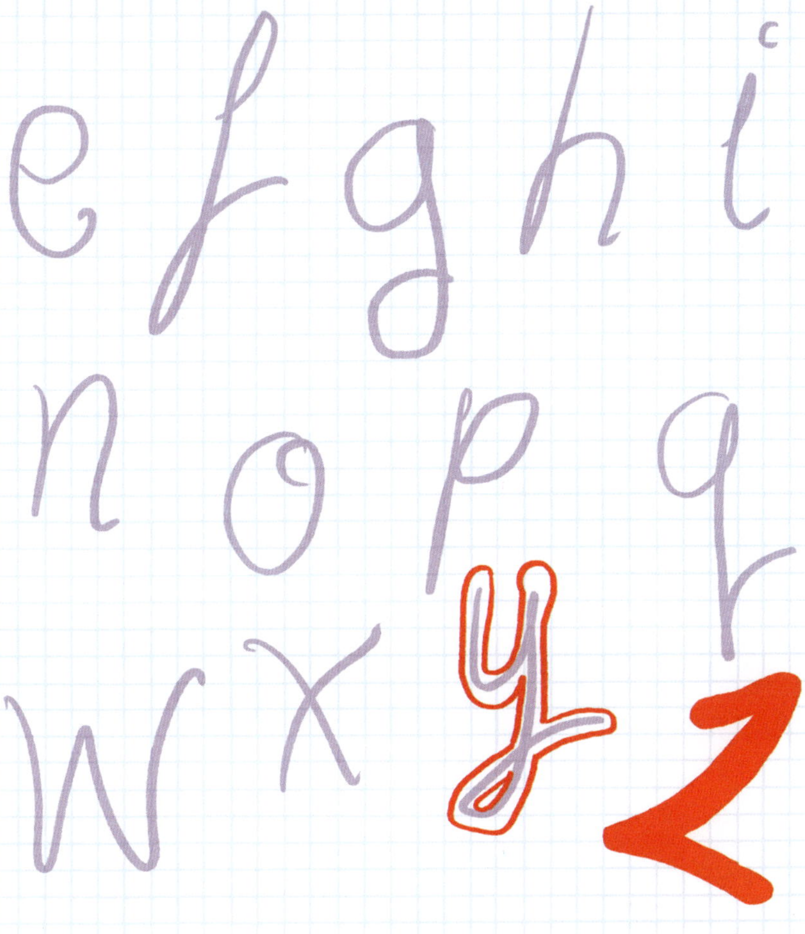

Start by drawing around these freehand letters and colouring them in.

Now draw
around some
of your own!

Freestyle letters are unique to you, so start developing your own! Here are two of my favourites.

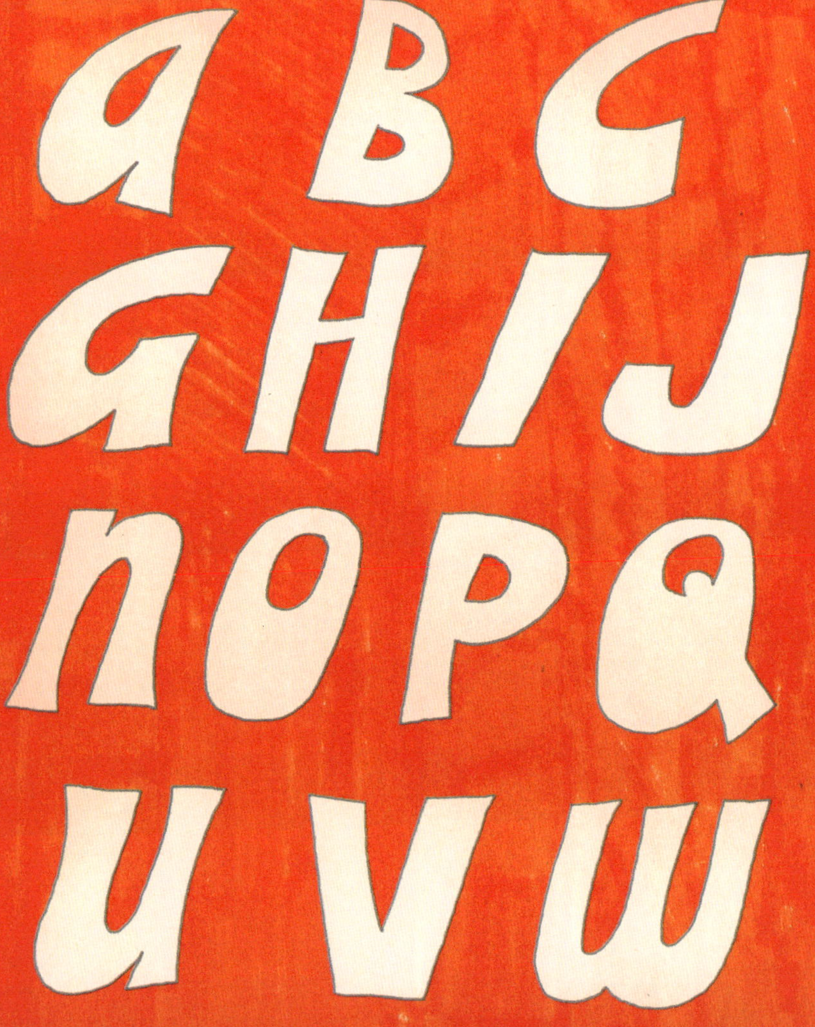

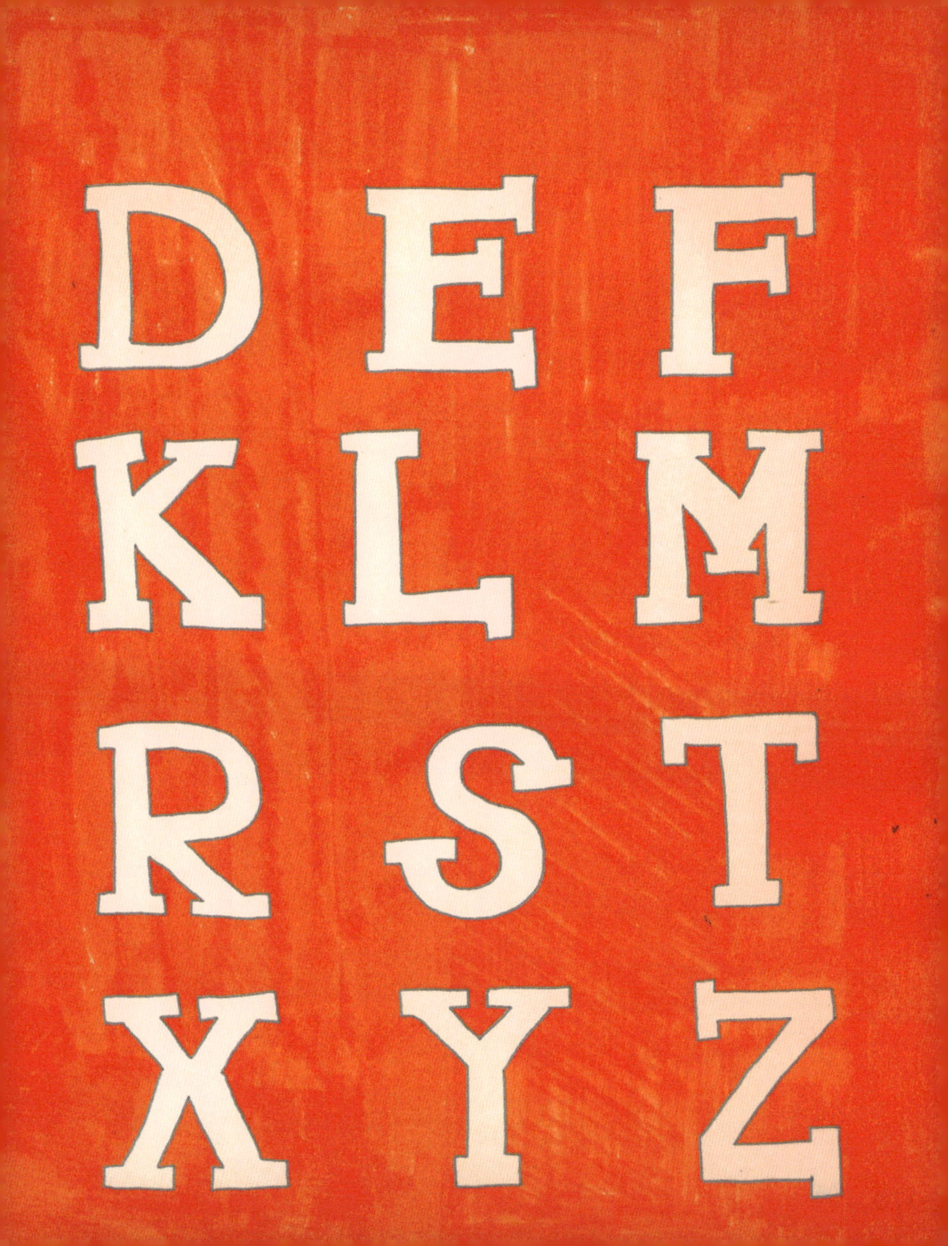
D E F
K L M
R S T
X Y Z

Use this space to design your own freestyle letters. Don't worry if they are upper or lower case – it's time to throw the rules out.

Yes, really...no rules. If you want your letters to look like mountains, then they can.

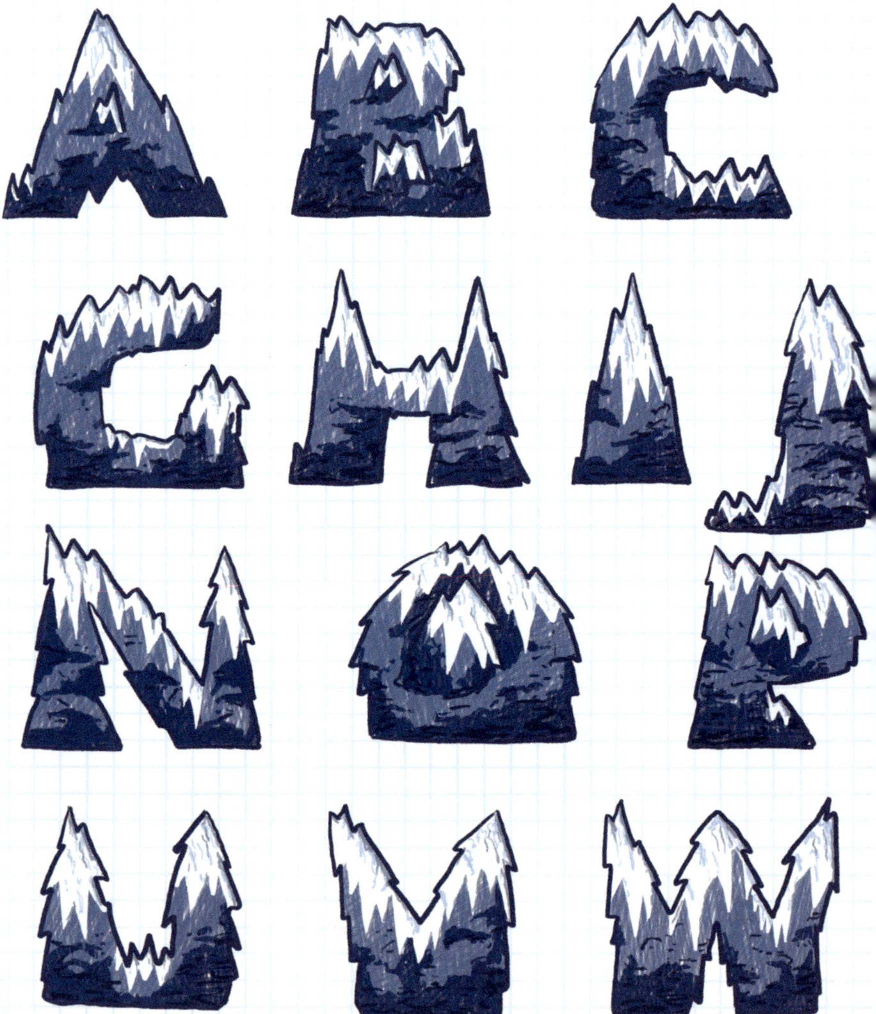

These ones need a bit of finishing off.

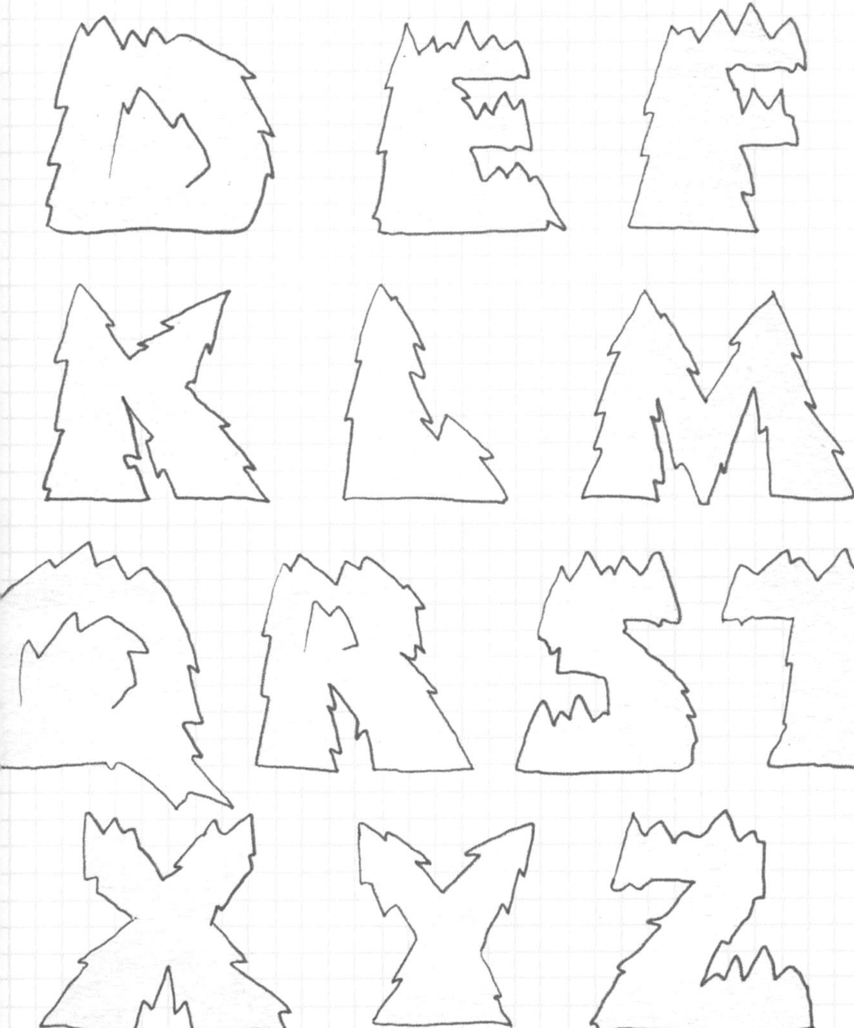

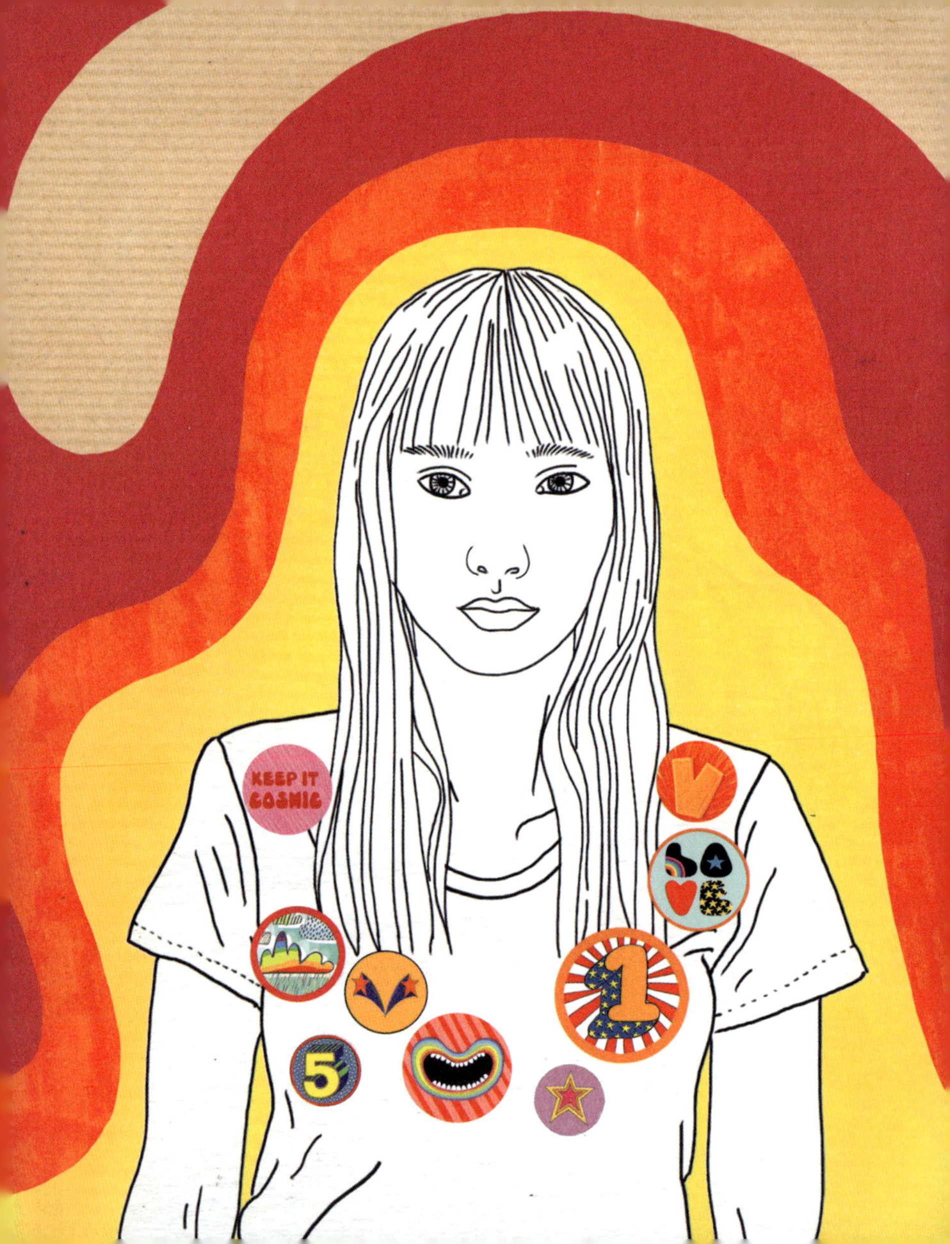
KEEP IT COSMIC

Be powerful!

Wear your beliefs with pride!

Pin badges are perfect for showing off your letter styles. Finish colouring these ones in.

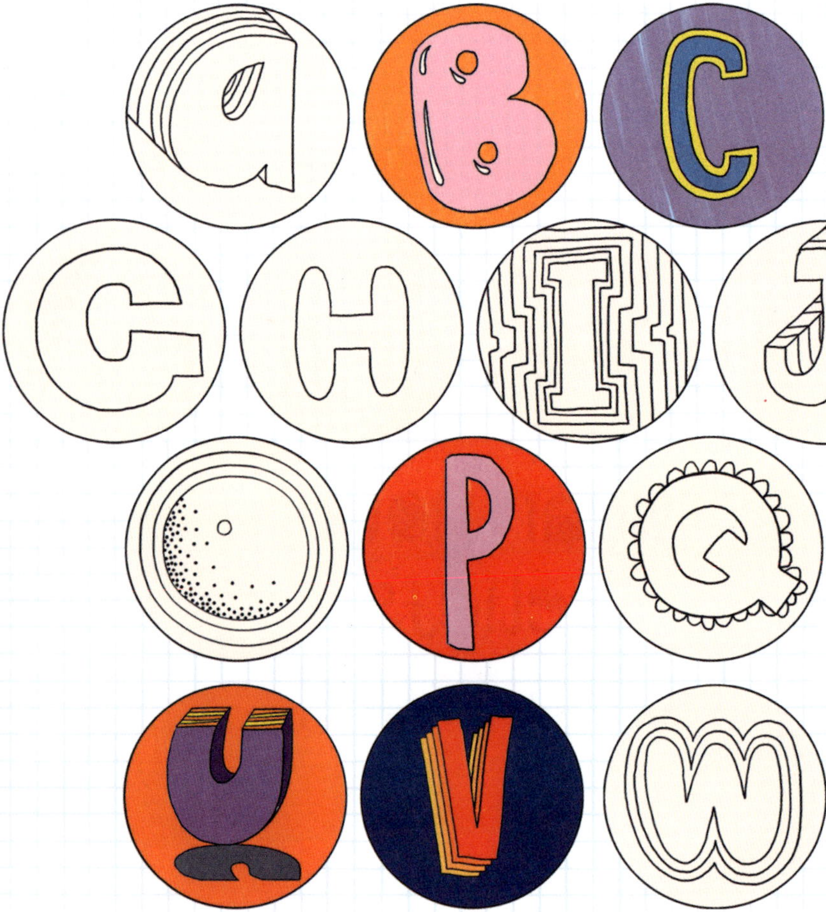

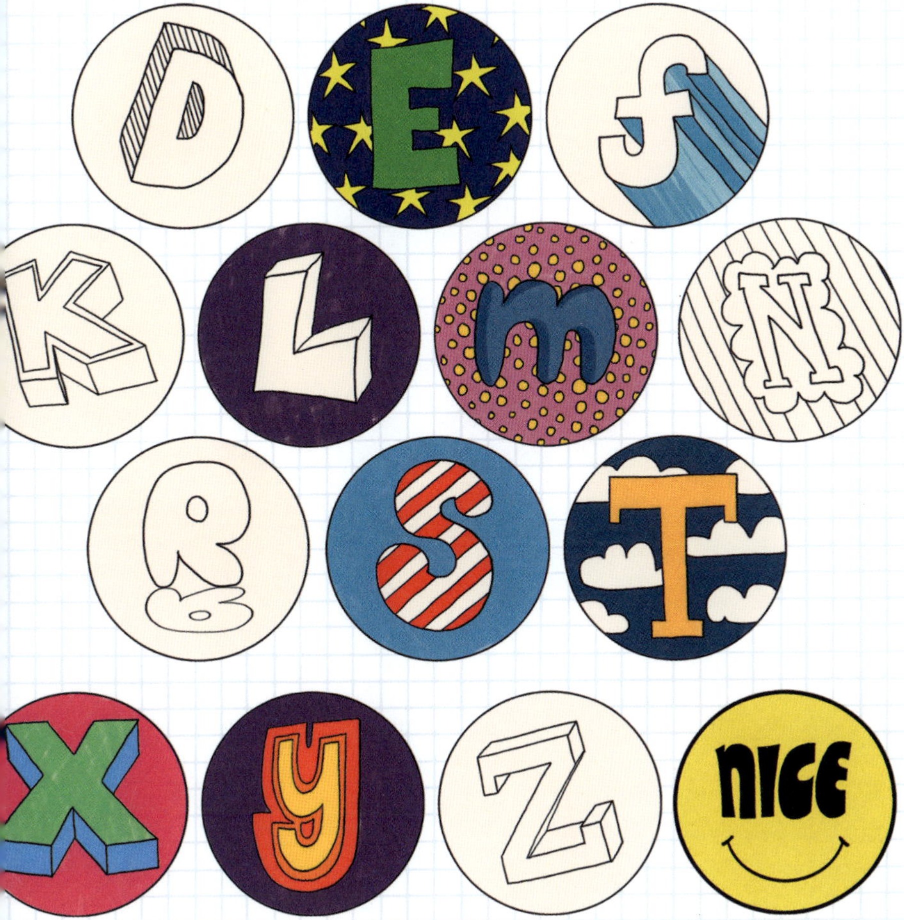
D E F
K L M N
R S T
X Y Z NICE

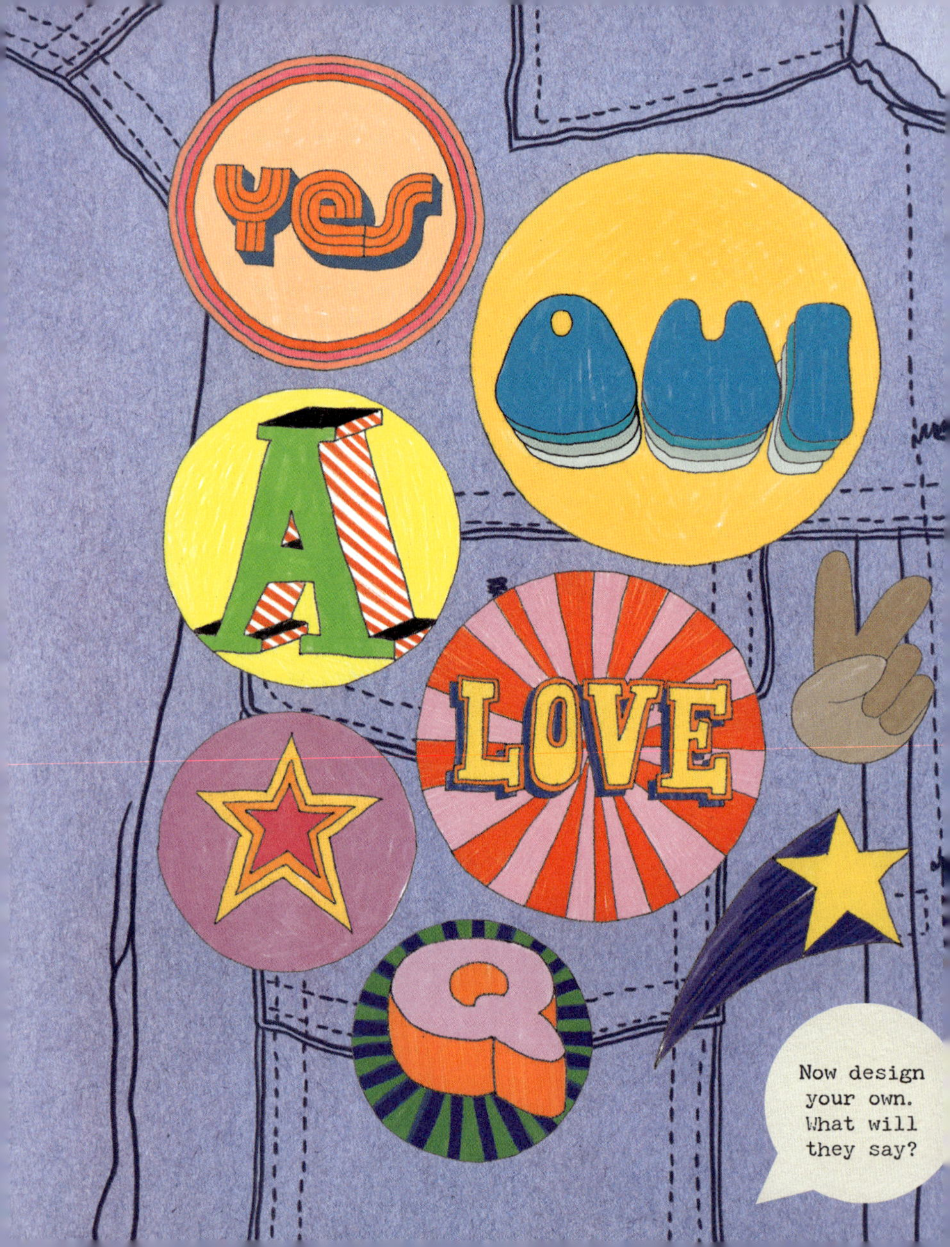
yes
OUI
A
LOVE
Q
Now design your own. What will they say?

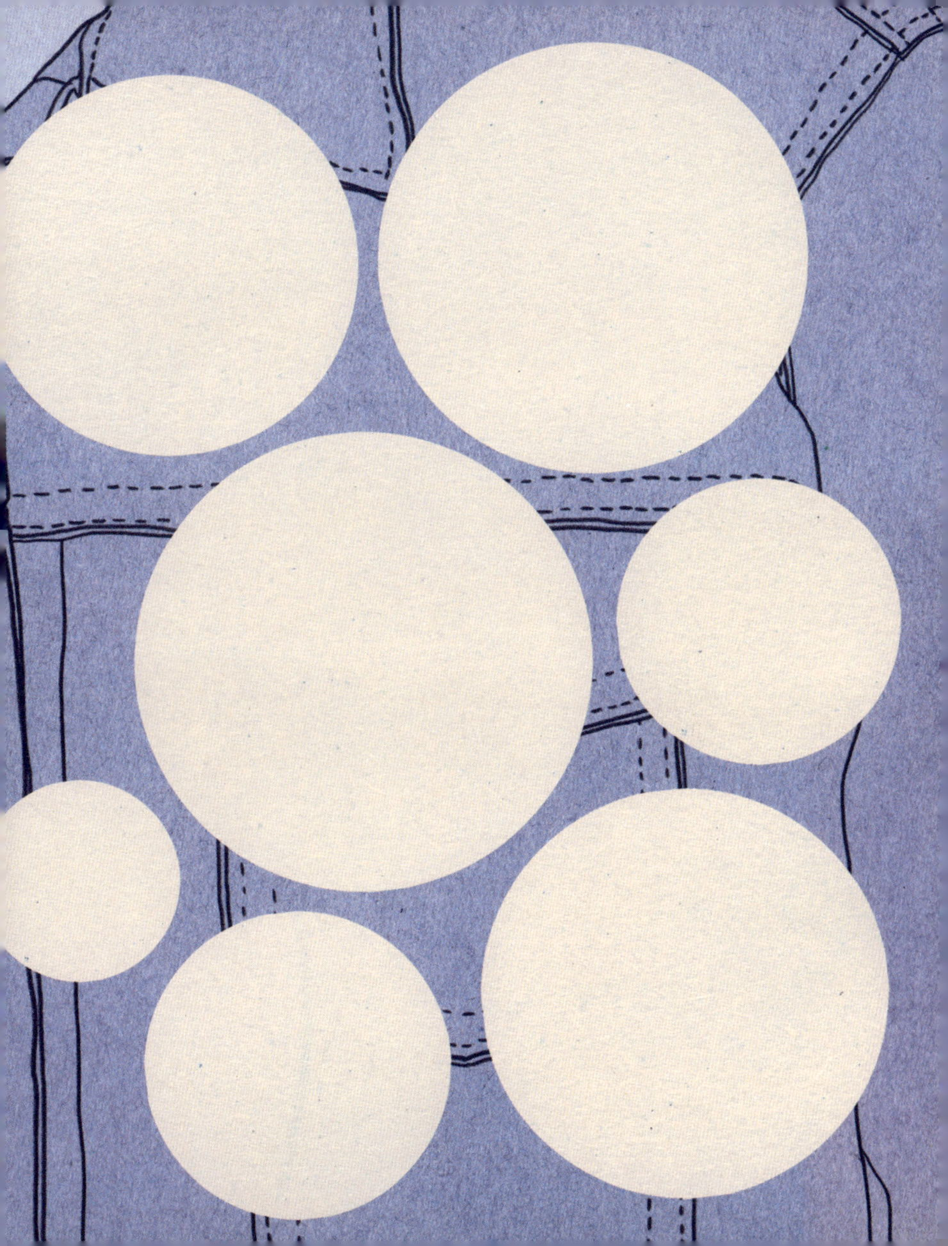

There's no such thing as too much practice!

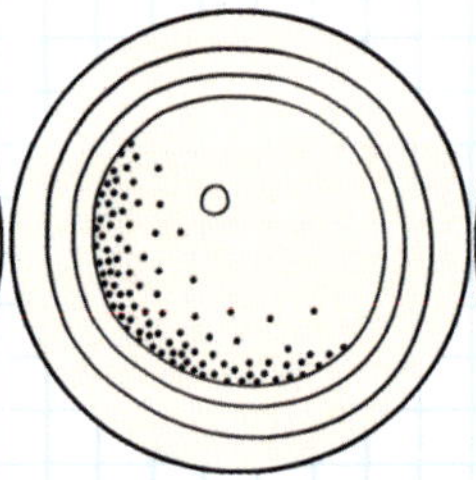

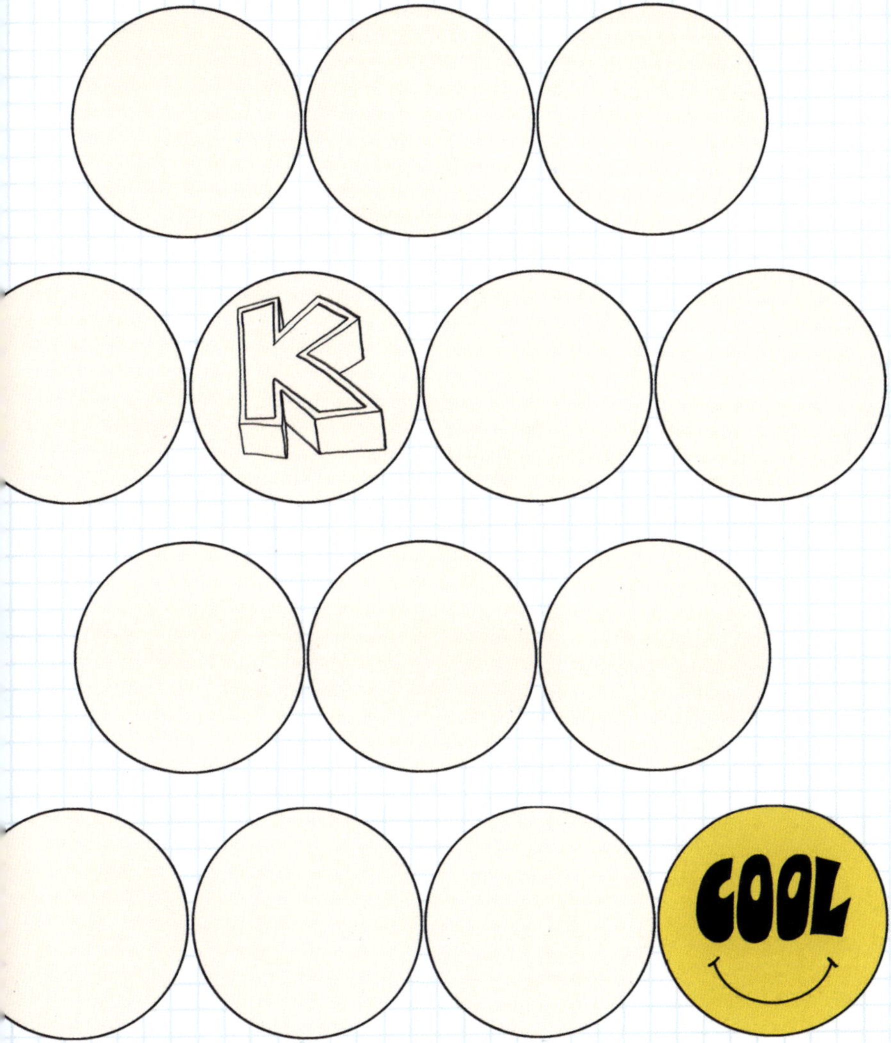
K
COOL

Keep it going: design badges to be proud of.

SAY IT ROUND

SAY IT **PROUD**

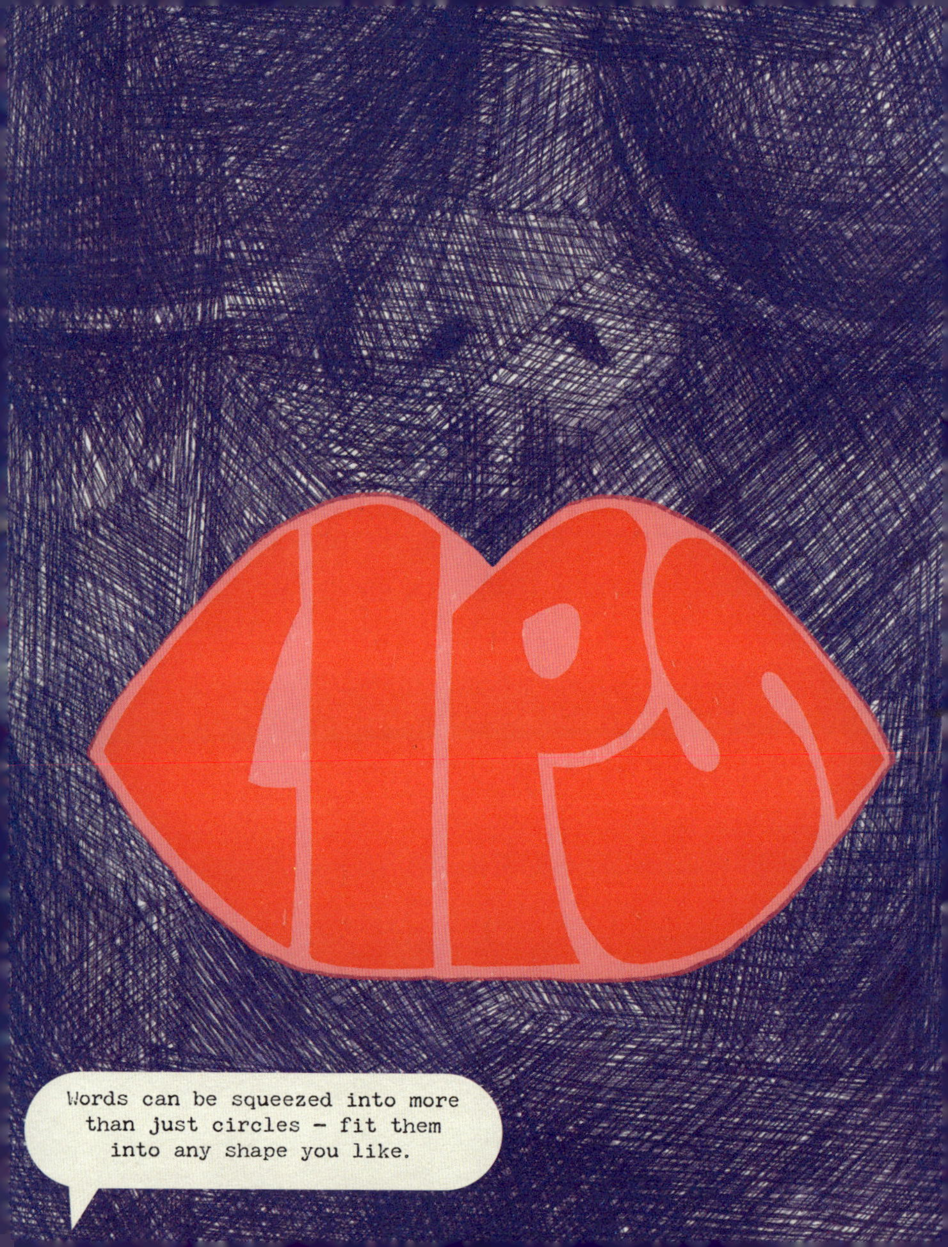
LIPS
Words can be squeezed into more than just circles - fit them into any shape you like.

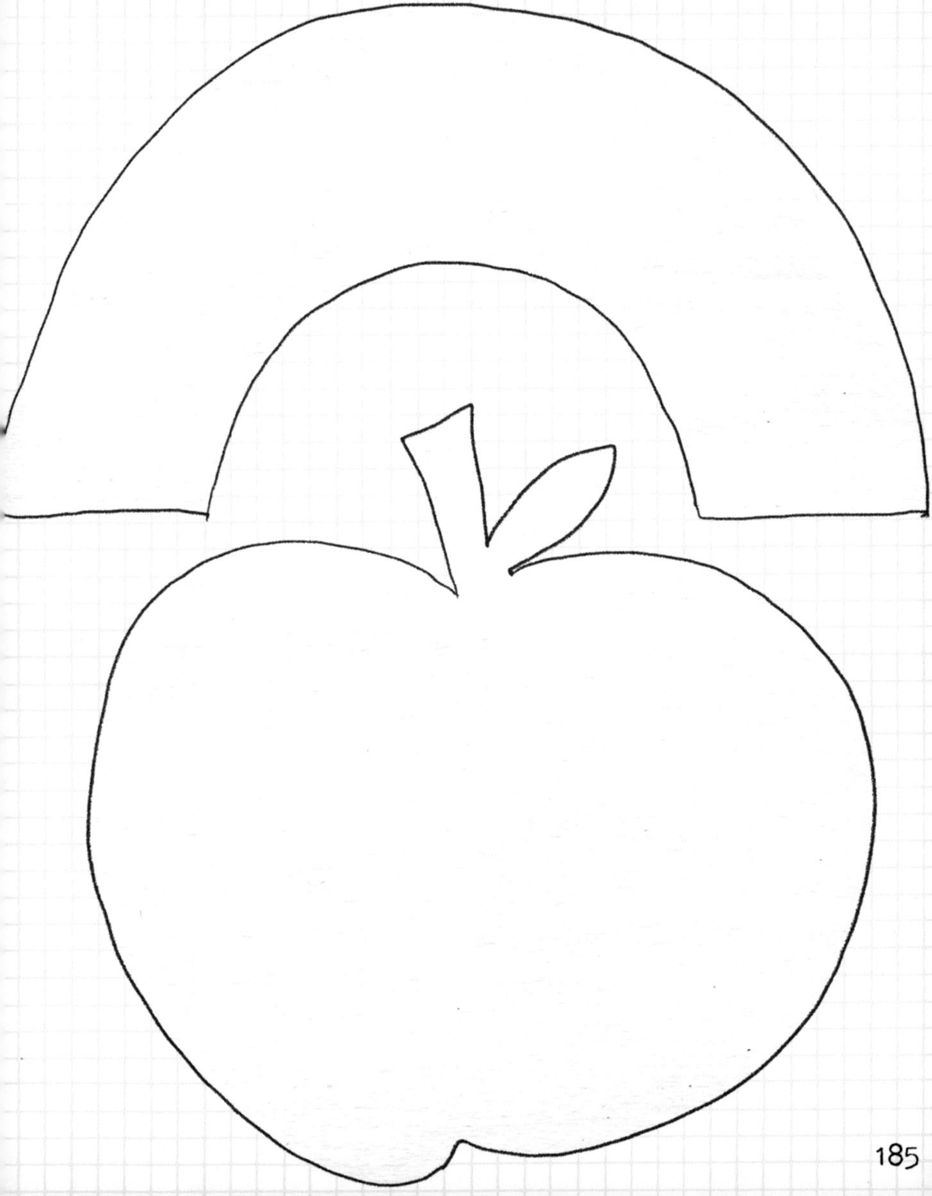

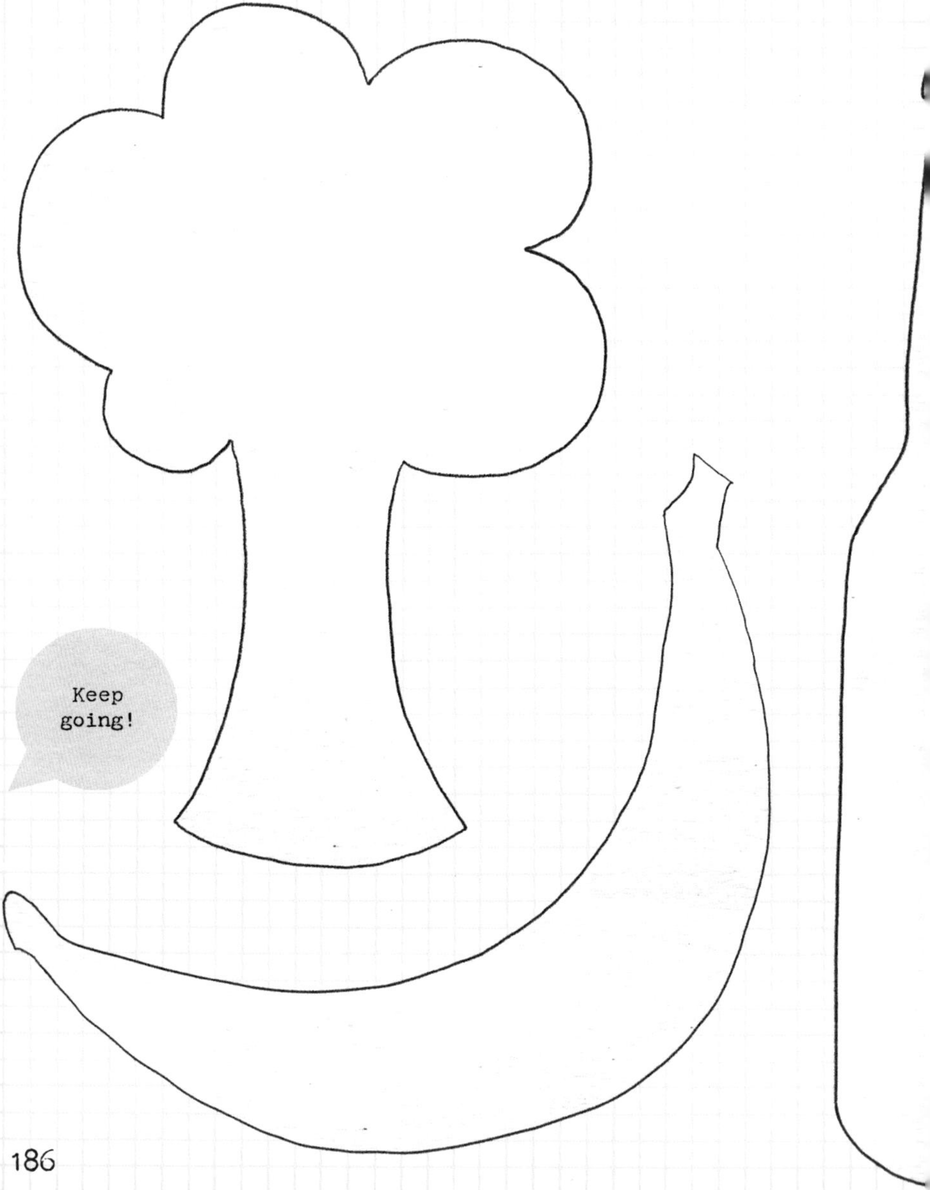
Keep going!

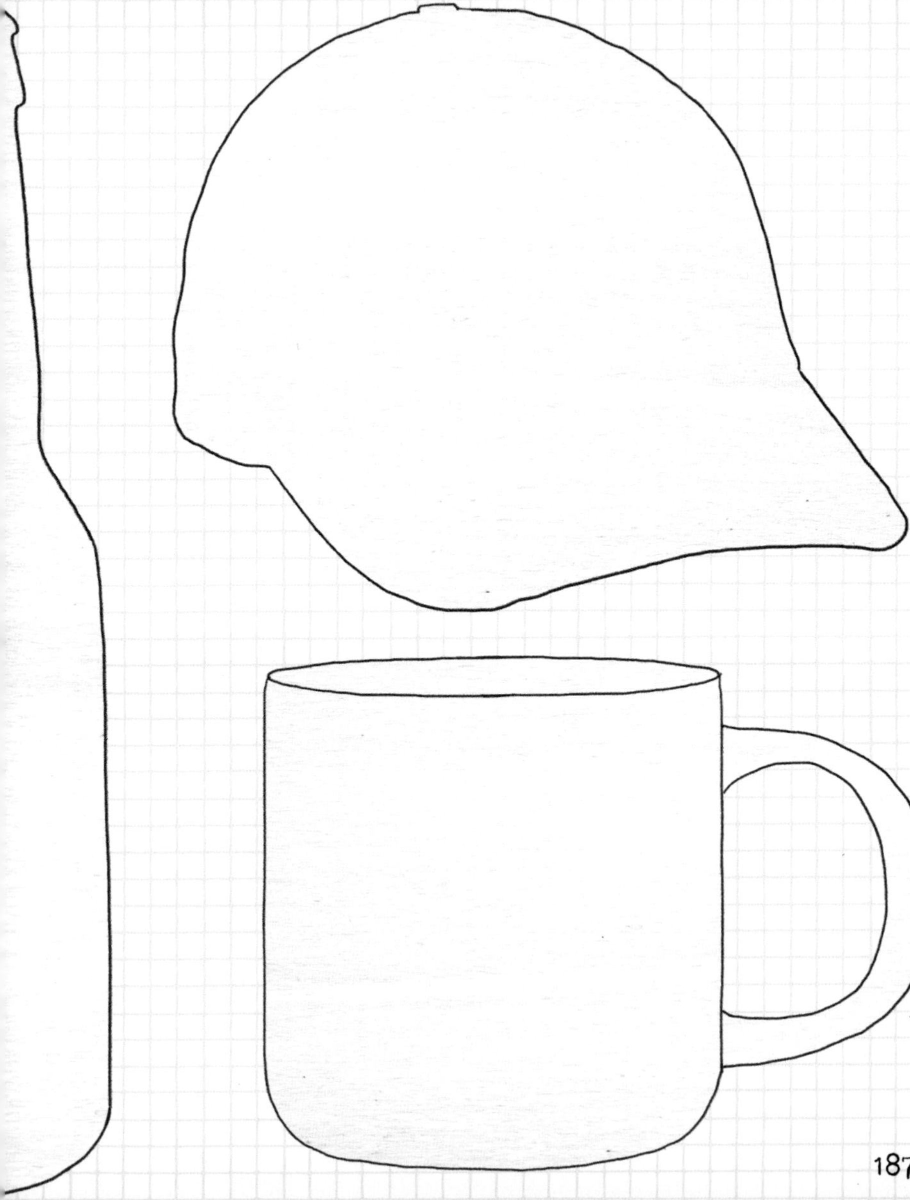

Colour me in!

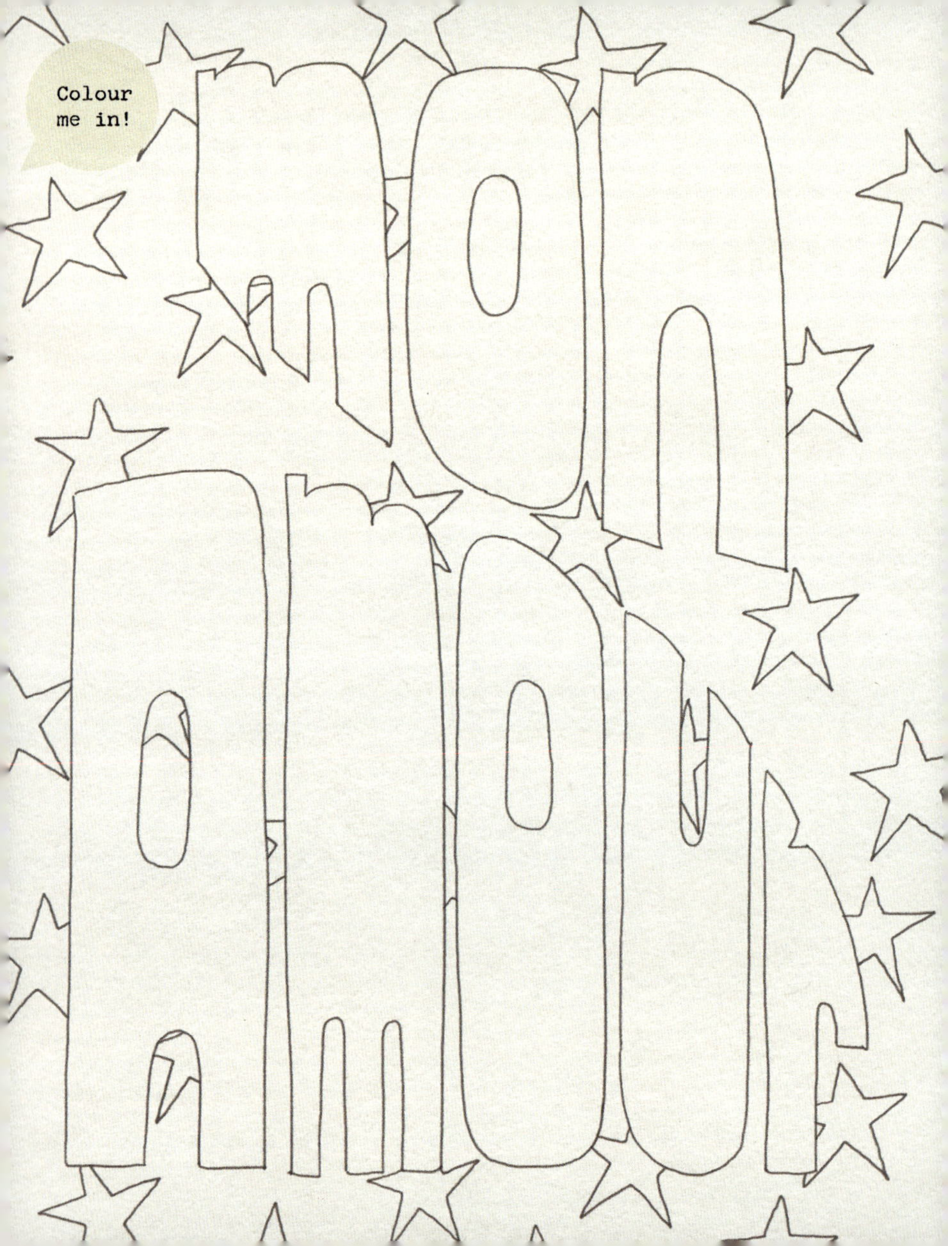

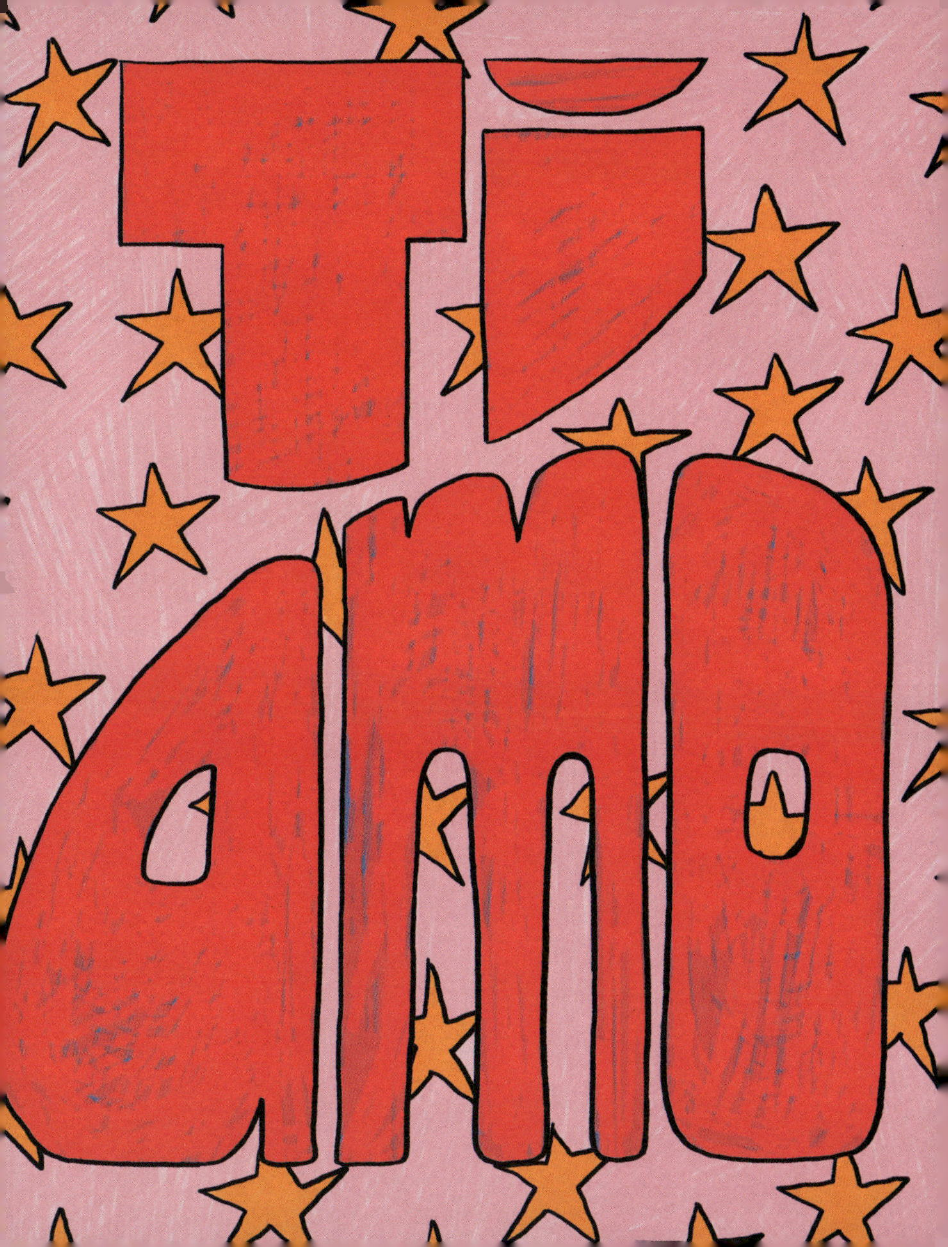
Ti
amo

The pen (or pencil) is mightier than the sword!
Finish off these bendy pencil letters.

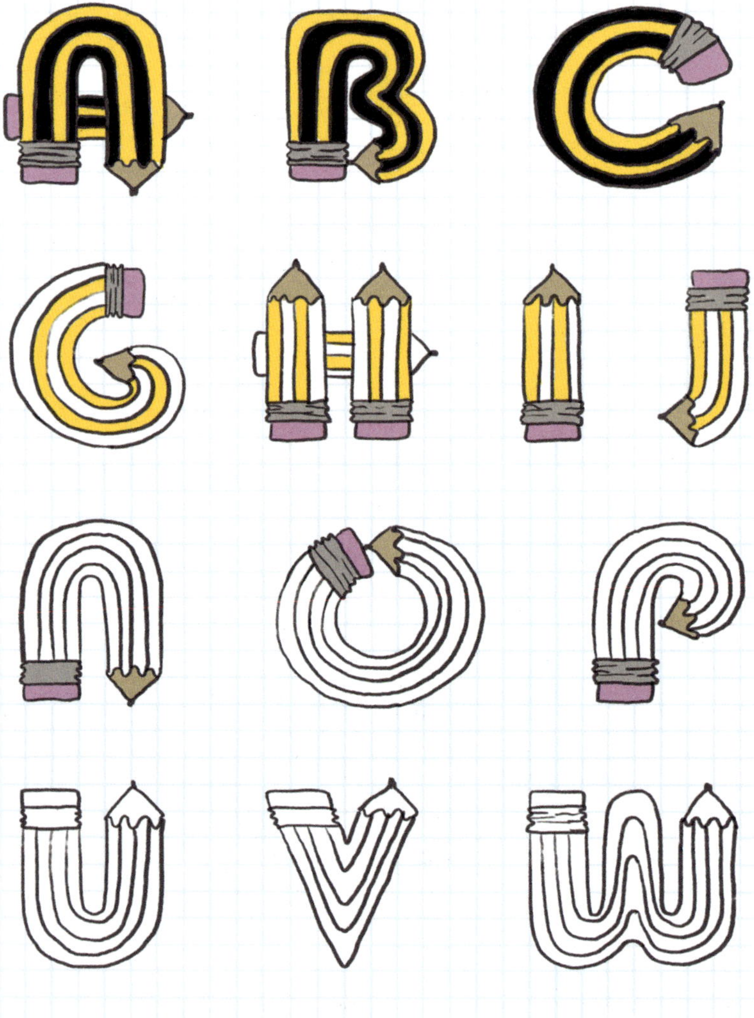

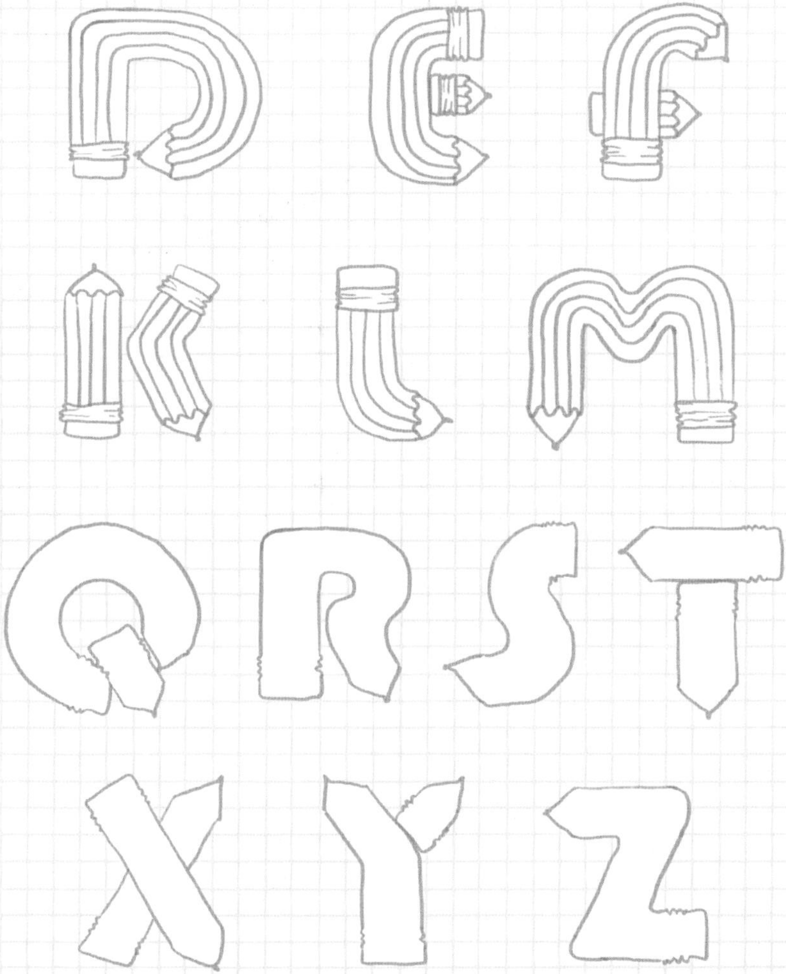
def
klm
qrst
xyz

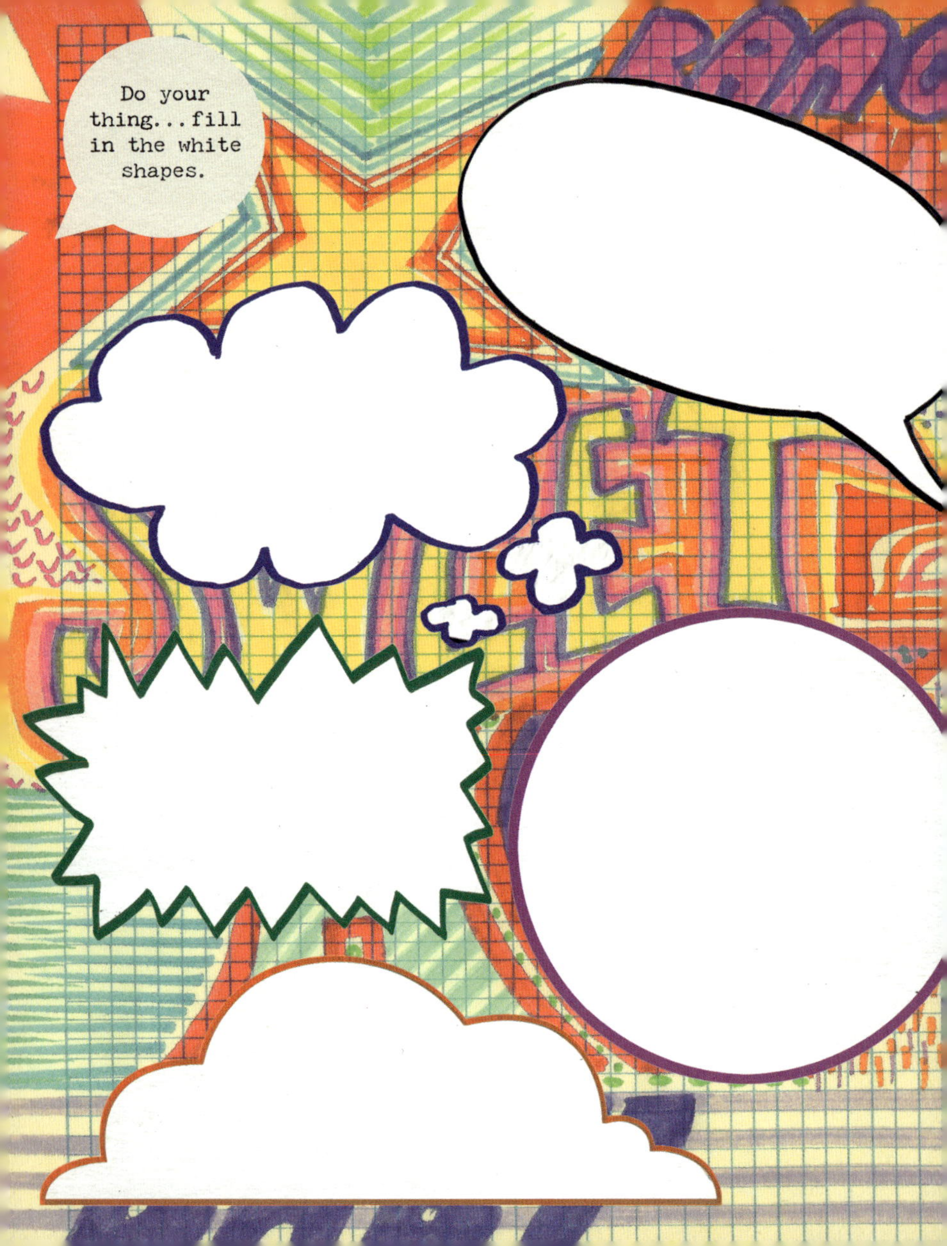
Do your thing...fill in the white shapes.

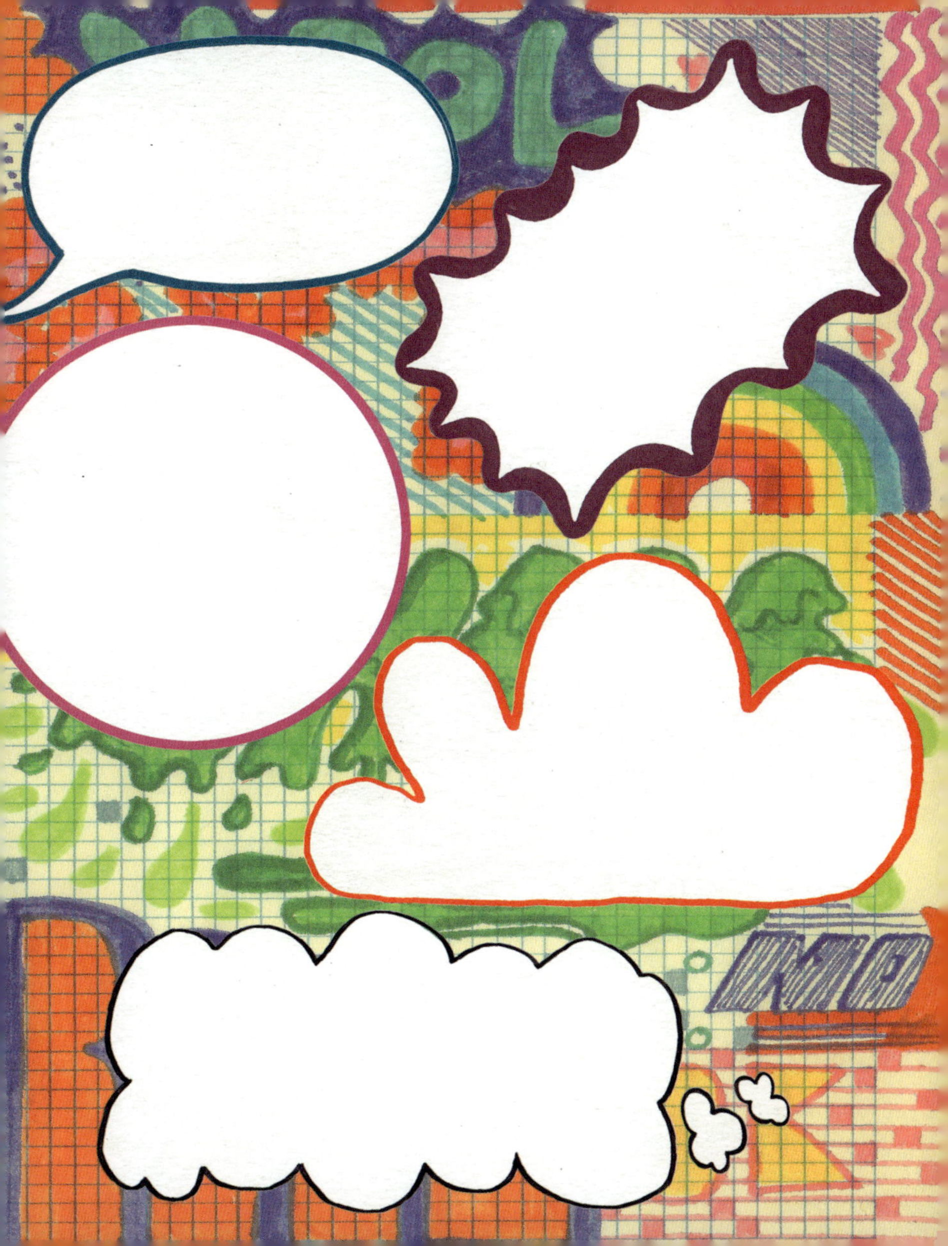

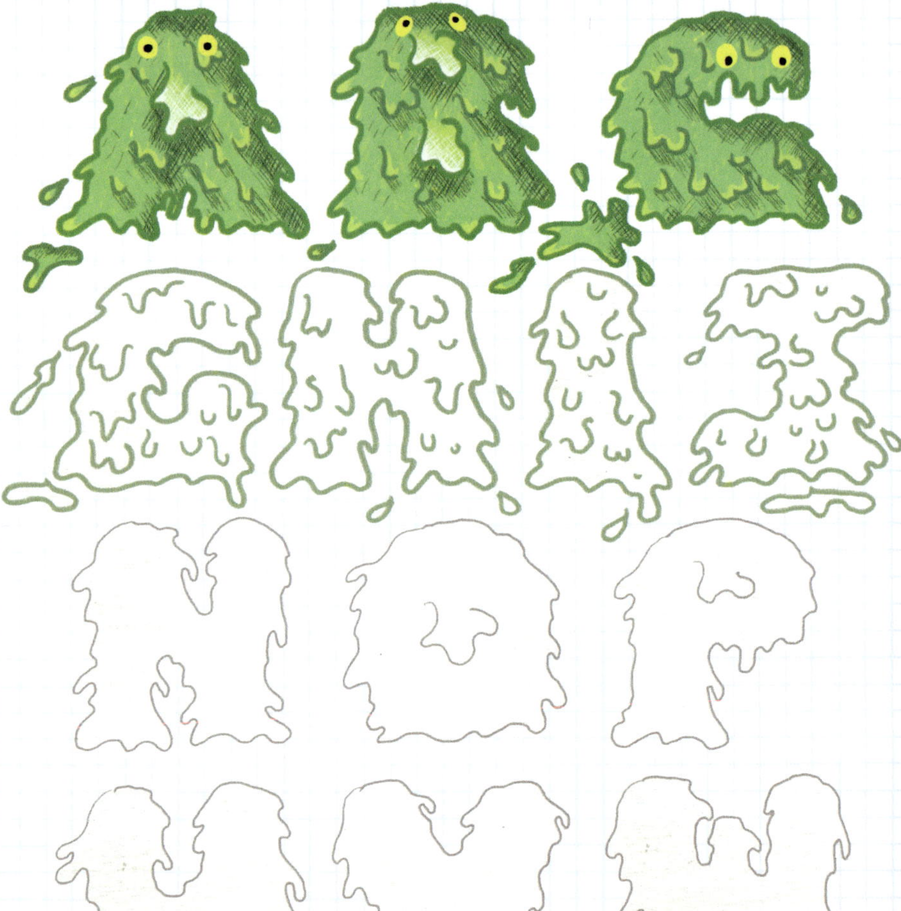

Make a sticky mess, and finish off these creatures with some more slime.

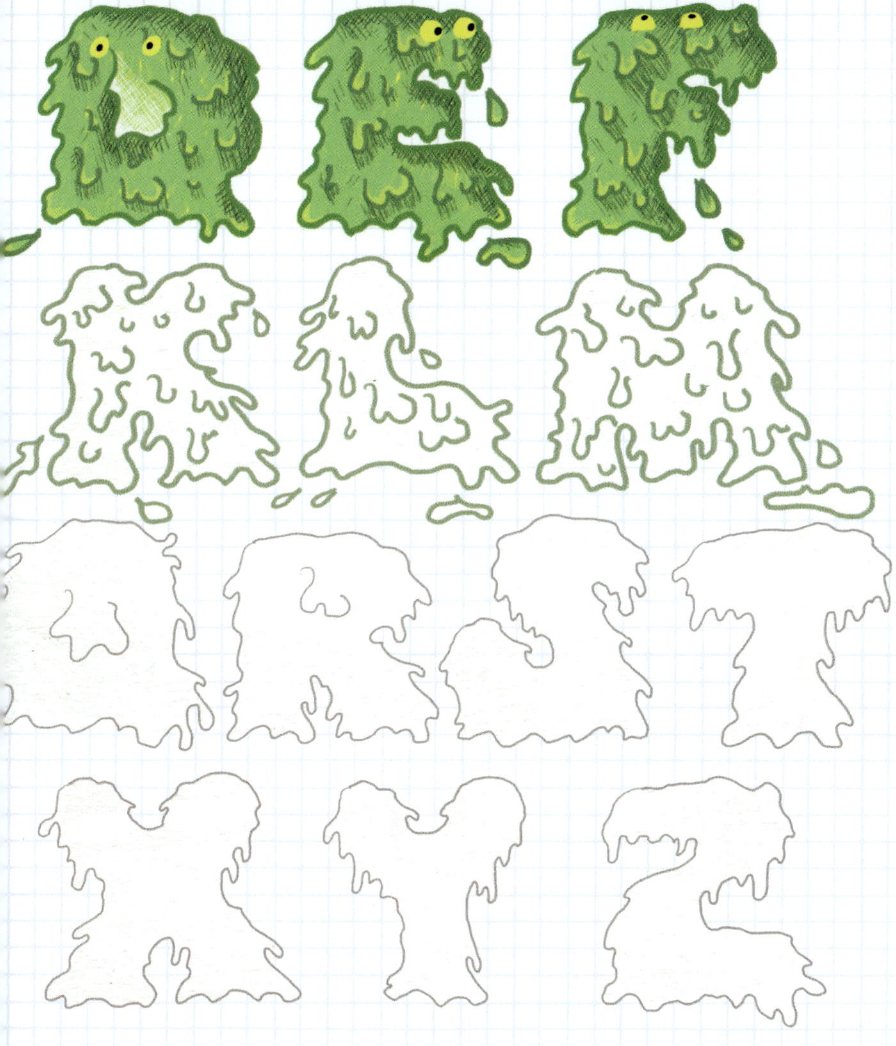

Write down what's on your mind...

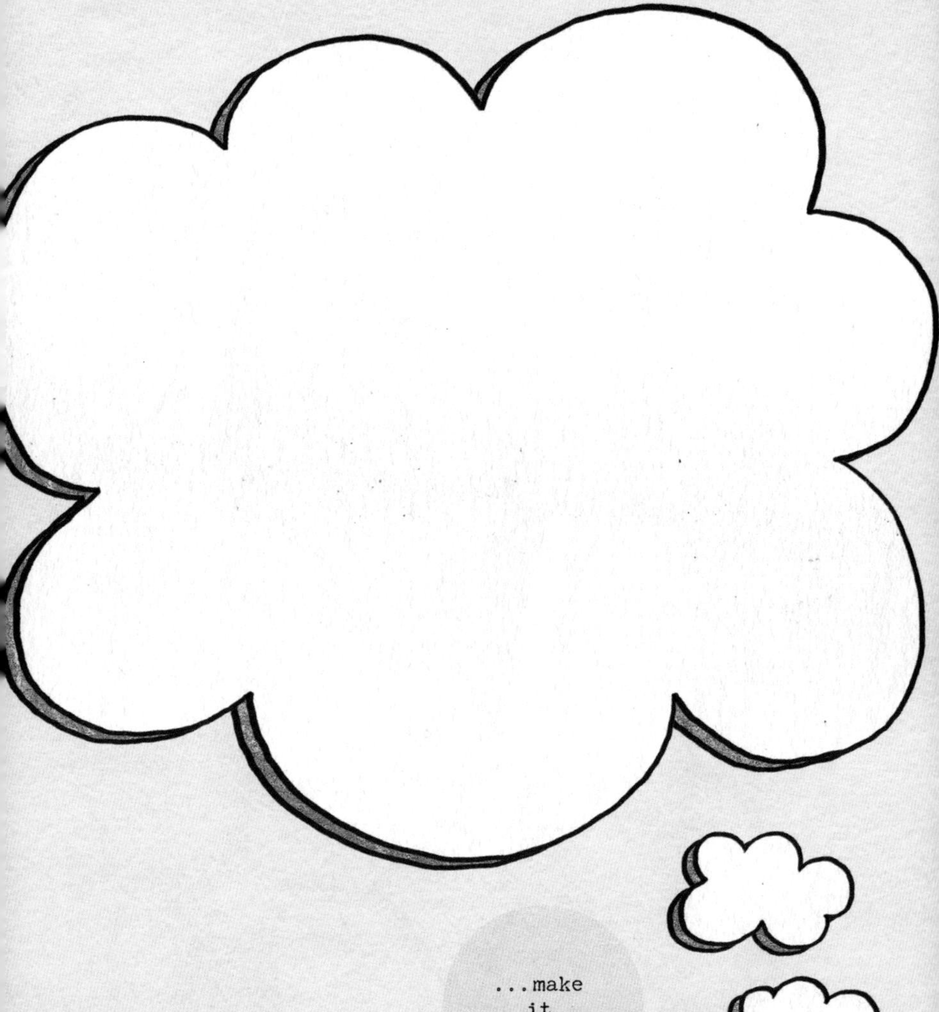

...make
it
matter.

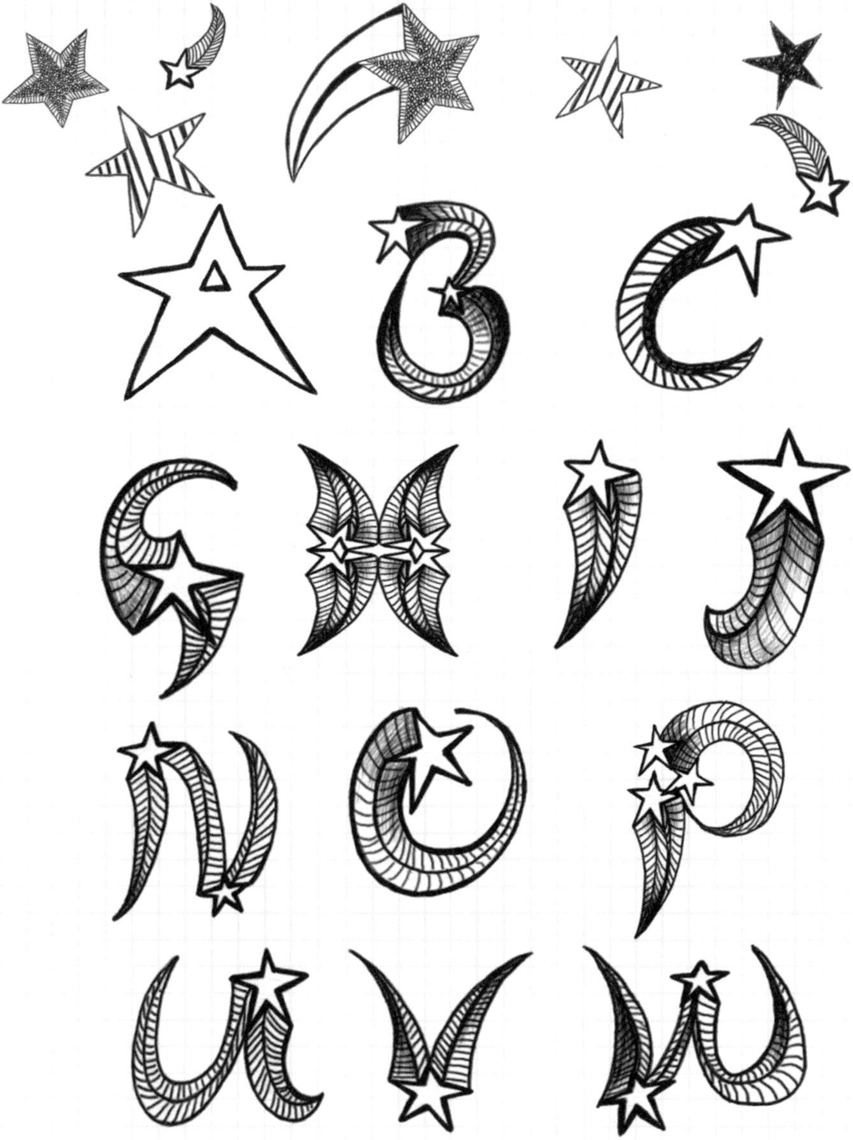

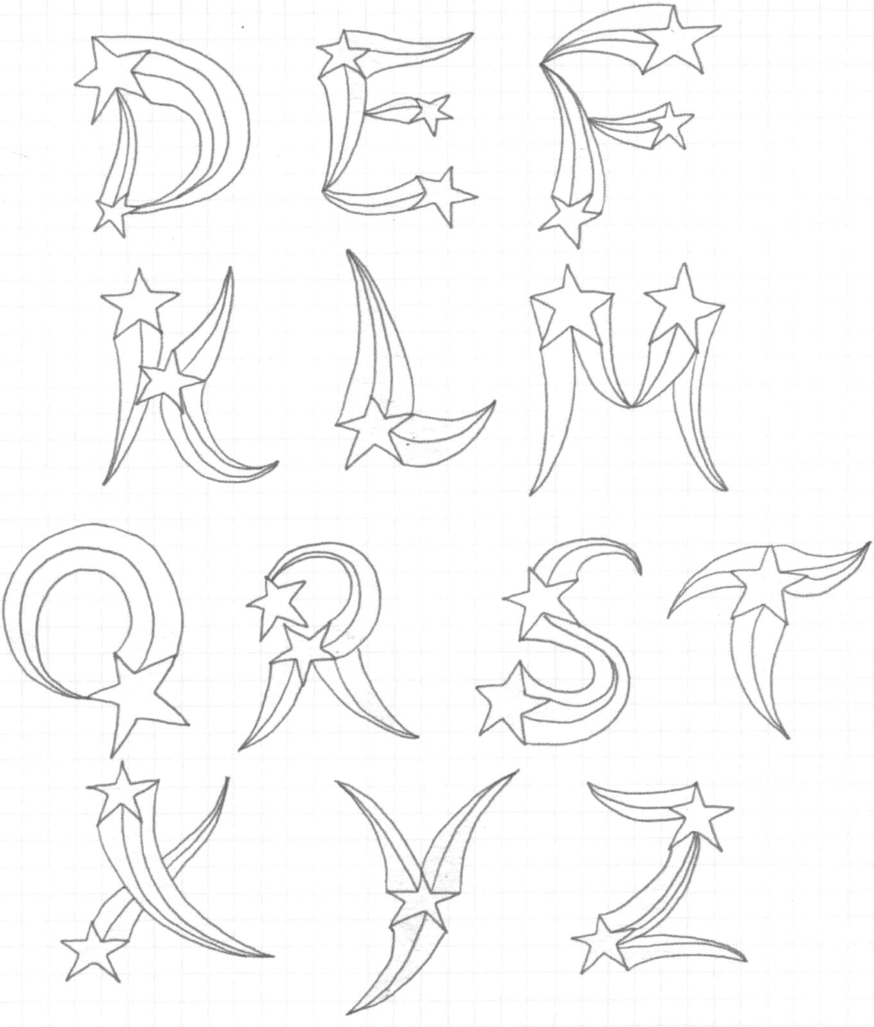

Fill in the tails of the shooting stars with ballpoint pen.

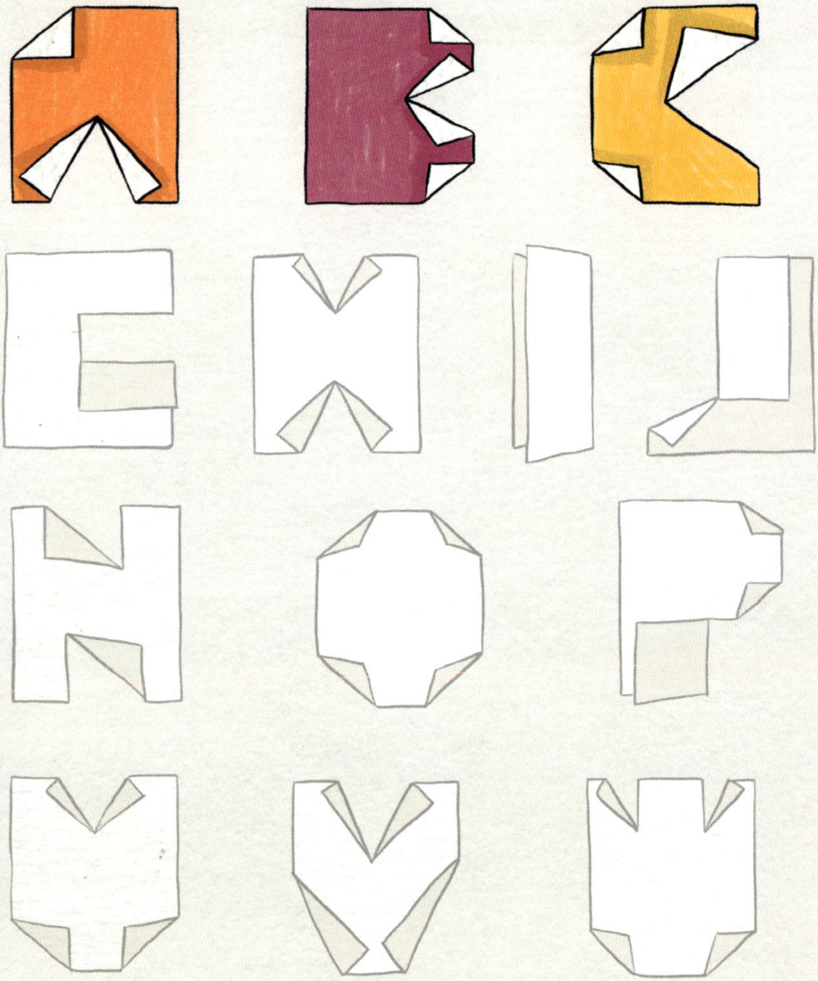

Have a go at the origami letters
- draw them or fold them!

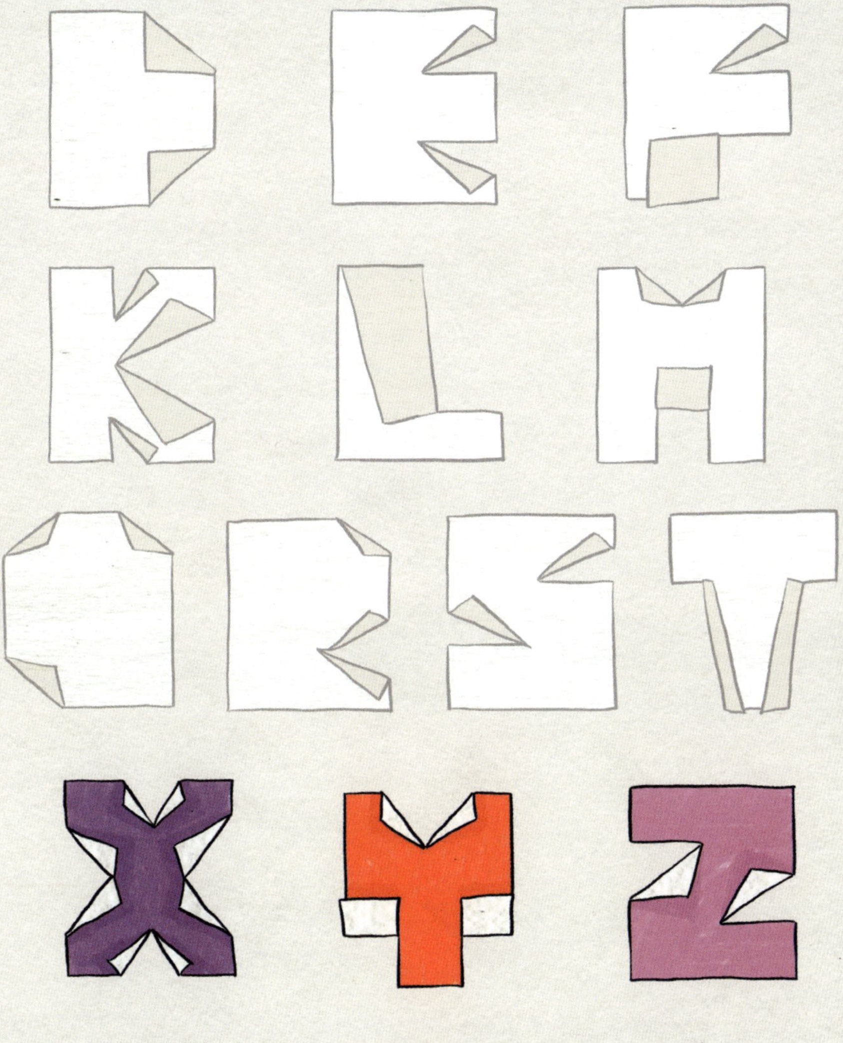

Imagine a letter in a square of paper then, with a combination of simple 'cuts and folds', draw the clearest version of that letter that you can.

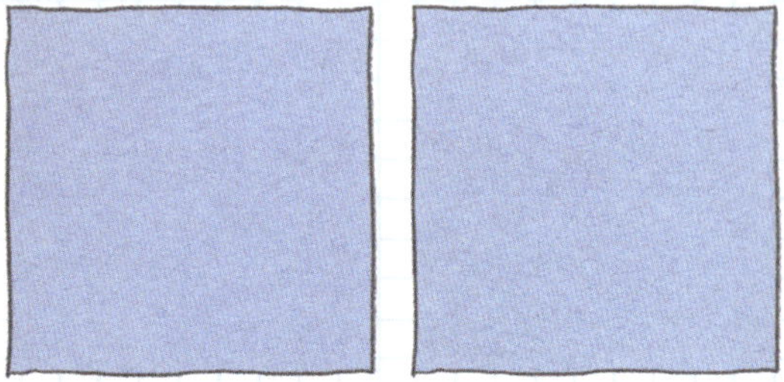

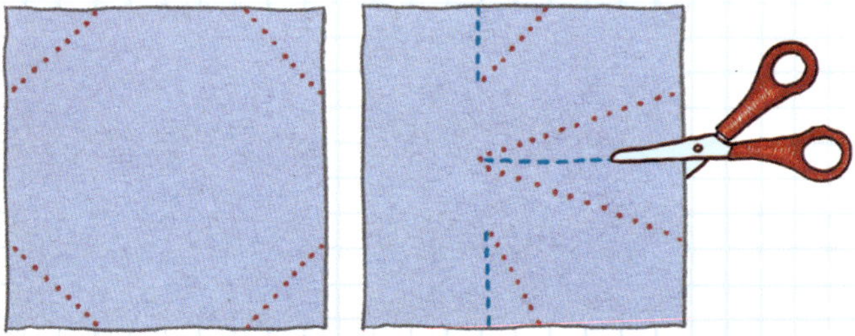

Actually cutting and folding real letters before you try to draw them will really help.

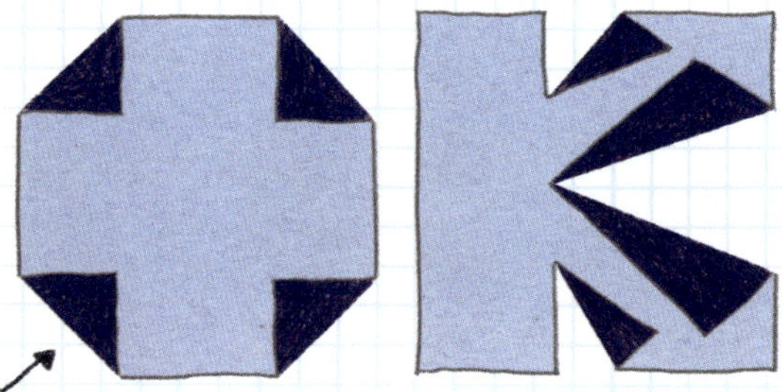

Colour the underside darker than the front of the paper to define the folds.

Draw or collage your letters onto the insides of old envelopes.

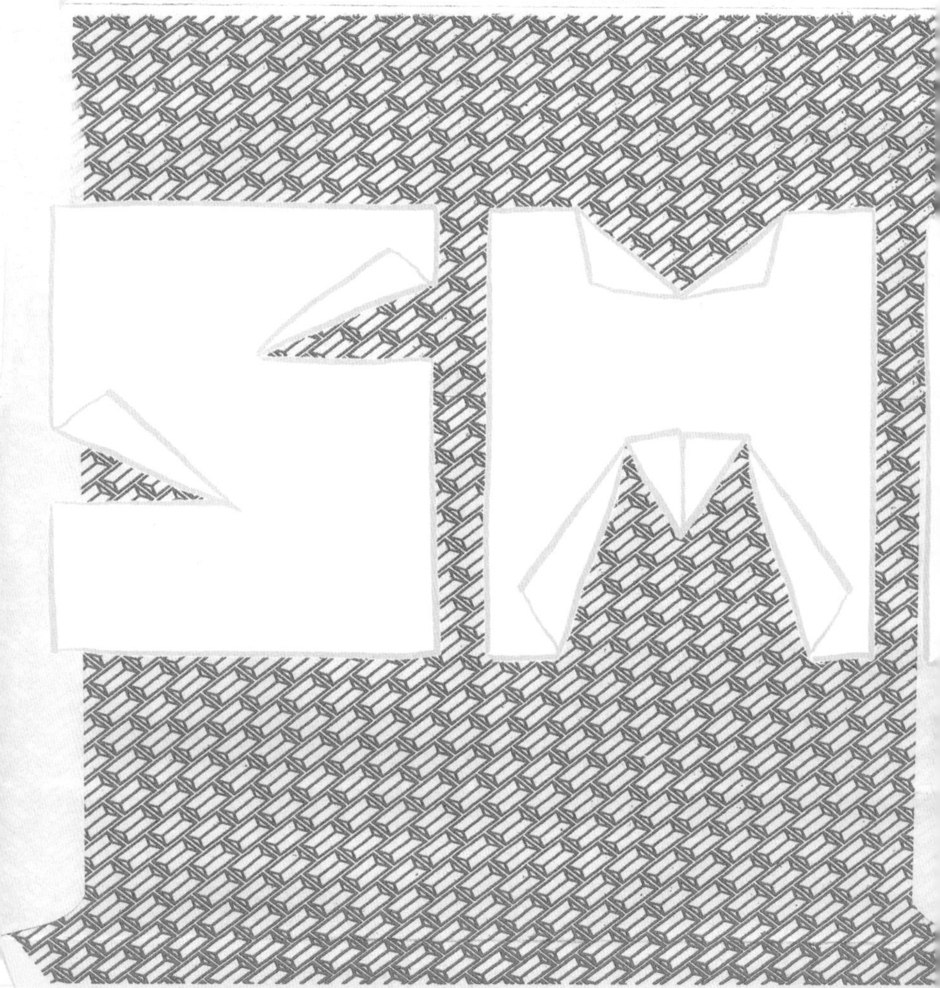

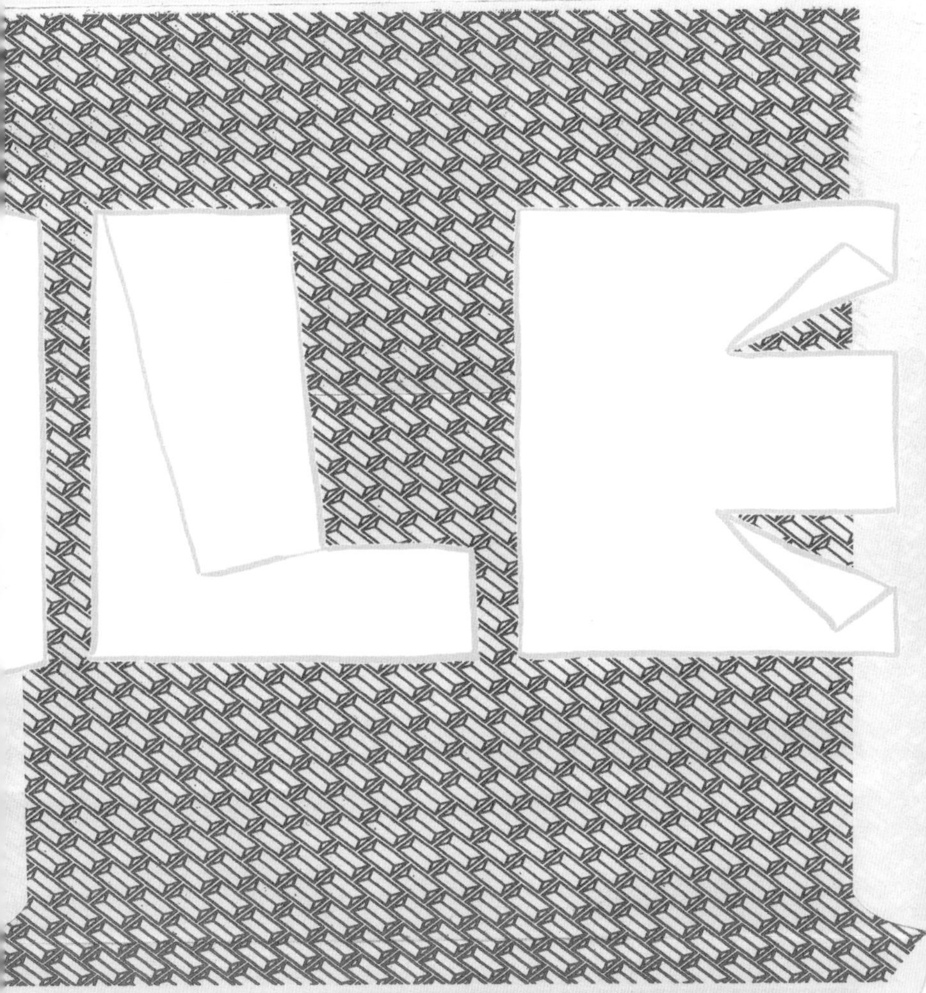

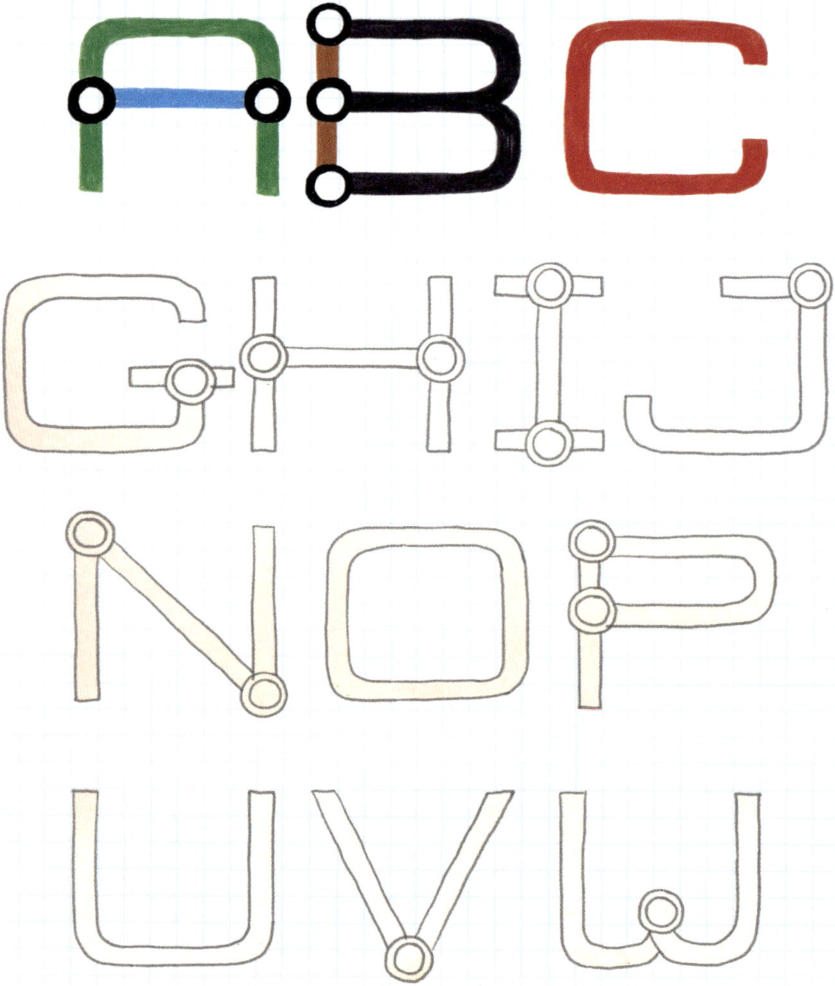

Finish off these transport map-inspired letters to reach your destination.

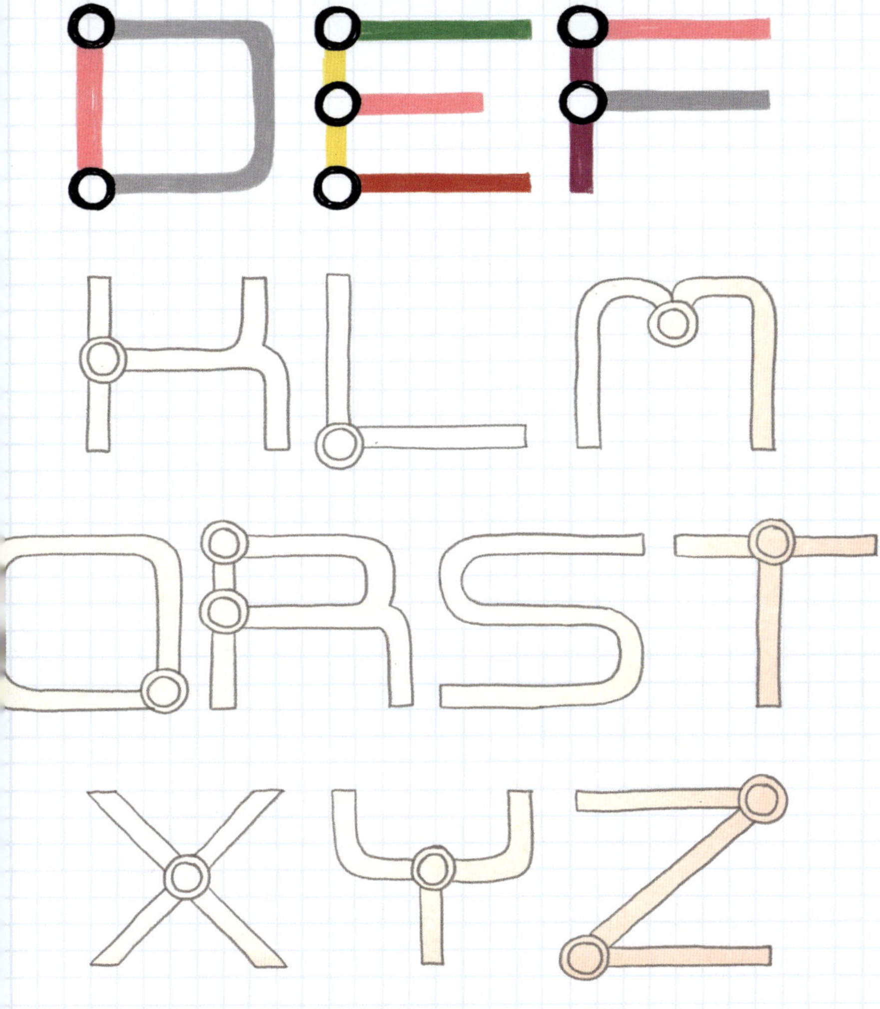
DEF
HLM
QRST
XYZ

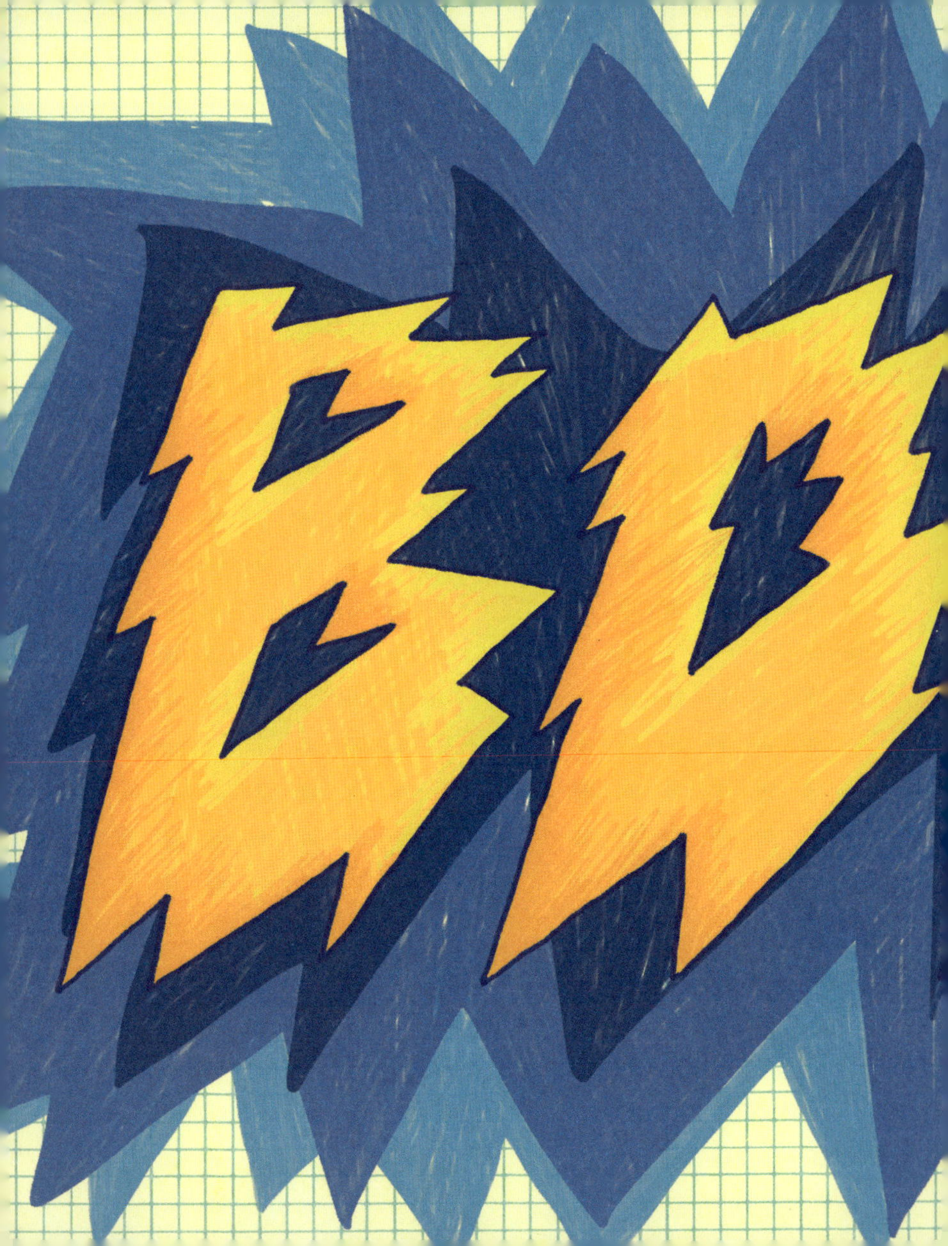

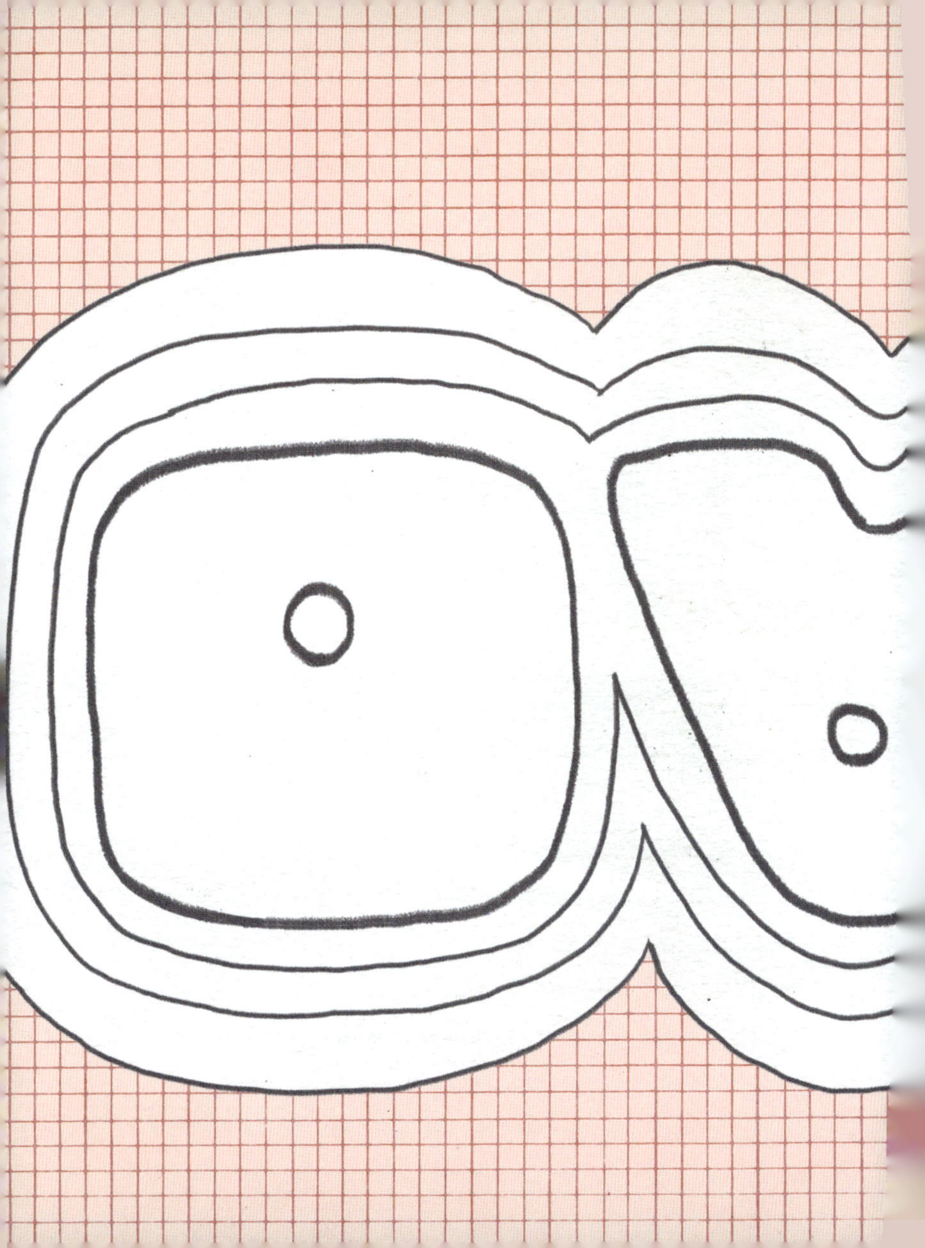

Skittledog

First published in the United Kingdom in 2026
by Skittledog, an imprint of Thames & Hudson Ltd,
6–24 Britannia Street, London WC1X 9JD

Senior Editor: Virginia Brehaut
Designer: Alison Guile
Production: Felicity Awdry

EU Authorized Representative: Interart S.A.R.L.
19 rue Charles Auray, 93500 Pantin, Paris, France
productsafety@thameshudson.co.uk
interart.fr

A CIP catalogue record for this book is available from the British Library

ISBN 978-1-83776-114-2
01

Printed and bound in China by C&C Offset Co., Ltd

MIX
Paper | Supporting responsible forestry
FSC www.fsc.org FSC® C008047

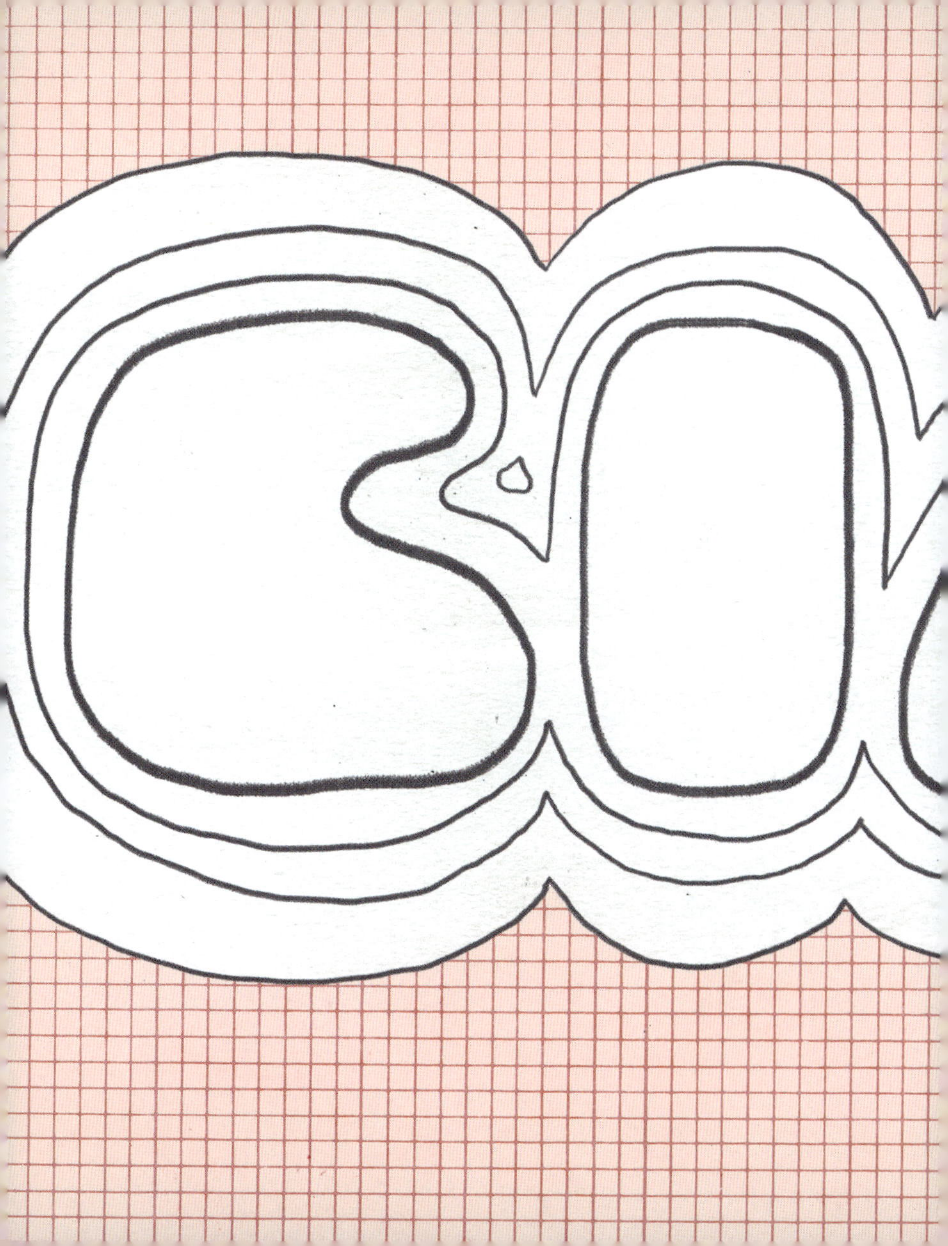

ABOUT THE AUTHOR

Linda Scott - also known as The Bubble Writer - is an all-round letters nut. An artist obsessed with words and typography, her hand-drawn images are instantly recognizable as nostalgic nods to 1970s peace and love, school exercise book graffiti, flower power, 1960s Californian surf culture and political posters. They will strike a chord with anyone with a taste for super-cool typography. She takes her inspiration from anything printed, such as old record sleeves, book jackets, posters and stickers, and she is a huge collector of retro typographic paraphernalia.

Linda has 20 years' experience in the creative industry, writing and illustrating children's books, exhibiting her work, collaborating with a host of creative partners, producing fashion and T-shirt graphics, badges, fonts, murals, neon lights, and anything at all that captures her heart and imagination.

She lives and works in London.

Instagram @lindascott
bubblewriter.com

THANKS!

To the Skittledog Angels
and all-round Dream Team:
Zara Larcombe,
Virginia Brehaut
and Alison Guile
x

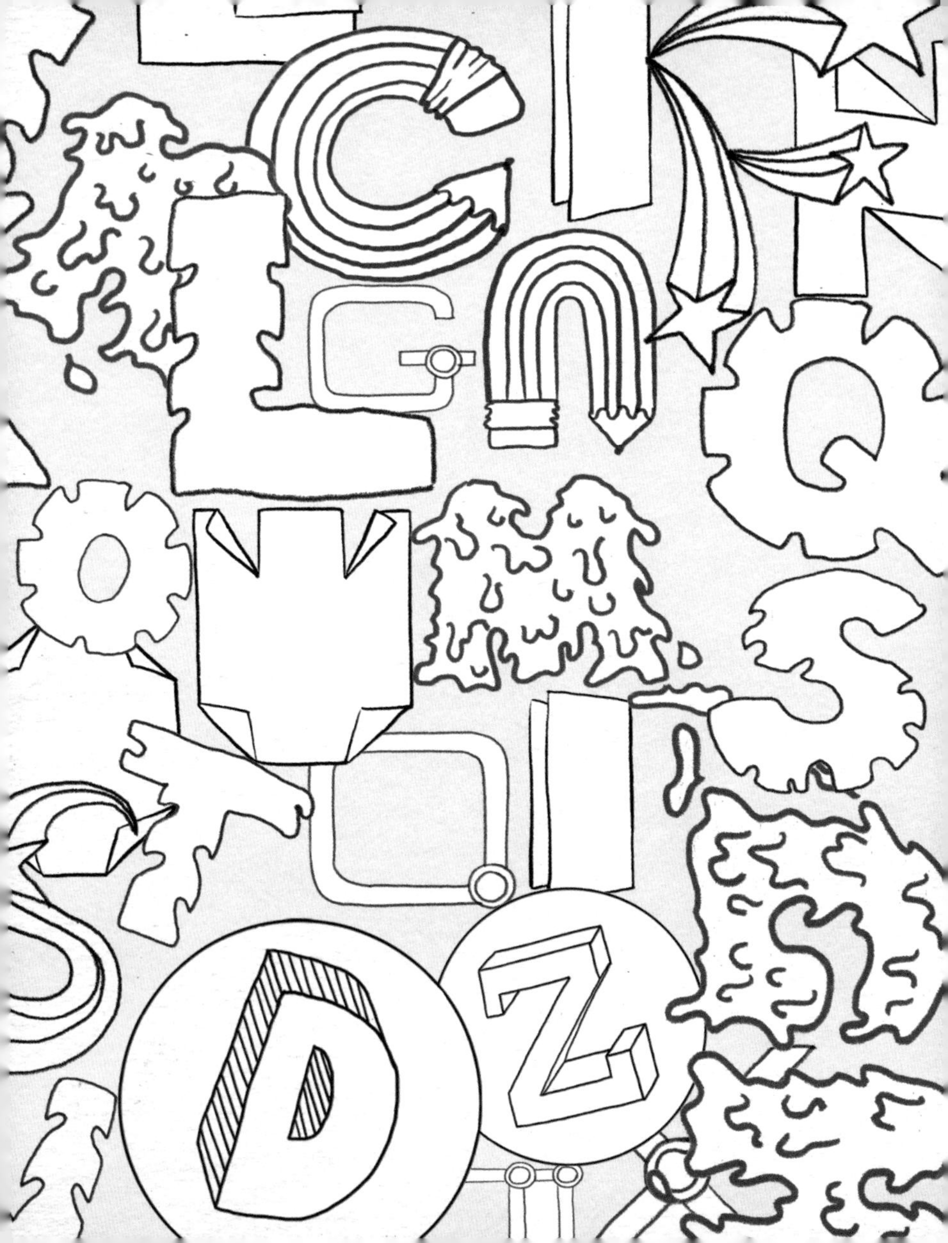

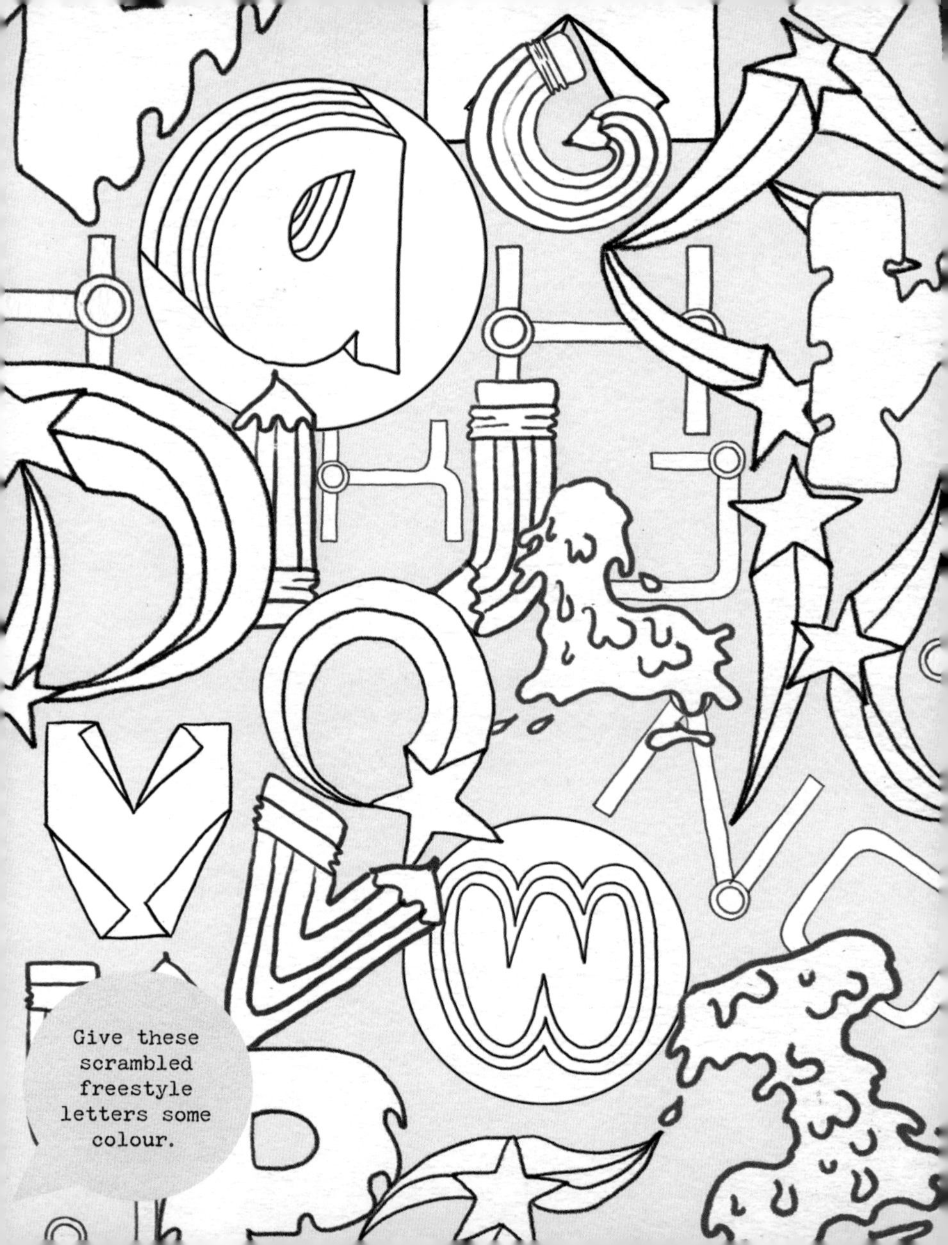

Give these scrambled freestyle letters some colour.

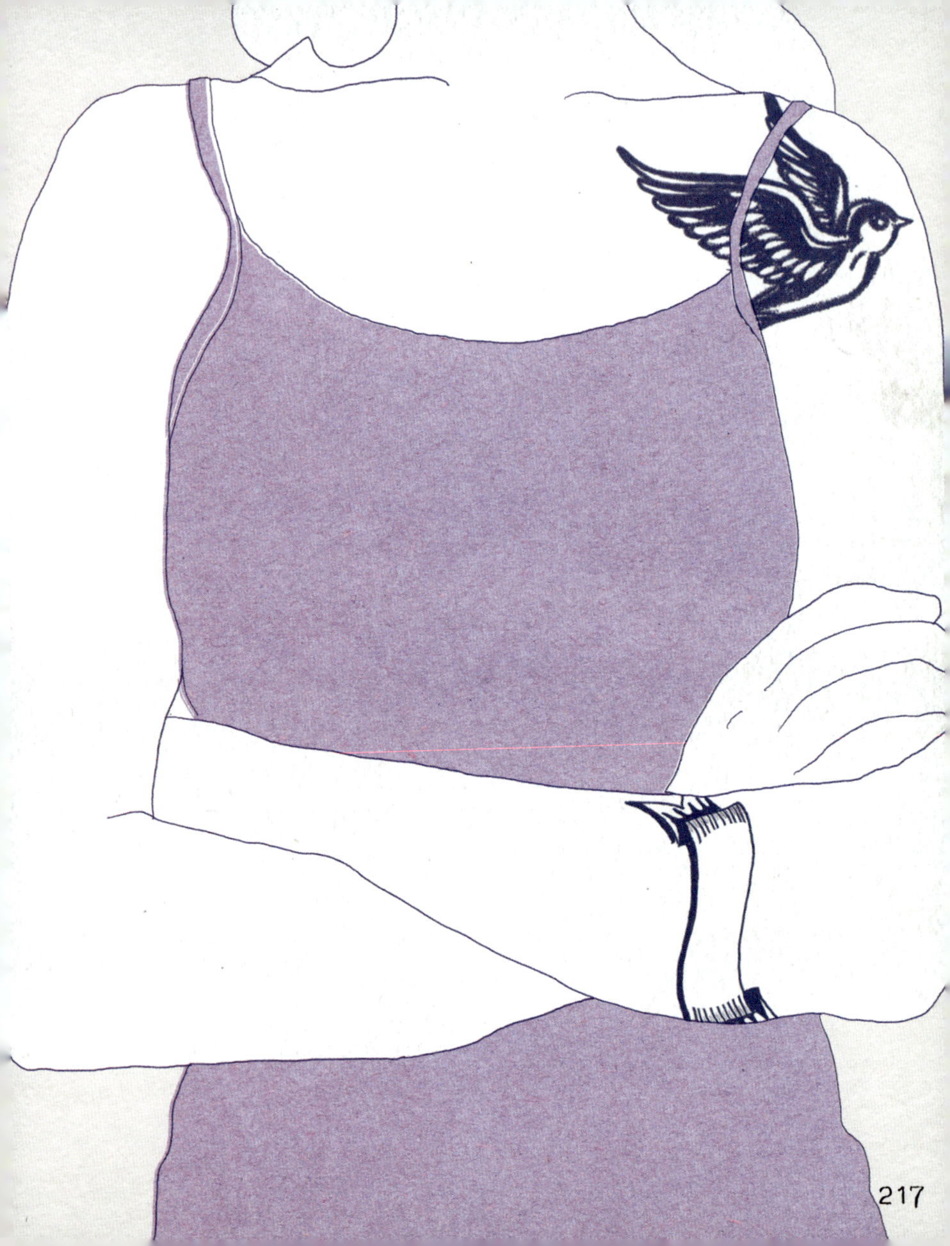

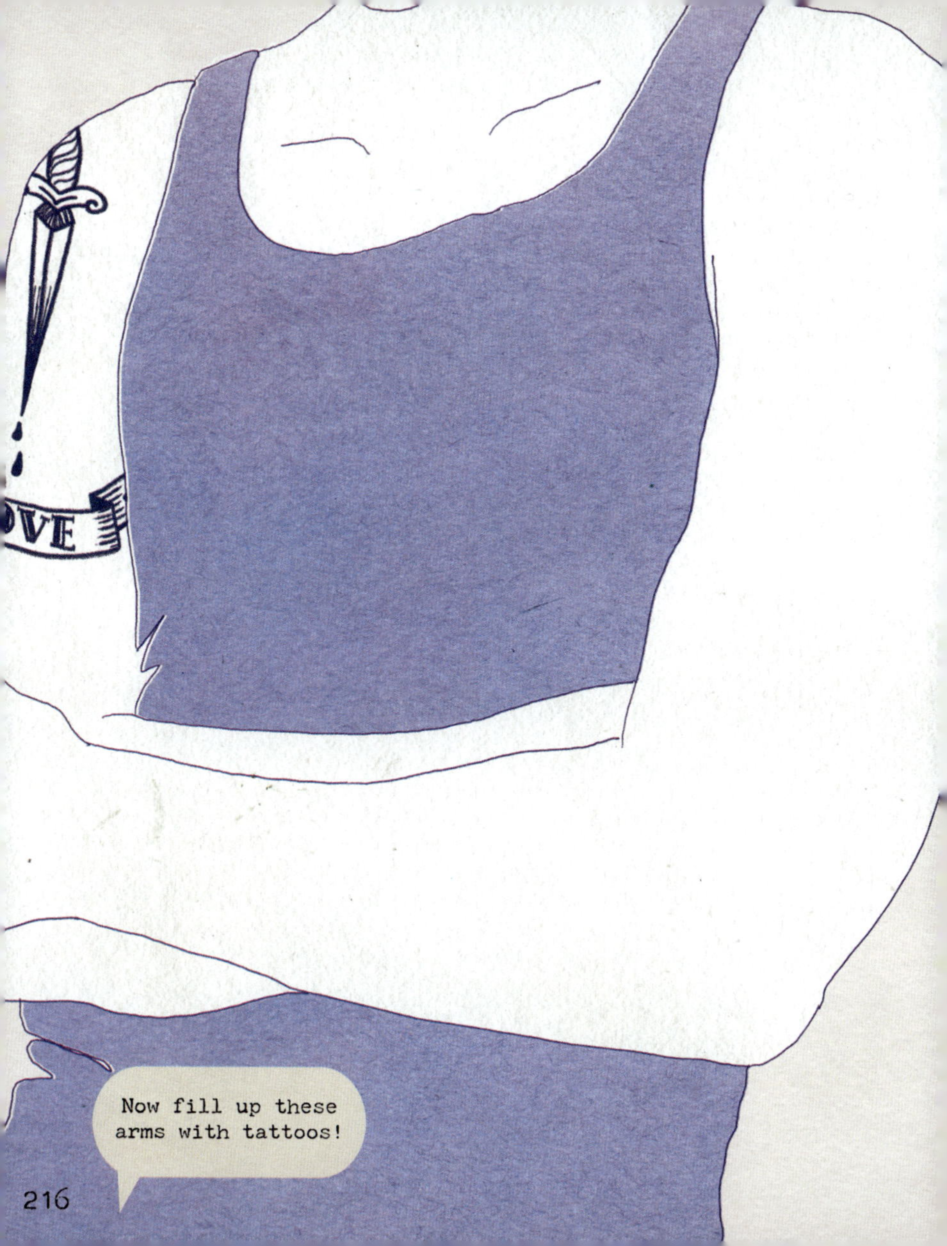
Now fill up these arms with tattoos!

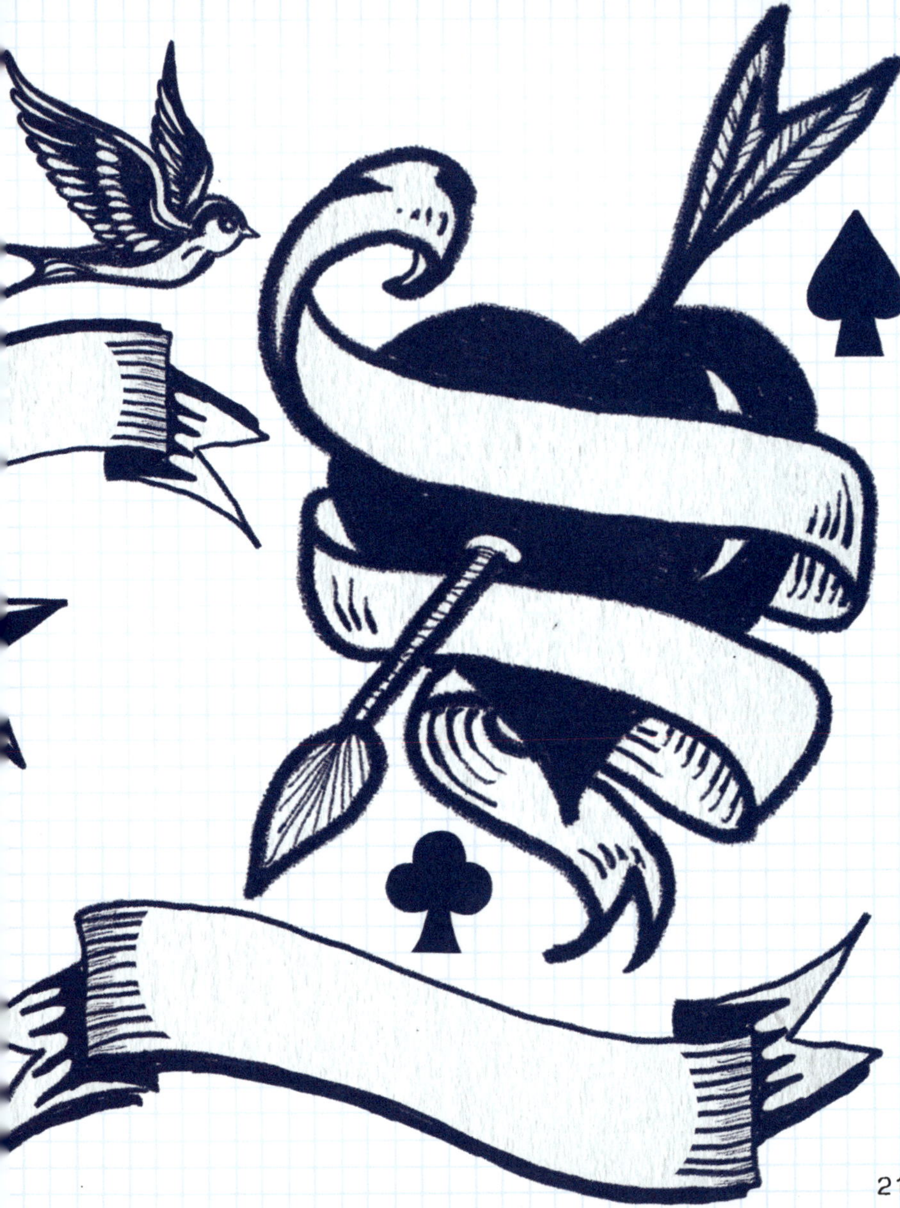

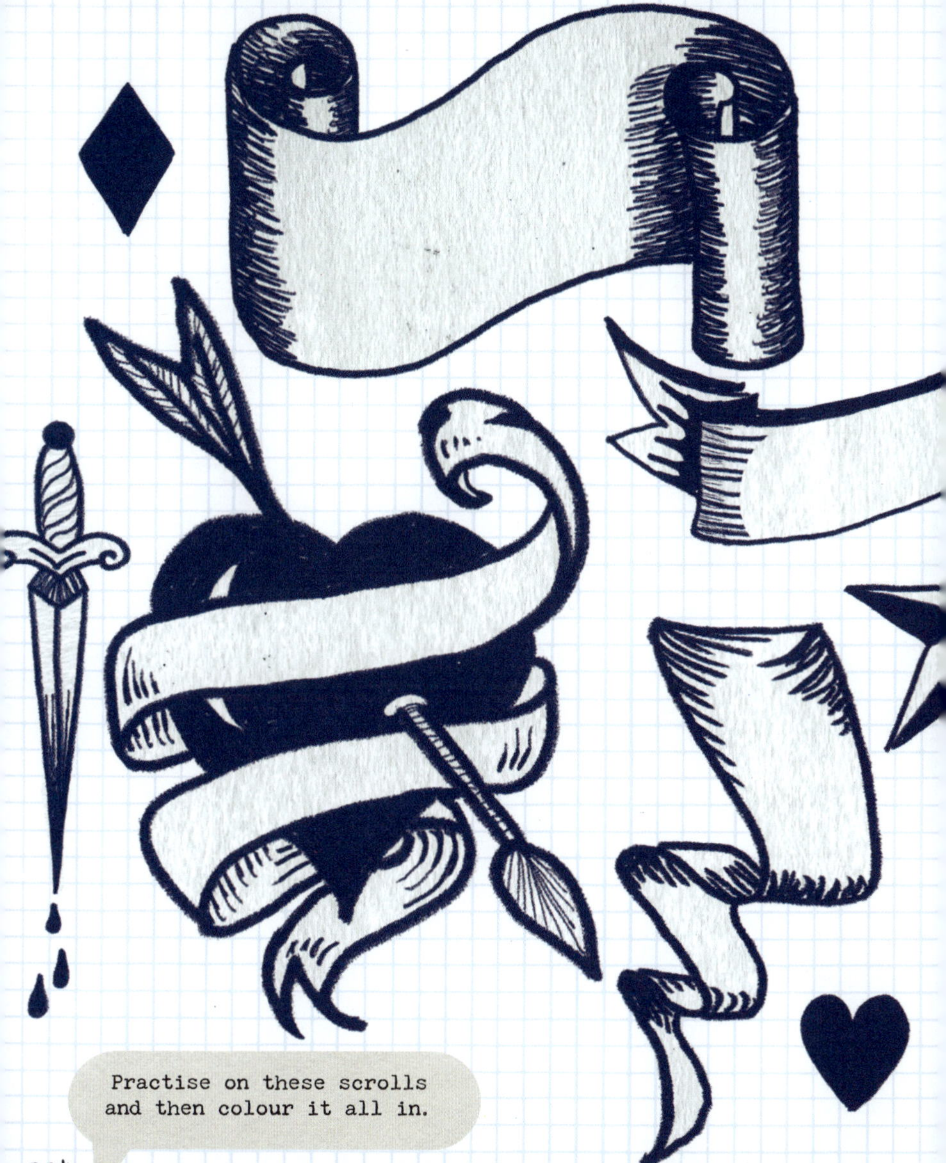

Practise on these scrolls
and then colour it all in.

Add a diamond pattern and choose two colours to blend. Be as flamboyant as you like!

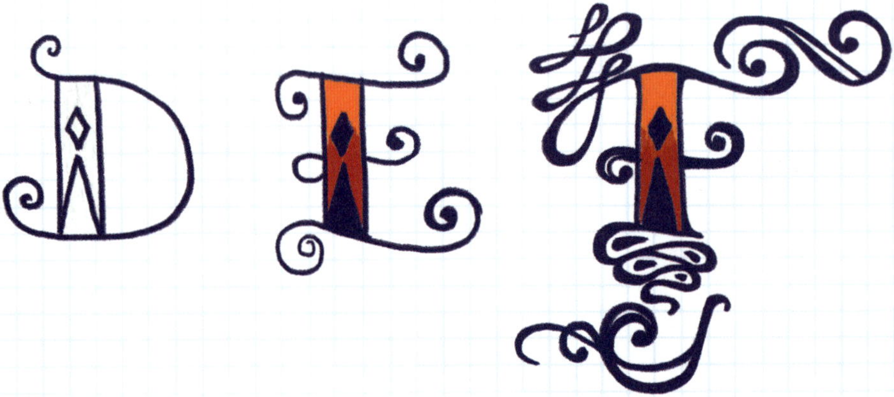

Start with a simple, hand-drawn letter, then add a column and some swirls.

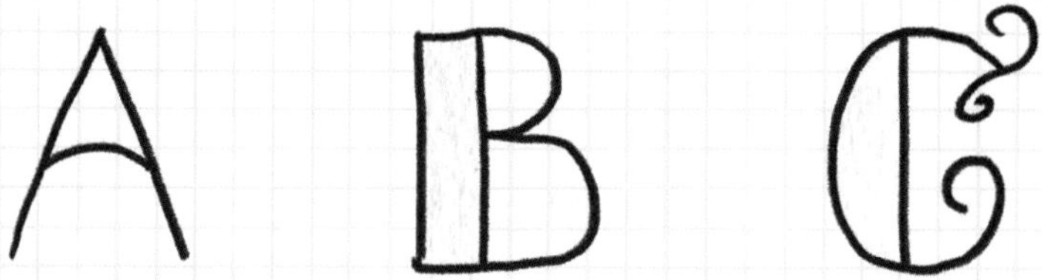

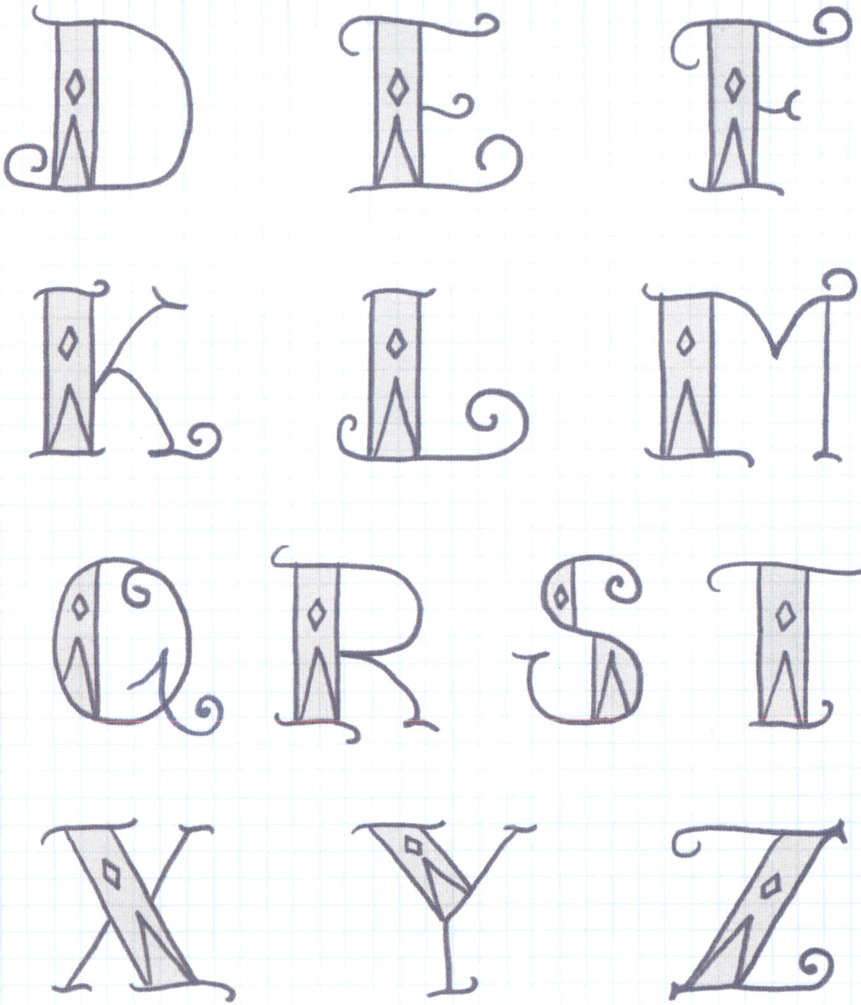
D E F
K L M
Q R S T
X Y Z

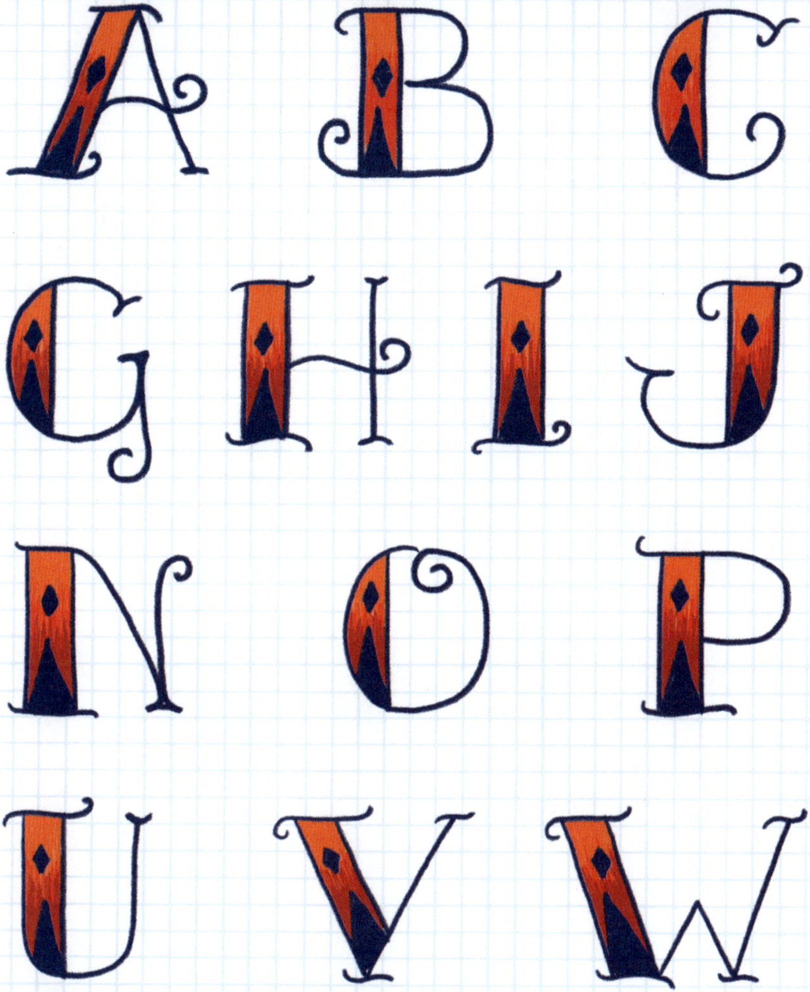

Tattoo-style letters add attitude. Colour these blank ones in and turn over to draw some from scratch.

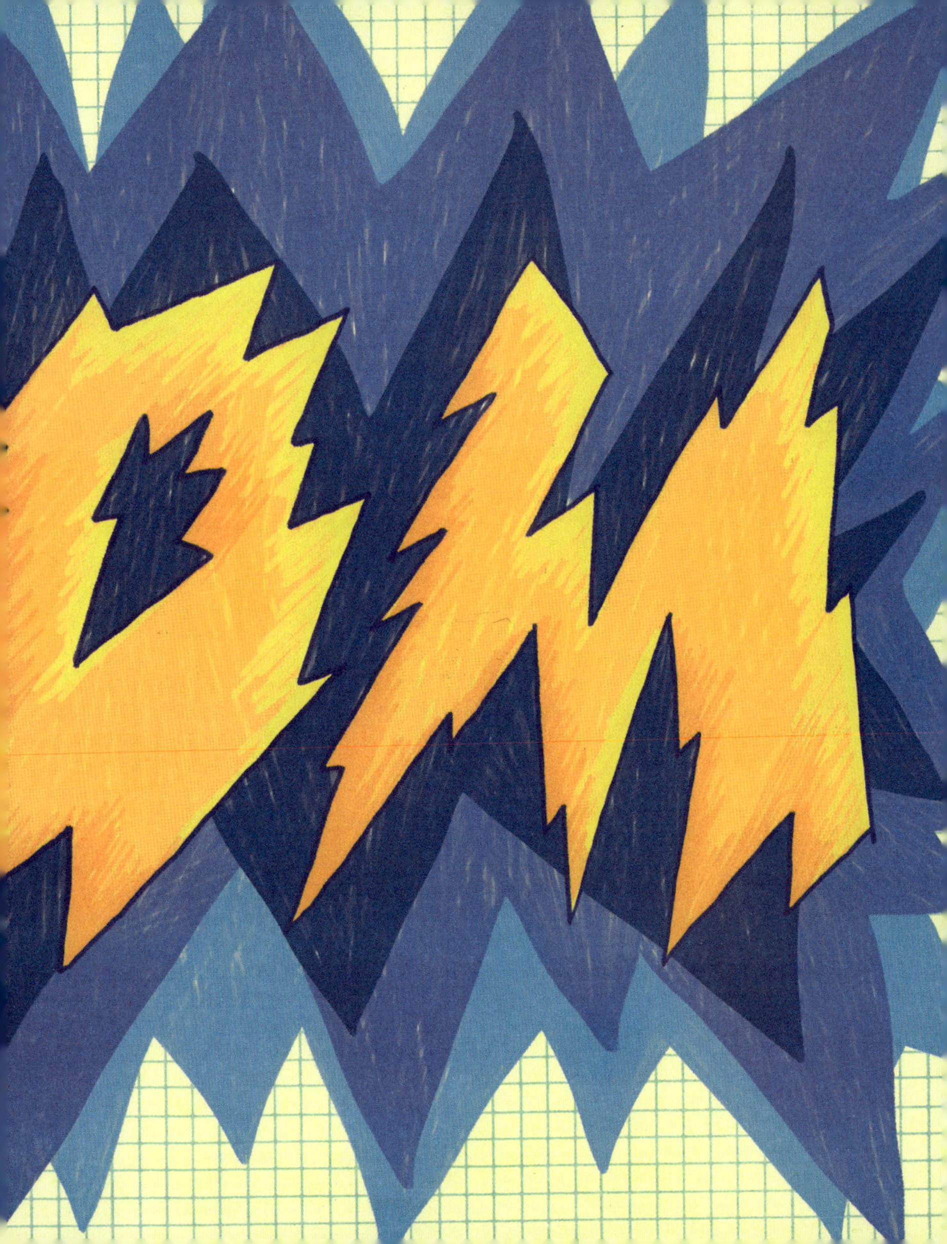